French Newspaper Opinion on the American Civil War

Recent Titles in
Contributions in American History

Federal Antitrust Policy During the Kennedy-Johnson Years
James R. Williamson

The Home-Front War: World War II and American Society
Kenneth Paul O'Brien and Lynn Hudson Parsons, editors

Portrait of an Abolitionist: A Biography of George Luther Stearns
Charles E. Heller

No King, No Popery: Anti-Catholicism in Revolutionary New England
Francis D. Cogliano

James Glen: From Scottish Provost to Royal Governor of South Carolina
W. Stitt Robinson

The Journalist as Reformer: Henry Demarest Lloyd and *Wealth Against Commonwealth*
Richard Digby-Junger

Reconciliation and Revival: James R. Mann and the House Republicans in the Wilson Era
Herbert F. Margulies

Varieties of Southern History: New Essays on a Region and Its People
Bruce Clayton and John Salmond, editors

A Utopian Experiment in Kentucky: Integration and Social Equality at Berea, 1866–1904
Richard Sears

A Mythic Land Apart: Reassessing Southerners and Their History
John David Smith and Thomas H. Appleton, Jr., editors

The Corporate City: The American City as a Political Entity, 1800–1850
Leonard P. Curry

Democracy Reformed: Richard Spencer Childs and His Fight for Better Government
Bernard Hirschhorn

French Newspaper Opinion on the American Civil War

George M. Blackburn

Contributions in American History, *Number 171*

GREENWOOD PRESS
Westport, Connecticut • London

Library of Congress Cataloging-in-Publication Data

Blackburn, George M. (George McCoy), 1926–
French newspaper opinion on the American Civil War / George M. Blackburn.
p. cm.—(Contributions in American history, ISSN 0084–9219 ; no. 171)
Includes bibliographical references and index.
ISBN 0–313–30261–8 (alk. paper)
1. United States—History—Civil War, 1861–1865—Foreign public opinion, French. 2. Public opinion—France—History—19th century. 3. United States—Foreign relations—1861–1865. I. Title. II. Series.
E469.8.B6 1997
973.7—dc20 96–30583

British Library Cataloguing in Publication Data is available.

Library of Congress Catalog Card Number: 96–30583
ISBN: 0–313–30261–8
ISSN: 0084–9219

First published in 1997

Greenwood Press, 88 Post Road West, Westport, CT 06881
An imprint of Greenwood Publishing Group, Inc.

Printed in the United States of America

The paper used in this book complies with the Permanent Paper Standard issued by the National Information Standards Organization (Z39.48–1984).

10 9 8 7 6 5 4 3 2 1

To Mary Ellen

Contents

Introduction		ix
Chapter 1	France in 1861	1
Chapter 2	The 1860 Election and Secession	23
Chapter 3	The *Trent* Affair	45
Chapter 4	Changing Military Fortunes and Emancipation	57
Chapter 5	The Cotton *Crise*	73
Chapter 6	French Official Actions through Mediation	91
Chapter 7	1863 and 1864	109
Chapter 8	The End of the War	127
Bibliographical Essay		141
Index		147

Introduction

Any study of French newspaper opinion about the American Civil War inevitably tells as much about France as it does about America. "French observers, in their writings on American democracy," stated one scholar, "ultimately may reveal more about France than about the United States." Perceiving alternating periods of pro- and anti-Americanism from 1834 to 1870, another scholar attributed such changes in sentiment not to alterations in American society, but rather to political changes in France.[1]

At least some rudimentary knowledge of French government and society in the 1860s seems, therefore, to be essential to understand French reactions to the Civil War. The first chapter provides a brief introduction to the French government, the French economy, French society, and the French press. Later chapters deal with the specific attitudes of French newspapers regarding various aspects of the Civil War. Organized basically in a chronological manner, these chapters describe French attitudes toward the causes and early stages of the Civil War, French views on the *Trent* affair, the economic impact of the war on France, French efforts at mediating the conflict, and French views about events in the last years of the war. Space in the book about these various topics reflects the emphasis accorded by the French press, not their intrinsic importance in the Civil War.

Some of the treatment the French press gave to those topics was colored by marked pro-Confederate sentiments, a point of view that might surprise many Americans. Almost all of my colleagues and friends, when I told them about this study, for example, assumed that Frenchmen were sympathetic toward the North because the North was fighting to abolish slavery. How could Frenchmen support Southern efforts to preserve a slaveholding society? Indeed, many Americans have frequently asked why the French have not supported goals that Americans deemed worthwhile. Part of the answer, of course, is that Frenchmen supported goals that *they* perceived as worthwhile. That was as true for the France of Napoleon III during the 1860s as it was for the France of Charles de Gaulle. Rather than postulating a perverse negativism by the French toward American goals, Americans could more profitably examine the reasons for French attitudes. That is the perspective of this study.

Three book-length studies have examined French attitudes regarding the Civil War. W. Reed West, in *Contemporary French Opinion on the American Civil War* (Baltimore, 1924), found that conservative imperialists, supporters of the French emperor Napoleon III, favored the Confederacy not because they approved of slavery but because they were "enemies of the Union." For liberals, however, in West's view, slavery was the "determining issue." Donaldson Jordan and Edwin Pratt, in their *Europe and the American Civil War* (Boston, 1931), divided the Parisian newspapers into two categories: conservative followers of the Emperor, who were supporters of the South because "the Northern cause and Imperialism were fundamentally incompatible" and the "more modern" supporters of the North, who were "the spiritual successors of those who supported American independence in 1775." Serge Gavronsky, in *The French Liberal Opposition and the American Civil War* (New York, 1968), argued that internal concerns rather than the slavery issue led French liberals to support the North. Unable to criticize the government directly, French liberals supported democracy and the Union as an indirect means of attacking the oppressive regime of Napoleon III. David H. Pinkney, in an article-length study, "France and the Civil War," in Harold Hyman, ed., *Heard Round the World: The Impact Abroad of the Civil War* (New York, 1969), emphasized that Frenchmen, rather than France, reacted to the Civil War.

An examination of French reaction or attitudes toward the Civil War involves two major aspects. One aspect is the *desired* outcome of the war: some Frenchmen championed the Northern cause while others championed the Southern cause. A second aspect is the *anticipated* outcome of the Civil War: a belief that the North would triumph militarily and maintain the American Union or a belief that the South would achieve independence.

My thesis is that ideology was of crucial importance in shaping French attitudes toward the *desired* outcome of the Civil War. French conservatives favored a Southern victory because they opposed democracy, believed democracy to be inherently unstable, and hence regarded the dissolution of American democracy as both desirable and inevitable. The failure of American democracy would also provide justification for authoritarian regimes in France. French liberals and opponents of Napoleon III, on the other hand, favored a Northern triumph because they wished to see democracy triumph. The success of American democracy would also provide justification for a more democratic government in France. Thus, politically aware Frenchmen perceived the American Civil War as an acid test of the legitimacy and viability of democratic institutions not only in America, but also in France.

Assessment of the American military and political situation was crucial in influencing beliefs in the *anticipated* outcome of the Civil War. Some French journalists changed their assessment of the outcome in accordance with changing military fortunes. Typically, however, Conservatives, professed confidence in a

Confederate victory even in the face of Southern adversity, while Liberals were much less consistent in their assessment of the outcome of the war.

French newspapers frequently discussed two other major concerns that affected their attitudes toward the Civil War. One was the question of slavery, and the other was the economic impact of the Civil War on the French economy.

Just as Abraham Lincoln said that slavery was "somehow" the cause of the Civil War, so, also, slavery somehow influenced the attitude of Frenchmen toward the American conflict. The role of slavery in determining attitudes is, however, difficult to determine because no Frenchmen publicly defended slavery and every French newspaper claimed to be antislavery. Pro-Northerners continually argued that the North was fighting an anti-slavery crusade and a Northern triumph would result in the extinction of that evil. Pro-Southerners, on the other hand, argued that the North was not genuinely antislavery and had blocked Southern efforts to free their slaves; some concluded that the best way to achieve emancipation was through an independent South! While perhaps the slavery issue strengthened existing pro-North sentiment, the endless debate on slavery and consistent expressions of antislavery sentiment by all elements of the French press suggest that the institution did not so much influence the views of French journalists toward the Civil War, but rather served as a debating device to justify an existing attitude.

The impact of the Civil War on the French economy seems to have played a similar role. In order to raise the blockade and thus secure cotton and restore trade, pro-South newspapers argued for French intervention to end the war on the basis of Southern independence. Pro-North newspapers argued for non-intervention and a Northern victory to achieve precisely the same goals. While economic hardship may well have intensified pro-South sentiment, economic issues probably served as a debating device rather than as an issue that changed journalistic views on the Civil War.

French newspapers described other concerns or interests which they used as justification for their Civil War stance. French national interest, the desirability of a powerful American navy to counterbalance Britain's navy, the presumed racial affinity of Southerners with Frenchmen, the heritage of French assistance in the American Revolution, varying interpretations of the constitutionality of secession, the causes of the war, the legitimacy of a people to seek independence—French journalists discussed these matters and others to elicit support for their stance on the American conflict. Often they used a variety of reasons as explanations for their posture. Typically, their reasons were part of recurring patterns, and a major purpose of this study is to describe those patterns.

Footnotes for citations to French newspapers follow certain forms. First appears the author of an article—if available, since the author was usually but not always given. Then follows the city (in parentheses) where the newspaper was located—except that the city is not given for Parisian newspapers and for provincial newspapers where the name of the city is in the title of the newspaper.

The name of the newspaper is italicized without a definite article. Finally, the footnote includes the date of the newspaper citation.

For assistance in various stages of this project I am grateful to many individuals. Most important were those persons at various institutions that house materials essential for this study: Bibliothèque Nationale at Paris (and the annex at Versailles); Centre Georges Pompidou, Paris; Archives Nationales, Paris; department archives, La Rochelle; Park Library, Central Michigan University (CMU), as well as libraries at the University of Michigan, Michigan State University, and the University of Rochester. Susan Conner, History Department, CMU, xeroxed many essential documents for me at the Archives Nationales, Paris, as did Kathleen Attwood, Bowling Green State University. My daughter, Margaret Blackburn, Maumee Valley Country Day School, Toledo, Ohio, enjoyed correcting her father's French errors. My colleagues at the History Department at CMU critiqued a draft of a portion of the topic. Central Michigan University generously supported the research and writing of this book through sabbatical leaves and research professorships. The Faculty Research and Creative Endeavors Committee at CMU provided financial support for various phases of research. An early study of this topic, "Paris Newspapers and the American Civil War," appeared in *Illinois Historical Journal*, 84 (autumn, 1991), 177–93. Finally, I am especially grateful to my wife, who endured several trips to France for research and who also patiently accepted the endless hours of writing and rewriting.

NOTE

1. Stephen J. Whitfield, "A Century and a Half of French Views of the United States," in *The Historian*, 56 (spring, 1994), 542. Durand Echeverria,"L'Amérique devant l'opinion française, 1734–1870; Questions de méthode et d'interprétation," *Revue d'histoire moderne et contemporaine*, 9 (1962), 60–61. For an historical sketch of French views of Abraham Lincoln, see Cyrille Arnavon, "Images français du Président Lincoln," *Études Anglais*, 12 (January–March, 1959). Arnavon demonstrated clearly that French images of Lincoln varied according to the values and the beliefs of French authors. I am grateful to Professor Mark Neely, of St. Louis University, who informed me of the article and kindly furnished me a copy of it. Further evidence of the relationship between ideology and views about Abraham Lincoln may be found in Gordon S. Boritt, Mark E. Neely, Jr., and Harold Holzer, "The European Image of Abraham Lincoln," *Winterthur Portfolio*, 12 (1986), 153-83.

Chapter 1

France in 1861

> There is no point of collision between the two countries [France and the United States], rather everything in their past history and present relations tend to unite them in bonds of unity.
>
> Napoleon III, 1860

> Controlled, if polite, hostility was the dominating tone of French-American relations as America stepped toward its most anguishing national experience, the War between the States.
>
> Marvin Zahniser[1]

Franco-American diplomacy during the Civil War reflected more than the events in that conflict. By then sporadic clashes and hostility, as well as friendship, characterized their relationship. French reaction to events in the Civil War also reflected the peculiarities of the economic structure and political institutions of the Second Empire under Napoleon III. Finally, French public opinion found expression in newspapers, which possessed certain pronounced characteristics.

Since 1776 many Americans have warmly viewed France with a "Lafayette, we are here" spirit, which reached a peak in World War I. Many Americans have also viewed France with a mixture of anger, distrust, and contempt. During the Charles de Gaulle era, Americans faulted the French as an unfaithful ally and as ungrateful for American contributions to the liberation of France. Such ambivalence is not simply a twentieth-century phenomenon; rather, it was characteristic of American attitudes toward France, as well as French attitudes toward America in the nineteenth century.[2]

Americans were grateful for French assistance during the American Revolution, when the absolutist government of Louis XVI sent arms, munitions, and men to help the Patriot cause. Many Americans then and since that time, in particular during the Civil War era, considered that assistance to be of critical importance in the Patriot triumph.

Nevertheless, less friendly sentiments emerged a few years after American independence. The immediate catalyst was the French Revolution of 1789, which transformed the social and political structure of that country. Americans displayed a range of attitudes toward the stirring events in France. Particularly in the early stages of the French Revolution, followers of Thomas Jefferson were notably sympathetic toward efforts to create more democratic and republican governments, while the more conservative Federalist followers of Alexander Hamilton feared mob rule.

The culminating government of the French Revolutionary era, the Empire under Napoleon, took important actions regarding the United States. Napoleon's sale of Louisiana to America in 1803 guaranteed American greatness, claimed the French emperor; yet, curiously, in the relations between the two powers that action was "unimportant as a bearer of love or hatred, gratitude or regret."[3] Napoleon's Continental System in his war with Great Britain, on the other hand, aroused American anger and nearly led to war with France. During the War of 1812, when both America and France fought against Great Britain, a common foe did not bring about warm feelings between the Napoleonic regime and the United States. Each fought its own separate war.

The end of the Napoleonic wars in 1815 led to the restoration of the old French ruling family, the Bourbons. Americans noted with approval that the government of Louis XVIII did have constitutional aspects. Louis' death in 1824 led to the accession of his brother, Charles X, to the throne. Reactionary and distrustful of democracy, Charles ruled with such a heavy hand, restricting the suffrage and abolishing the secret vote, that Frenchmen rose in revolt in 1830 and threw out the Bourbon leader. The Bourbons never regained power in France, but the Legitimists, as their followers were called, were a force in French political life for many years. In particular, they played a distinctive role in the Civil War era.

As a result of the Revolution of 1830, Louis Philippe, a member of the Orleanist branch of the royal family, ascended to the throne with the support of Lafayette. In that era of Jacksonian democracy, Americans hailed this "glorious revolution"[4] and the strengthening of constitutionalism in France, though Louis Philippe clearly was more concerned about the preservation of public order and private property than extension of democratic principles. In addition, Louis Philippe's wealthy bourgeois supporters were not numerous, the economy did not improve substantially, and his reign was not very exciting. As a result, Louis Philippe's regime fell in the revolutionary disturbances that swept Europe in 1848.

His Orleanist followers still were active during the 1860s, however, and played an important role in French politics.

The democratic revolution of 1848 and the establishment of the Second Republic naturally delighted Americans. Subsequently Americans were keenly disappointed when the President of the Republic, Louis Napoleon, the nephew of the great Napoleon, proclaimed himself Emperor Napoleon III as a result of a *coup d'état* in December, 1851.[5]

The frequent changes of regime in France in the sixty-year period from 1789 to 1851 led many Americans to question the stability of French political institutions. Such a concern affected Americans of whatever views about France, from the Francophiles who admired the clarity and logic of enlightened France to the ardent democrats who decried the lack of constitutionalism and democracy in French government.

Likewise, Frenchmen exhibited a range of views toward America. Was America a model or a *bête noire*? Proponents of democracy pointed to the United States as embodying the beneficial results of democracy, including freedom, the opportunity for individual development, and remarkable economic growth. Conservative Frenchmen, on the other hand, were appalled at what they viewed as secular values, unbridled individualism, mobocracy, and an inevitable descent into anarchy. These political conservatives saw the American Civil War and the disruption of the United States as the long-predicted and inevitable result of democracy. Occupying a middle ground between these two positions, Alexis de Tocqueville and others argued that, whether they approved or disapproved of American democracy, Europeans should study the New World society because it was the wave of the future and would serve as a model for Europe itself.[6]

While ideology influenced attitudes, particular issues also marked the relationship between the two countries. Of primary importance was French assistance during the American Revolution, which was a very lively memory during the Civil War in both France and the United States. Napoleon's sale of Louisiana, as already noted, had little consequence in shaping respective attitudes, although Frenchmen during the Civil War were very much aware of the French heritage in Louisiana and other states, such as South Carolina.

Friction continued after the Bourbon restoration in France, particularly in issues regarding the New World. The United States aggressively expanded at the expense of its neighbors and promoted the independence of the former Spanish colonies in Latin America. At the same time, America sought to exclude European, including French, influence from the New World, a policy that was embodied in the Monroe Doctrine. Strongly resenting the pretensions of that Doctrine, France attempted to block American expansion, for a time seeking to keep Texas independent, meddling in the Oregon question, and formulating plans for intervention in Mexico before the Mexican War, 1846–1848. By the time of that war, French ministers to the United States were warning of the existence of a "unique national instinct that drove Americans to violate the territorial integrity of their neighbors by any suitable means, including conquest, purchase, infiltration, and revolution."[7] In addition, France made no secret of diplomatic efforts in the 1850s to keep Cuba out of American hands. Indeed, the French, alarmed over reports that the United States would expand in Central and South America, explicitly warned the United States that France would not be indifferent to such developments. Predictably, Americans reacted with anger to Napoleon III's efforts to assume guardianship over affairs in the New World.[8]

Partly as a result of conflicts with France, Americans viewed Russia sympathetically during the Crimean War, 1854–1856. A British-French victory in that conflict, Americans feared, might lead the *entente* to police not only the Middle East but other parts of the world as well, including the New World. Thus, on the eve of the Civil War relations between France and the United States were characterized by traditional friendship, multiple points of friction, and divergent ideological attitudes toward democracy and constitutional government.

French reaction to the momentous events of the American Civil War must also be understood in the light of the political institutions of France. The structure of the government under the Second Empire, 1852–1871, was *sui generis*.[9] The background to that regime included the revolution of 1848, which overthrew the rule of Louis Philippe, the subsequent creation of the Second Republic, the election of Louis Napoleon as its president, and finally the *coup d'état* in 1851, which led to the Empire with Louis Napoleon as Emperor Napoleon III. Fearful of excesses of mob rule and enchanted with the magic name of Napoleon, Frenchmen through a plebiscite gave their approval to the creation of the Second Empire.

Despite Napoleon's ceremonial bow toward democracy in utilizing a plebiscite, his enthusiasm for that form of government was restrained. While the constitution which he proclaimed did make provision for universal manhood suffrage in electing the *Corps législatif*, or lower house of the national legislative body, the emperor appointed most members of the more important upper chamber or Senate. In addition, the powers of these legislative bodies were severely limited. They could discuss issues, vote taxes, and recommend legislation, but the Emperor retained an absolute veto over legislative actions. Indeed, the real power of government rested with high administrative officials. Because of the highly personalized style of government in the Second Empire, the roles of Napoleon III and his immediate advisers or cabinet were of critical importance.[10]

Limiting the power of the legislature seems to have been scarcely necessary because the emperor largely controlled elections to the lower chamber through a process of gerrymander and manipulation. Such maneuvers themselves were also unnecessary in view of the popularity of the emperor. The regime was popular for many years because the French people, especially those in rural areas, reveled in the sacred name of Napoleon and had genuine fears of mob rule and disorder.[11]

Despite the emperor's personal popularity, political opposition to his regime emerged over time. While France had no political parties in that era, certainly none in the American sense of that term, persons with common ideas, ideologies, and goals coalesced into various political groups. Such political groups may be classified as 1) supporters and opponents of the regime of Napoleon III or as 2) Liberals and Conservatives.

Conservatives were by no means a simple, homogeneous group. On the far right were the Legitimists, those who wished to restore the Bourbon family to the throne in France. Some very conservative Roman Catholics also favored restoration of the Bourbons.[12] Often the same persons, Legitimists and traditional Roman Catholics made up a reactionary opposition to the government of Napoleon III. The largest number of Conservatives, however, were Imperialists, supporters of Napoleon III and the Second Empire.

Although they held divergent views about the government of Napoleon III, all three Conservative groups held—or came to hold—similar ideas regarding issues relating to the Civil War. All three favored rule by monarchy; all three opposed democracy and, indeed, believed that democracy contained within itself the seeds of its own destruction because of its inevitable degeneration into anarchy. Certain Roman Catholics, in particular, saw American democracy as doomed because it was so profoundly secular. Thus all three of those Conservative groups expected and came to favor a rupture of American democracy, which in practice meant a Southern triumph in the Civil War.[13]

The Liberal political opposition to Napoleon III included three major groups. The Orleanists, followers of the deposed Louis Philippe, favored an orderly, constitutional government with a strong leader. They found much to admire in an America governed by the firm hand of a George Washington; at the same time, though, they were worried about mob tendencies in an unbridled democracy. The Republicans, on the other hand, inheritors of the traditions of 1789 and ever conscious of French contributions to American independence, were unabashed admirers of popular rule and American democracy. Finally, Liberal Catholics, supporters of a free church in a free state, found much to admire in an America characterized by separation of church and state. It is not surprising that the Orleanists typically and Republicans and Liberal Catholics consistently hoped for the success of American democracy, which meant in practice a Northern victory.

Throughout this book the capitalized word "Conservative" will refer to defenders of monarchy and opponents of democracy. In France during the Civil War era Conservatives included Legitimists, supporters of Bourbon restoration; traditional Roman Catholics; and Imperialists, supporters of Napoleon III. The capitalized word "Liberal" will refer to those who favored a democratic or constitutional government, including Orleanists, supporters of the deposed Louis Philippe; Republicans, heirs of the republican tradition of the French Revolution; and Liberal Catholics, supporters of constitutionalism and a free church in a free state.

In addition to ideological filters, Frenchmen viewed the American Civil War in the light of French foreign policy goals. In formulating those goals

Napoleon III played a crucial role. "Historians generally agree," wrote a biographer of the French leader, "that, notwithstanding autonomous foreign and domestic pressures which shaped imperial foreign policy, the major plans and ultimate decisions were the Emperor's."[14] While scholars are by no means unanimous about what motivated that policy, there is substantial agreement on many aspects. Most of all, Napoleon wanted to reestablish French greatness and break the restraints imposed in the peace settlement of 1815.[15] Napoleon III's efforts to promote French influence were notably evident in his efforts to create and support the ill-fated empire of Maximilian in Mexico. This endeavor coincided in time with the American Civil War and absorbed an enormous amount of French official attention.

Napoleon III was also a nineteenth-century nationalist, who genuinely sympathized with the aspirations of people for national self-determination. Thus he intervened more than once to promote Italian unity, advocated Polish independence, and supported efforts to promote German unity. His belief in nationalism was consistent with Southern efforts to create an independent Confederacy.[16]

In addition, Napoleon was interested in exerting French influence and expanding French power outside of Europe. Besides Latin America, France intervened in the Middle East, in the Holy Land and Syria. France's attempts to block Russian expansion in the Middle East led to the Crimean War. France also expanded her colonial empire in Central Africa, in Algeria, and in Indochina.[17] Thus the same Napoleon III who supported nationalism in Europe was also an exponent of Eurocentric colonialism.

In all of these endeavors Napoleon was acutely aware that Frenchmen desired success and *gloire* in foreign policy; triumphs in foreign policy would bring luster—and security—to his regime. Consequently, Napoleon III chose among foreign policy actions those which showed the highest likelihood of success. In practice, this meant that Napoleon could undertake major initiatives only with the support of Great Britain, the dominant naval power. "French policy," observed Case and Spencer in their definitive study of Franco-American relations during the Civil War, "had always been one of only moving in cooperation with the British."[18] Napoleon reportedly complained that "Other countries are my mistresses, but England is my wife."[19] The conflict inherent in these two imperatives—the desire to assert French power and the necessity of acting with Britain—must have been frustrating to Napoleon III during the Civil War, as his desire to help the South foundered against the rock of British reluctance to act.

In all of these diplomatic activities Napoleon III was very much concerned about public opinion. As a result, the autocrat realized and responded to very specific interests of particular French groups. Perhaps the most notable example was Napoleon's retention of French troops in Rome to preserve Papal secular authority in central Italy, an objective much desired by some French Catholics. With his keen awareness of public opinion, it is not surprising that Napoleon acted in response to French economic distress brought about by the Union blockade in the Civil War.

This brief survey of French diplomatic interests and constraints in the first decade of the Second Empire shows that Franco-American relations must be put in context. For both France and the United States, their diplomatic relations on the eve of the Civil War were of minor concern.[20] While the American Civil War was a significant event for French foreign policy, it was but one of many foreign policy issues during the 1860s, and during much of the conflict it was not the most important. In addition, the French government was scarcely a free agent in dealing with issues arising from that conflict.[21]

Besides diplomatic considerations, the particular structure of the French economy and French society affected French attitudes toward the American Civil War. With a stable population of some 38 million persons, France was still essentially an agricultural society. Almost three-fourths lived in rural areas, and over 50 percent of the population derived their income from agriculture. French peasants, who existed barely above the poverty level, scrimped and saved to buy tiny parcels of desperately desired land. As a result, they were a conservative element, willing to accept authoritarian government in return for law and order and the opportunity to purchase land.[22]

While peasants focused their attention on agricultural pursuits, many other Frenchmen were occupied with industrial and commercial activities. These included cotton textile workers, who were clustered in Normandy, Alsace, and northern France. The Union blockade severely affected the cotton textile industry because French industrialists, like their British counterparts, utilized almost exclusively the high-quality cotton produced in the American South. The Civil War also disrupted the American market for such luxury goods as wine, silks, clothes, and perfumes; the important Southern markets were particularly impacted.[23]

The disastrous economic affects of the Civil War were especially distressing because under Napoleon III the French economy had expanded and prospered in the 1850s. Major developments included an extensive program of railroad construction; as a result, today's network of French railroads was basically in place by 1860. In addition, French entrepreneurs actively expanded iron and steel manufacturing. Finally, the French merchant marine industry was important and profitable, as was the ship construction industry.

Napoleon III was very interested in these developments and conspicuously promoted industry through favorable economic policies. With many French city dwellers adversely affected by the Union blockade and—unlike their rural cousins—articulate, interested in politics, and willing to demand government action to relieve their distress, it is not surprising that Napoleon felt constrained to undertake diplomatic initiatives to reduce the economic distress brought on by the Civil War.

Certainly the views of citizens were important during the Second Empire. "Public opinion," observed Lynn Case, "was one of the chief concerns of Napoleon III," who instructed certain officials to report views of his subjects on a variety of topics. The most important of these officials, the *procureurs généraux*, public prosecutors for Imperial courts, were appointed by the minister of justice. The latter specifically charged the prosecutors with accurately reporting the state of public opinion in their jurisdictions. Case reported that the *procureurs* realized the importance of their responsibility and accurately reported public opinion, even when it was opposed to certain government policies. Further, said Case, the Emperor relied upon those reports.[24]

Unlike the reports of the *procureurs*, which were unpublished documents and bear something of a presumption of validity precisely because of their confidentiality, commentary by newspapers was very public, and judgment about the validity of press views requires careful examination. Any study of journalism during this period, for example, must distinguish between the Parisian press and the provincial press. Typically, Paris newspapers provided broader national and international coverage. They also enjoyed far more prestige: Provincial journals frequently quoted Paris sheets; the reverse occurred much less often. In addition they also differed in political orientation and in their treatment of Civil War issues.

Fortunately for historians, the imperial government carefully gathered detailed information about both provincial and Parisian newspapers. The names, political affiliations, and number of subscribers in August, 1861, for Parisian newspapers utilized in this study appear in Table 1.1.[25]

Newspaper supporters of Napoleon III included *Moniteur*, the official organ of the French government, and *Constitutionnel*, *Pays*, and *Patrie*. The latter three were commonly called the "semi-official press," because, while not officially sponsored, they were widely believed to reflect the views of Napoleon III. The French government repeatedly declared that *Moniteur* was the only official journal, and that there were no semi-official journals. Yet one skeptical newspaper said that was perhaps the twentieth such statement in recent years,[26] and repeated references to the "semi-official" press continued during the Civil War. In any event, the "semi-official press," like Napoleon III, opposed Southern secession efforts in the early phases of the conflict. Within a month after the outbreak of hostilities, however, in May, 1861, they changed from support of the Union to support of the Confederacy—a transition which paralleled that of the emperor.[27]

Legitimist and Clerical newspapers, which favored the restoration of the Bourbons to the throne of France and supported conservative Roman Catholic doctrines, were pro-South and also reactionary political opponents of Napoleon III. Such Parisian Legitimist/Clerical journals as *Union* and *Monde* were perhaps more virulently anti-North than they were enthusiastic supporters of the South. Sometimes they applauded specific policies of Napoleon III looking to Southern independence; more often, though, they believed that the emperor should show more initiative and act alone, rather than acting jointly with Great Britain.[28]

Republican or Progressive newspapers advocated the principles of 1789, a free press and constitutional government. Republican journals included *Siècle*, an ardent supporter of the North, whose circulation of 52,000 was the largest of any French newspaper. Equally firm in its support of the North was *Opinion nationale*. Though also devoted to republican ideals, *Presse* was less consistent in its support of the Northern cause.

TABLE 1.1
PARISIAN NEWSPAPERS:
POLITICAL AFFILIATION AND CIRCULATION

Official newspaper		
	Moniteur	17,242
Governmental newspapers		
	Constitutionnel	19,448
	Patrie	22,904
	Pays	7,000
Progressive (Republican) newspapers		
	Opinion nationale	17,252
	Presse	17,740
	Siècle	52,300
Legitimist newspapers		
	Monde	13,982
	Union	7,732
Orleanist newspapers		
	Courrier du dimanche	5,039
	Journal des débats	12,842
	Revue des deux mondes	13,400
	Temps	3,178
Liberal Catholic newspaper		
	Correspondant	3,290

Some pro-North periodicals were Orleanist, that is, supporters of the house of Orleans, one of whose members, Louis Philippe, had been forced to abdicate as a result of the revolution in 1848. *Journal des débats* was the most important Orleanist daily, and *Temps* was strong in its coverage of business activities, while the weekly *Courrier du dimanche* attracted many prominent writers for its columns. *Revue des deux mondes*, a publication that appeared twice a month, was the greatest review in France, if not in the entire world; that review and *Journal* were the principal Orleanist organs. The newspaper spokesman for Liberal Catholics was *Correspondant*. This newspaper was consistently pro-North throughout the Civil War.[29]

Any discussion of the political persuasion of newspapers must be understood in the light of the close relationship between politics and journalism during the Second Empire. Newspapers extensively reported and analyzed political events in very partisan terms. Indeed, specific newspapers were widely viewed as spokesmen for particular political factions or leaders. Some journalists actively engaged in political life, with a few even elected to the *corps législatif* in the 1863 elections. Newspapers and political organizations were similar in terms of their constituencies. Political parties in the American sense of that phrase simply did not exist; rather, politically active persons coalesced around relatively small factions. Likewise, French newspapers had a small number of subscribers, thus reflecting the views of a comparatively small number of persons. Finally, the relationship between journalism and politics is demonstrated by the 1863 election for members of the *corps législatif.* Parisians voted overwhelmingly for opponents of the government. Liberal opponents of Napoleon III in Paris enjoyed a substantial margin over their Conservative peers, both in numbers of newspapers and numbers of subscribers. In rural areas, the vast majority of newspapers were supporters of the regime, and the 1863 elections were a landslide for followers of Napoleon III.[30]

As the compilation of Parisian newspapers shows, individual Parisian political newspapers did not enjoy a large number of subscribers. The twenty-two political journals in Paris sold 236,000 copies daily in 1861; circulation was one million in 1870. *Siècle*, an opposition paper, could claim 52,000 subscribers, by far the largest circulation of any Parisian newspaper, while other important journals scarcely had 5,000.[31] The number of subscribers was not the only measure of a newspaper's influence, however. Though difficult to calculate, readership was much broader than circulation. A journalist was "very celebrated" when his paper had a circulation of 7,000–8,000 copies.[32] Nor did a low number of subscribers reflect a lack of interest in current issues; French street popular opinion has always been spirited and influential.

Regardless of their circulation, Parisian newspapers shared certain characteristics. They were four-page journals with international and national news featured on the first two pages, often local news and government reports on the third page, and advertisements on the fourth. Editors frequently filled their columns with copies of official reports, including verbatim extracts of the proceedings of the *corps législatif.* Newspapers also utilized "scissors and paste" techniques, copying extensively from other newspapers. Along with quoting other newspapers, sharp-tongued journalists engaged in frequent polemics with one another. This characteristic was helpful in determining attitudes toward Civil War issues, since Parisian newspapers explicitly described sharp differences of opinion with colleagues about American events. *Opinion nationale*, for example, virtually read fellow Republican *Presse* out of the Progressive fellowship of Parisian newspapers, charging that *Presse* had strayed from devotion to the Union cause on too many occasions.[33]

Whatever their views on the conflict, Paris newspapers made significant efforts to report the Civil War. Often they copied articles that had appeared in American newspapers.[34] At irregular intervals certain journals printed long letters from American correspondents. All Paris newspapers published signed columns of opinion about the American conflict. Each had a *Bulletin du jour* or its equivalent, which interpreted and summarized major news stories, and which frequently treated Civil War events and issues.

During the course of the conflict, Parisian newspapers varied in the amount of space they devoted to Civil War questions. While specific events, such as a battle, a Presidential proclamation, or an election, elicited discussion, nevertheless coverage was most extensive in the first two years of the war. The "interminable" war was "a little forgotten" in 1863 and 1864, when French diplomatic activity in relation to the war also declined, though interest and coverage increased again toward the end of the war. Grant's Wilderness campaign, *Presse* reported, profoundly moved Europe. "The wars of Marius and of Sulla, of Pompey and of Caesar, of Mark Anthony and of Augustus," the newspaper remarked, "have not offered an interest as powerful."[35] The assassination of Abraham Lincoln fascinated Frenchmen, and for days column after column described the assassination and the funeral in painstaking detail.

While the provincial press was very similar to Paris journals in format, provincial newspapers differed from their Parisian counterparts in many ways. Certainly they did not enjoy as much prestige. The hinterland journals, related an historian of the press during the Second Empire, were "uniformly gray and governmental," "provincial, ignorant of political questions, distrustful in regard to foreign policy, and without personality." Lucien Prévost-Paradol, a prominent contemporary Parisian journalist, sneered that "We read, for example, in some newspaper of the North, *The disastrous effects*, we continue in a newspaper of the Center *of parliamentary government* and we finish in a newspaper of the South *are felt in England.*"[36]

Some provincial journals, however, did enjoy star status in journalistic circles. *Phare de la Loire,* at Nantes, epitomized Republican sentiments and was frequently cited by the Paris press. Liberal *Gironde* of Bordeaux, reportedly with the largest circulation of any provincial newspaper, "has greatly favored our [Union] side. . . . and made many friends" for the North, reported the American consul at Bordeaux.[37] Certain Lyons and Marseille newspapers, among others, also enjoyed national stature.

Republican *Phare* and Liberal *Gironde* were not typical of provincial newspapers, which were overwhelming conservative in their political stance. A government document from the early 1860s lists 262 provincial political newspapers, of which only 60 were opposition journals. The 202 governmental journals counted 207,071 subscribers. For the opposition, the thirteen Orleanist newspapers claimed 20,069 subscribers; thirty-four Legitimist, 31,134; thirteen Republican, 22,981. Thus there was not only a small number of opposition journals in the provinces; in addition, the very conservative Legitimist newspapers (which also included Clerical) enjoyed the largest number of opposition journals and largest circulation among the opposition. The sixty opposition newspapers were housed in only thirty-five of the eighty-eight departments. Each of twenty departments had one opposition journal; nine had two opposition journals; four (Côte d'Or, Côtes du Nord, Meurthe, Yonne) had three opposition journals; one (Gironde, which included the city of Bordeaux) had four; another (the heavily industrialized Nord) had six opposition journals. In the eighty-eight departments all had at least one governmental journal, except for one department (Hautes Alpes) with no political newspaper at all and two (Bas Rhin and Sarthe) where there were opposition journals but no supporter of Napoleon III.[38] Thus the provincial newspapers were overwhelmingly conservative, with opposition newspapers in less than one-half the departments, and most of the opposition newspapers were of the very conservative Legitimist persuasion.

Just as opposition journals reflected Parisian opinion, provincial journals reflected the views of their readers with most of the Liberal provincial journals located in cities, where the opposition tended to cluster. Scholars agree that the countryside and small towns were strongholds of support for the government of Napoleon III.

Finally, provincial newspapers were less ideologically pure—or more pragmatic and flexible—than Parisian newspapers. One Clerical editor quite frankly stated that he did not care which side won the Civil War; he was only interested in the abolition of slavery.[39] Certain provincial journals switched support in 1862. Early in the year, as Union general George McClellan advanced on Richmond and the North seemed on the verge of victory, they were enthusiastic supporters of the Union. Later in the year, as Confederate general Robert E .Lee invaded the North and the South seemed on the verge of victory, the same editors became enthusiastic supporters of the South.[40] There was no such comparable switch among the more consistent Paris journals.

But how accurately did these provincial and Parisian newspapers reflect French public opinion? Lynn Case, co-author of the definitive study of Franco-American diplomacy during the Civil War, claimed that the press was "an even sorrier instrument for registering popular thought" than the packed, shackled, legislative body. Not only was the press subject to government censorship and control, but it was also thoroughly corrupt. According to Case, "Nearly all writers and journals had their price." Further, charged Case, if Liberal journalists praised Northern democracy, it was only for the purpose of criticizing by implication the autocratic government of Louis Napoleon.[41] Hence, Case concluded that "Any resemblance between press opinion and public opinion was largely coincidental." Thus, Case's assertion that the French press did not accurately reflect French opinion regarding Civil War issues rests upon three arguments: 1) the press was not free, 2) the press was corrupt, and 3) the press utilized Civil War issues for domestic political reasons.

In regard to the first point—that the French journalists were not free to print as they wished—it is clear that the government did exercise considerable control over the press. Newspapers could not attack the state, the principles of the government, or the dynasty.[42] Government approval was necessary for the establishment of new newspapers and the appointment of editors. The government had the authority to censor the press, and through administrative action to issue warnings to the press for journalistic "irresponsibility," usually for defaming an official acting in his official capacity. Three such warnings led to a two-month suspension. Administrative officials issued five such warnings to Parisian newspapers in 1861, six in 1862, twelve in 1863, five in 1864, and nine in 1865.[43] Suspensions and warnings, it should be noted, were far more common in the provinces than in Paris. As a result of these restrictions, freedom of the press, charged the Liberal *Siècle*, was "only a dream."[44]

The press was far more free than a mere reading of the law indicates, however, and the government found it impossible or unwise to utilize all possible legal weapons to control the press. Only one Parisian newspaper was actually suspended during the Civil War; *Courrier du dimanche* suffered this penalty for two months on two occasions.[45] Limited use of suspension led one scholar to hypothesize that suspension was not effective in controlling the press, especially when the owner was wealthy. Indeed, instead of employing the threat of massive repression, the government approved two avowedly opposition papers on the eve of the Civil War—*Courrier* in 1858 and *Temps* in 1861—as a device to dilute opposition influence. It is even possible that Napoleon III may have found an opposition press useful. The existence of anti-Clerical newspapers, especially *Siècle* with the largest number of subscribers of any French newspaper, may have been a not-so-subtle hint to Roman Catholics that they needed Napoleon III on the throne of France to stem anticlerical assaults.[46]

Even the frequent and extended discussions about the desirability of freedom of the press provide intrinsic evidence of press freedom. While complaints about restrictions on the press provide transparent evidence of limitations on freedom of expression, nevertheless, repeated demands for more freedom also provide palpable evidence that journalists felt free to criticize the government's press policy.

Explicitly taking cognizance of political criticism, the Minister of State, Eugène Rouher, one of Napoleon III's most influential advisers, provided persuasive evidence that editors were free to express their opinions. Sounding like a modern Washington official grumbling about negative media coverage, Rouher complained that of the twenty political Parisian newspapers, sixteen belonged to the "most ardent opposition," while two defended the government "resolutely and sincerely"; for one or two newspapers, he said, it was necessary every morning to resolve the enigma whether they were friends of the government.[47]

Finally the specific restrictions by the Second Empire on the press—no criticism of the state, the principles of the government, or the dynasty—may, paradoxically, have encouraged French journalists to devote attention to Civil War issues that were not subject to restrictions. Indeed, one prominent journalist of the time, Lucien Prévost-Paradol, complained that the provincial press for reasons of security avoided discussion of local matters and focused on European and world matters.[48] A student of French attitudes toward slavery suggests that French newspapers, restricted in their coverage of domestic issues, found a certain liberty of discussion on the problem of slavery in America, which encouraged treatment of that issue.[49] Certainly the most superficial examination of French newspapers demonstrates that they expressed openly and often a wide variety of views about the American Civil War.

Finally, a wry comment by a French journalist highlights a universal truth about a journalist's freedom of expression. "For a writer," claimed this journalist writing in a Conservative organ,

> if one wishes to speak truly in good faith, there is only one day, there is only one hour of absolute personal liberty. It is the day, it is the hour when, after long and sincere reflections, he makes, in full knowledge of the situation, the choice of a newspaper where he wishes to write.[50]

It would be fair to conclude that French editors or owners of newspapers, restrained as they were in treating domestic questions, felt free to discuss Civil War issues. Indeed, for the very reason that there were restraints on discussion of domestic issues, French editors were more likely to express their views on the American conflict.

A second reason for Case's assertion that French newspapers were a "sorry instrument" for registering public opinion rests upon his charges of journalistic corruption. Certainly both the Union and the Confederacy made efforts to influence French journalists. In May, 1861, William L. Dayton, American minister to France, requested the appointment of a consul in Paris to devote himself to cultivating the French press, which he thought was hostile to American interests. "If a little money were judiciously expended here," he wrote to Washington, "it would go far to put public sentiment right in certain quarters." Subsequently John Bigelow, an experienced journalist, was appointed American consul at Paris.[51]

The Confederacy also sought to influence the French press. Edwin de Leon was the first of two Confederate propaganda agents in France. Arriving in France in July, 1862, he "lavished funds on a venal press," according to Charles Cullop's study of Confederate propaganda. By September, 1862, de Leon reported that Parisian and provincial semi-official journals supported the Southern cause. He also reported awarding "a handsome subsidy" to Felix Aucaigne, editor of the Paris *Patrie*, a Conservative newspaper that reputedly served as a Confederate publicity organ until early 1864.[52]

Yet Cullop's evidence scarcely proves that bribery influenced the French press in their treatment of Civil War issues. The Parisian semi-official press had become pro-South in mid-1861, *Patrie* included, long before de Leon arrived in France. In fact, *Patrie* became even more virulently pro-South in 1865, many months after that journal was no longer fulfilling its alleged role as a Confederate publicity organ. Most of the Governmental provincial press was pro-South before the summer of 1862; as will be seen later, some provincial journals did switch allegiance in 1862, but military operations in that year provide a more than adequate explanation for that change.[53]

Felix Aucaigne is an egregious example of a corrupt journalist, yet his sins of venality do not show that bribery changed an editorial position. When his subsidy from the Confederates dropped substantially, Aucaigne went to John Bigelow, then American minister to France, and offered *Patrie* to the Federal cause. Bigelow refused the offer because, he explained, *Patrie* was defending slavery, precisely "the issue we wished to make." Since Confederate money "did our work so satisfactorily," Bigelow said that it was not worth his while to spend his money on *Patrie*. Bigelow had at least three conversations with Aucaigne and in a book he described the conversations under the title of "Newspaper parasites." He also told of refusing an offer to purchase one-half a Clerical journal and lending the editor 50,000 francs; Bigelow explained that "our government allowed nothing for such purposes. . . ."[54] Bigelow, however, did encourage and subsidize the publication of pamphlets by pro-Union advocates.

A second Confederate propaganda agent, Henry Hotze, did not attempt bribery of the French press; rather, he persuaded officials of the Havas news agency to distribute news concerning the South and the Civil War that Hotze furnished. Hotze first had the news published in a British newspaper, and Havas subsequently distributed the news to French newspaper without any pecuniary consideration.[55]

It seems clear that venality is not a good explanation for the editorial stance of Parisian newspapers toward the Civil War issues. In fact, Parisian newspapers rather consistently followed their political ideology in expressing their sympathies in the conflict. Changes in their views regarding the outcome of the conflict can be understood in the light of events in America.[56]

Finally, Case charged that Liberal French journalistic views did not reflect their genuine opinion on Civil War issues; rather, they praised American democracy as a device to criticize indirectly the autocratic regime of Napoleon III. It is true that one can find examples of praise for American democracy, particularly in the columns of the very Liberal *Siècle* and *Journal du dimanche*. Yet the Civil War issue that dominated discussion was the slavery question. When discussing the Civil War, pro-Northern papers cited *sans cesse* the slavery issue. Ceaseless harping on the slavery issue, which pro-Northern journalists emphasized far more often than the virtues or faults of democracy, suggests that Liberal journalists were seeking support from anti-slavery Frenchmen rather than merely trying to make points against an autocratic French regime.[57] In any event, not all discussions of the American conflict by Liberal journals were motivated by a desire to discredit the government of Napoleon III. Even a cursory examination of the files of French newspapers reveals countless examples of very frank discussion and bitter controversies about specific Civil War issues that had no relevance to French politics.

At heart the question raised by Case can be stated simply: How genuine were the views of French newspapers regarding the Civil War? Any answer to that question must take into account the fact that journalistic stances on Civil War issues typically were related to their orientation on internal French political issues. Pro-Southern journals held distinct political orientations: either they were 1) Conservative supporters of Napoleon III, 2) Legitimist supporters of a Bourbon restoration, and/or 3) conservative Clerical supporters of the Roman Catholic church. Pro-Northern journals held equally distinct political orientations: 1) supporters of Republican principles of 1789; 2) Orleanists, who favored restoration of the deposed house of Orleans to the throne; and 3) Liberal Catholics.[58]

The relative consistency of French journalists provides convincing evidence that expressions of opinion regarding the Civil War were genuine. In addition, the general political stance of French newspapers—largely Liberal in Paris and Conservative in the provinces—is evidence that the views of French newspapers about the Civil War roughly reflected the views of their subscribers.

A French scholar provided a succinct judgment on the role of the press. The French press, he wrote, "became in the nineteenth century the principle means of molding public opinion." Its political importance was judged to be so great, he claimed, that governmental efforts to control it did not cease until 1878.[59]

NOTES

1. Napoleon III made the remark in a conversation with Charles J. Faulkner, American minister to France, on October 6, 1860; Faulkner to Cass, Paris, October 8, 1860, quoted in Lynn M. Case and Warren F. Spencer, *The United States and France: Civil War Diplomacy* (Philadelphia, University of Pennsylvania Press, 1970), p. 19. Marvin R. Zahniser, *Uncertain Friendship: American-French Diplomatic Relations Through the Cold War* (New York, Wiley, 1975), p. 124.

2. Ambivalent American attitudes toward France are the major theme of Crane Brinton, *The Americans and the French* (Cambridge, Harvard University Press, 1968). Yves-Henri Nouailhat, "Franco-American Relations: French Perspectives," in *Reviews in American History,* 14 (December, 1986), 663, stated that "the history of Franco-American relations is that of an alternation between great moments of enthusiasm and affection, all the more outstanding since they have been short, and long periods of resentment, crises, and disappointments." Jean-Baptiste Duroselle, *France and the United States: From the Beginnings to the Present Day* (Chicago, University of Chicago Press, 1976), pp. 46–82, described "A Century of Distant Relations (1815–1914)." Zahniser, *Uncertain Friendship*, and Henry Blumenthal, *A Reappraisal of Franco-American Relations, 1830–1871* (Chapel Hill, University of North Carolina Press, 1959) and *France and the United States; Their Diplomatic Relations, 1789–1914* (Chapel Hill, University of North Carolina Press, 1970), emphasized conflicts between France and the United States. Henry Blumenthal, *American and French Culture, 1800–1900: Interchange in Art, Science, Literature, and Society* (Baton Rouge, Louisiana State University Press, 1975), p. 483, noted that while government-to-government relations were usually strained, person-to-person interactions between Frenchmen and Americans "worked out beautifully." In a recent survey, Stephen J. Whitfield, "A Century and a Half of French Views of the United States," *The Historian*, 56 (spring, 1994), 531–42, emphasized fluctuations between approval and disapproval on the part of Frenchmen toward the United States.

3. Brinton, *The Americans and the French*, p. 56. In the summer of 1862, Edouard Laboulaye, a noted writer and ardent friend of American democracy, wrote two articles in the *Journal des débats*, which were subsequently published in pamphlet form by John Bigelow, American consul at Paris. In the pamphlets Laboulaye quoted Napoleon as saying "In ceding Louisiana, I strengthen forever the power of the United States, and give to England a rival upon the sea, which sooner or later shall abase her pride." Laboulaye was arguing for French neutrality in the Civil War and urging France to remain faithful to "the grand traditions of Louis XVI and of Napoleon." John Bigelow, *Retrospections of an Active*

Life (5 vols., New York, The Baker & Taylor Co., 1909–1913), I, 535.

4. Blumenthal, *France and the United States, 1789–1914*, p. 47.

5. Henry Casper, *American Attitudes toward the Rise of Napoleon III* (Washington, D.C., Catholic University of America Press, 1947).

6. Guy Sorman, "United States Model or Bête Noire?" in Denis Lacorne, Jacques Rupnik, and Marie-France Toinet, *The Rise and Fall of Anti-Americanism: A Century of French Perception* (New York, St. Martin's Press, 1990), pp. 213–18. A similar view may be found in René Rémond, *Les États-Unis devant l'opinion française, 1815–1852* (2 vols., Paris, A. Colin, 1962), cited in Nouailhat, "Franco-American Relations," 654–65. Alexis de Tocqueville, *Democracy in America* (2 vols., New York, Vintage Books, 1990). One of the most influential of pro-American intellectuals in France during the Civil War, Edouard Laboulaye, is perhaps best known for his role in raising funds for the Statue of Liberty. Laboulaye wrote a history of the United States praising American political institutions; he was a leading figure in the Liberal opposition to the Second Empire. Walter D. Gray, "Liberalism in the Second Empire and the Influence of America: Edouard Laboulaye and His Circle," in Joseph Klaits and Michael H. Haltzel, *Liberty/Liberté: The American and French Experiences* (Baltimore, Johns Hopkins University Press, 1991), pp. 71–85. For French sentiment critical of America, see David Strauss, *Menace in the West: The Rise of French Anti-Americanism in Modern Times* (Westport, CT, Greenwood Press, 1978).

7. Blumenthal, *France and the United States*, p. 63.

8. *Ibid.*, pp. 64, 67. For an example of French anger over American efforts to expand in Latin America, see M. F. Belly, "La Question de l'Isthme Américain, épisode de l'histoire de notre temps," in *Revue des deux mondes*, July 15, 1860, 328–68.

9. Roger Magraw, *France 1815–1914: The Bourgeois Century* (New York, Oxford University Press, 1986), p. 164, stated that the "regime's political system was *sui generis*, without contemporary European parallel."

10. For a discussion of the roles of the legislative bodies and ministers of the emperor, see Alain Plessis, *The Rise and Fall of the Second Empire, 1852–1871* (Cambridge, Cambridge University Press, 1985), pp. 25–42, and J. M. Thompson, *Louis Napoleon and the Second Empire* (New York, W. W. Norton & Company, 1967), pp. 244–45.

11. Plessis, *Second Empire*, pp. 23–24, 38.

12. For the role of French Legitimism, see Steven D. Kale, *Legitimism and the Reconstruction of French Society, 1852–1883* (Baton Rouge, Louisiana State University Press, 1992), and Robert R. Locke, *French Legitimists and the Politics of Moral Order in the Early Third Republic* (Princeton, Princeton University Press, 1972).

13. Donald Bellows, "A Study of British Conservative Reaction to the American Civil War," *Journal of Southern History*, LI (November, 1985), 506–26, found a similar pattern in Britain, where conservatives reacted ideologically to Southern secession. Because of their views of history and their political values, they believed that democracy, a defective form of government that led to anarchy and despotism, had caused such turmoil and violence as secession and civil war. As a result, British conservatives favored the Confederate cause.

14. Alan B. Spitzer, "The Good Napoleon III," in *French Historical Studies*, II (spring, 1961), 324.

15. William H. C. Smith, *Napoleon III: The Pursuit of Prestige* (London, Collins & Brown, 1991).

16. Case and Spencer, *Civil War Diplomacy*, p. 597.

17. For concise accounts of Napoleon's early foreign policy, see George P. Gooch, *The Second Empire* (London, Longmans, 1960), pp. 20–26, and J. M. Thompson, *Louis Napoleon and the Second Empire* (New York, W. W. Norton, 1967), chs. VI, VII.

18. Case and Spencer, *United States and France*, p. 335.

19. Unfortunately for the Emperor, France needed Britain more than Britain needed France. Smith, *Napoleon III*, p. 75.

20. For France, the United States in 1860 was not as important as it had been in the past because it was "no longer the great counterweight, the balancing force against Britain" while European matters were far more important. When Henri Mercier, French minister at Washington during the Civil War, learned of his appointment to that position, he was "thunderstruck . . . thrown into gloom" at an assignment to a "distant and fruitless" country. In American eyes, France in 1860 "had become a sort of minor irritant, an imperial monarchy whose friendship with Great Britain and dabbling in Latin America could annoy the expanding republic but not threaten her life"; Daniel B. Carroll, *Henri Mercier and the American Civil War* (Princeton, Princeton University Press, 1971), pp. 3–4, 8–9.

21. Thompson, *Napoleon and the Second Empire*, p. 216, made but a passing reference to the Civil War, simply noting that Napoleon could intervene in Mexico because of American preoccupation with internal differences and difficulties with Britain.

The more important role of other European countries in French eyes was reflected in newspaper treatment of foreign topics. In France, German topics received more coverage, no doubt because of geographic proximity. Jürgen Wilke, "Foreign News Coverage and International News Flow over Three Centuries," in *International Journal for Mass Communication Studies*, 39 (1987), 147–80.

22. Plessis, *Second Empire*, pp. 58, 105.

23. For a discussion of the French economy during the Second Empire, see Plessis, *Second Empire*, pp. 58–97.

24. Lynn M. Case, *French Opinion on the United States and Mexico, 1860–1867: Extracts from the Reports of Procureurs Généraux* (Hamden, CT, Archon Books, 1969), pp. ix–xx.

25. The compilation is based on an undated manuscript in Archives Nationales, F18 295, which classified Parisian newspapers in five groups. (The government document classified the Liberal Catholic *Correspondant* in the same category as the Legitimist and ultramontane newspapers.) The document gives circulations for October, 1860 and August 22, 1861. The following are the 1861 figures:

Official journal: 17,242
Governmental newspapers: 52,832
Progressive newspapers: 91,292
Legitimist and ultramontane newspapers: 38,285
Orleanist and liberal newspapers: 36,859

Claude Bellanger et al., *Histoire générale de la presse française (5 vols., Paris, 1969–76)*, II (1969), 259–60, gave identical figures and cited the same Archives Nationales source.

26. "Bulletin du jour," *Temps*, November 1, 1861.

27. For the change in position of the "semi-official" press, see W. Reed West, *Contemporary French Opinion on the American Civil War* (Baltimore, Johns Hopkins University Press, 1924), pp. 26–30.

28. David Pinkney, "France and the Civil War," pp. 99, 105–108, cited various reasons for pro-Confederate sentiment. They included anti-Northern or anti-American sentiments: desire for the failure of American democracy as a vindication of Napoleon's authoritarian regime, fear that the Union would be hostile to the French intervention in Mexico, opposition to liberal democracy, and hostility to the presumed arrogance and claims of superiority by the United States. Pro-Southern reasons included support for self-determination, belief in the social superiority of Southerners, and admiration for gallant Southern warriors. Economic reasons included cotton shortages and loss of American

markets.

29. *Ibid.*, p. 111–15, summarized reasons for pro-Northern attitudes: hostility to slavery, belief in America as a model for free governments everywhere, Liberal Catholic support for a free church in a free state, use of a powerful United States as a maritime makeweight against Britain, and a cloak to attack the government of Napoleon III.

30. Francis Choisel, "La presse française face aux réformes de 1860," [the French press in relation to the reforms of 1860] in *Revue d'histoire moderne et contemporaine*, 27 (1980), 374–90, showed the close relationship between journalism and politics. Journalists reacted to the reforms of 1860, which gave the press more liberty of expression, along ideological lines. The Liberal press was profuse in its praise of the reforms; the Clerical press was silent on the substance of the reforms but criticized the reaction of Liberals. While the Conservatives treated the reforms as not without importance, they viewed them as the "better crowning the good."

31. The Minister of State, Eugène Rouher, based his analysis on twenty political Parisian newspapers; Grenier, *Pays*, December 19, 1863. For circulation figures from 1857 to 1863 based on government documents, see Pierre Albert, Gilles Feyel, Jean-François Picard, *Documents pour l'histoire de la presse nationale aux xixe et xxe siècle* (Paris, Centre de Documentation Sciences Humaines, n. d.), pp. 28–30, and Claude Belllanger et al., *Histoire générale de la presse française* (5 vols., Paris, 1969–75), II, (1969), 259–60. The population of Paris was 1,050,000 in 1846 and 1,800,000 in 1866.

32. For discussion of this point, see Roger Bellet, *Presse et journalism sous le Second Empire* (Paris, Colin, 1967), pp. 33–34.

33. Malespine, *Opinion nationale*, May 8, 1865.

34. Until 1864, American newspapers, the major source of information about the Civil War, took approximately two weeks to reach Paris, traveling via Great Britain. In June, 1864, with the establishment of direct postal service between France and America the time was cut to ten to twelve days. *Constitutionnel*, June 17, 1864.

35. *Pays*, March 23, 1864, complained of the "interminable" war. Bédollière, *Siècle*, March 16, 1863, claimed that Europeans turned to the Polish question because the North refused to take a stand of principle against slavery. *Siècle* was strongly anti-slavery. "Bulletin du jour," *Temps*, February 10, 1863, said that Poland always attracted the principal attention among foreign questions. Chatard, *Presse*, June 18, 1864, spoke highly of Sherman.

36. Bellet, *Presse sous le Second Empire*, p. 101; the quotation by Prévost-Paradol is from *Journal du Dimanche*, September 24, 1858, quoted in Bellet, p. 102.

37. C. Davisson to William Dayton, Bordeaux, July 24, 1863, quoted in Carl L. Lokke, "A Consular Report from Bordeaux: July, 1863," in *French Historical Studies*, 1 (1958), 102.

38. This analysis is based on a document in Archives Nationales, F18 294; the document is undated but undoubtedly dates from the early 1860s. Extremely useful for this study, the document lists newspapers by department, besides giving the name of each newspaper, the number of subscribers, and its political orientation (*Gouvernementaux*, *Orléaniste*, *Légitimiste*, and *Républicaine*).

39. Cumot, (Angers) *Ami du Peuple*, March 5, 1862.

40. Perroud, (Le Puy) *Moniteur de la Haute-Loire*, November 15, 1862, quite frankly stated that his newspaper had supported the North early in the war when it seemed to be winning; now events had shown that it was wrong. One should not argue with facts, added the editor.

41. Case and Spencer, *Civil War Diplomacy*, p. 605; Case, *French Opinion on War and Diplomacy during the Second Empire* (New York, Octagon Books, 1972), pp. x–xi. Serge Gavronsky, in *The French Liberal Opposition and the American Civil War* (New York, Humanities Press, 1968), argued the thesis that French liberals supported the North as a means of striking at the autocratic government of Napoleon III.

42. Francis Choisel, "La presse française face aux réformes de 1860," [the French press in relation to the reforms of 1860] in *Revue d'histoire moderne et contemporaine*, 27 (1980), 375.

43. For an extended treatment of government control of the press, see Irene Collins, *The Government and the Newspaper Press in France, 1814–81* (London, 1959), particularly pp. 118, 119, 125; Bellanger, *Histoire générale*, II, 249–53, 313–14; and Robert Justin Goldstein, *Censorship of Political Caricature in Nineteenth-Century France* (Kent, OH, Kent State University Press, 1989).

44. Jordan, *Siècle*, January 25, 1864.

45. *Courrier* complained that the second suspension was unfair and illegal since it was suspended twice on the basis of the same two warnings. For a report of the counsel on that issue, see the beginning of the microfilm roll for the year 1864, Bibliothèque Nationale; for the decree suspending the newspaper and a comment by the newspaper, see March 6, 1864. Collins, *Government and Press*, pp. 119, 125.

46. One government report explained that the regime approved the establishment of numerous rivals for the purpose of diminishing the importance of the great journals; quoted in Bellanger, *Histoire générale*, II, 318.

47. Grenier, *Pays*, December 19, 1863, claimed that it and *Constitutionnel* were the resolute defenders. For criticism of government policy during the war, see, for example, Millerin, *Courrier*, May 7, 1865. Delord, *Siècle*, October 7, 1863, explicitly criticized Imperial policy by charging that the French government was too disposed to undertake mediation and intervention.

48. Bellanger, *Histoire générale*, II, 264.

49. Barbara Karsky, "Les libéraux français et l'émancipation des esclaves aux États-Unis, 1852–1870," in *Revue d'histoire moderne et contemporaine*, 21 (1974), 575.

50. Grenier, *Pays*, December 19, 1863. A modern historian agreed that journalists suffered from a "narrow subordination," which was imposed by the hierarchical organization of journalism and considerably reinforced during the Second Empire; Marc Martin, "Journalistes parisiens et notoriété (vers 1830–1870)" [Parisian journalists and reputation (around 1830–870)], in *Revue historique*, 266 (1981), 73.

51. Beckles Willson, *America's Ambassadors to France* (New York, Frederick D. Stakes, 1928), pp. 262–63.

52. Charles Cullop, *Confederate Propaganda in Europe* (Coral Gables, FL, University of Miami Press, 1969), pp. 73–74, 119.

53. Frank Owsley, *King Cotton Diplomacy* (Chicago, The University of Chicago Press, 1931), pp. 182–85.

One scholar examined the question of the venality of the press in connection with the movement to abolish slavery in the French colonies, which occurred in 1848. In discussing planter efforts to bribe Paris newspapers into opposing abolition, he concluded that the press then was "blatantly venal"—with exceptions. While center, right-of-center, and monarchist newspapers succumbed to bribery by the planters, most liberal, leftist, or republican journals were "impervious" to efforts to bribe them to defend the slavery cause. Lawrence C. Jennings, "Slavery and the Venality of the July Monarchy Press," in *French Historical Studies*, 17 (July, 1992), 977–78.

54. Bigelow, *Retrospections*, II, 161, 165–66, 191–92.

55. Owsley, *King Cotton Diplomacy,* pp. 182–85.

56. David H. Pinkney, "France and the Civil War," in Harold Hyman, ed., *Heard Round the World: The Impact Abroad of the Civil War* (New York, Knopf, 1969), p. 108, wrote that both Union and Confederate officials attempted to influence French public opinion. John Bigelow, a journalist and consul at Paris, used various devices, including bribery, to plant articles and books. Confederate officials were much less effective, claimed Pinkney; Edwin de Leon wasted $25,000 in Paris. Henry Hotze, a Southern propaganda officer in London, was more successful; he supplied the Havas news agency with news stories favorable to the South. Blumenthal, *Franco-American Relations*, p. 133, cited evidence that while both Northern and Southern officials in Paris compensated certain members of the press, it would, he asserted, "obviously be improper" to charge the entire French press with intellectual prostitution.

57. For a contrary view, see Karsky, "Les libéraux français et l'émancipation des esclaves aux États-Unis," p. 576, who reported that antislavery writers put implicitly in parallel the violation of human rights by slavery and the repression of liberty in France by imperial institutions. Thus, the French scholar argued, the Liberals used the antislavery debate as an arm in the battle against an autocratic regime.

58. Views on the Civil War rested largely on long- standing political views, claimed Blumenthal: Liberal and Republican newspapers supported the North, while Conservative and Clerical newspapers supported the South. *Franco-American Relations*, p. 133.

59. Marc Martin, "Journalistes parisiens et notoriété (vers 1830–1870)," in *Revue historique*, 266 (1981), p. 31. Martin conceded that the importance of the press was "overestimated without doubt." He noted that journalists were respected neither by the French aristocracy nor by the government, who distrusted both journalism and democracy.

Chapter 2

The 1860 Election and Secession

> The South is right [in asserting] that the North has violated the Constitution. It is the North which is revolutionary, but in the best sense of word; the North has continued the revolution as the founders of the Republic intended, while the South has turned its back against the Revolution and deceived the hopes of 1776.
>
> Martin, *Constitutionnel*, January 24, 1861

> The first acts of Lincoln are as indecisive as his words. . . . The majority of independent American newspapers have levied judgments on Lincoln more severe than ours.
>
> Gaillardet, *Presse*, March 18, 1861

From the summer of 1860 until the end that year, the period from the political conventions until after the presidential election in November, French newspapers agreed that the major issue which divided the North and the South was the issue of slavery; likewise, Frenchmen concurred in hoping—and expecting—that Americans could successfully resolve their internal differences. With the secession of Southern states in the early months of 1861, Lincoln's inauguration in March, and the actual outbreak of hostilities soon after, French journalistic opinion became sharply divided. Liberal and Orleanist journals continued to express sympathy for the North, while Governmental and Legitimist journals now expressed sympathy for the South. Almost all did agree in the summer and fall of 1861, however, that the American Union was irreversibly sundered.

Devoting much less space to United States than to Europe, French newspapers nevertheless provided modest coverage of the American scene during the summer of 1860. This coverage prominently featured differences among Americans. Those from the North, explained a Liberal journalist, were descended from Puritans and were cold and pacific; indeed, Quakers were avowed pacifists. Persons from Virginia were descended from cavaliers, while those from Louisiana and Florida were of French and Spanish ancestry. More recent migrations populated the West, with the frontiersmen possessing a "warm head" and a bellicose temperament. They held the plow in one hand and the carbine in another and hunted in turn the wild beast, the Indian, or the Mexican.[1]

The French press also found certain traits common to all Americans, notably that the precocious inhabitants of the New World had developed overweening ambitions. In a characteristic observation one French journalist remarked that Americans "aspire modestly to the conquest of the universe [and] have made for several years some giant steps in that direction," especially in mechanical activities.[2]

French journalists also found paradoxes in American behavior. Although Americans lived a private life of silence and solitude, in public they were restless, active, and immature. Since all Americans loved a parade and excitement, militia service was not onerous; rather, it was a pleasure. If men of a ripe age loved to play soldier, so did boys at school. That alliance of "puerility and gravity," reported Liberal *Presse*,

> is one of the most remarkable of American traits. If children are suddenly men, the men always possess something of the infant. That leads to a precocious maturity of a people, who because of economy of time, skip youth, just as the climate skips spring.[3]

Despite these lapses into infantile behavior, Americans achieved remarkable economic growth, a development that was "without precedent in ancient and modern history."[4]

A Conservative journal also noted some disturbing social developments in America, particularly those involving women. Americans did not treat marriage with sufficient respect, according to the Conservative organ. One minister stood on a riverbank in Virginia and married a couple on the other side of the river, reported the obviously shocked newspaper. A railroad man married between stations, which the newspaper characterized as a "striking application of the maxim: *Goahead!*" *Constitutionnel* also unhappily reported that in America women aspired to high positions. Some demanded the right to vote, to sit in Congress, and to achieve public employment. Others had ambitions to become lawyers, doctors, and ministers. Several had succeeded. "It is difficult to suppose that these deviations from the natural role assigned to women," warned *Constitutionnel*, "might be turned to the advantage of a society, even a democratic one."[5]

Thus in 1860 there were abundant signs that Conservatives were critical of American society, a trend that became more pronounced during the course of the Civil War. As one scholar remarked, political attitudes influenced the ideas of Frenchmen about American society. The affirmation of Jacques Brissot, an ardent revolutionary leader in 1789, that there had never been a case of adultery in

Philadelphia, for example, was probably inspired more by political sympathies than by the chastity of American women.[6]

In addition to the social characteristics of the United States, French newspapers devoted much space to the American political scene. They were particularly zealous in reporting the activities of William Walker, the noted filibuster, who sought to create an empire in Central America. To many French journalists, Walker symbolized certain unlovely American traits. Walker's overweening ambition was characteristic of "that young republic [which] is so demanding!"[7] The grave Orleanist *Revue des deux mondes* perceived the insignificant figure and the metallic, cold eyes of Walker as reminiscent not only of the Frenchman Saint Just, but also as personifying hard-driving Americans. Americans in the North, in particular, had time only for an incessant and exclusive preoccupation with limitless ambition. The old societies of Europe with an intellectual or moral tradition differed markedly from America, which had no such tradition. Religion itself was only a hypocritical formality for Americans, who burned a slave by slow fire while treating all musical distractions on Sunday as a crime. Such were the people who supported the dogma of James Monroe that "America belongs to the Americans." Legions of individuals, claimed the Orleanist review, from New York to New Orleans were ready to play the role of Walker. Only weakness had prevented the realization of America's gigantic program to extend its sway over Latin America.[8]

The Liberal Catholic *Correspondant*, notably sympathetic with the North in the Civil War, nevertheless also found disturbing political symptoms in America. The electoral triumph of Thomas Jefferson and his followers of the "ultra-democratic party" had exercised a fatal influence over American society by granting absolute superiority to numbers and endorsing as a principle of government the sovereignty of brute force. Each election had testified to a progressive debasement of the level of political and social life. In social interaction utility had taken "the form and the place of honesty." In foreign policy, the United States had but one goal: the substitution, in the New World, of Yankee domination to that of other powers.[9]

Of all American topics, however, it was slavery that attracted the most attention. Frenchmen, who had emancipated the last of their slaves in their empire in 1848,[10] were well aware of the growing differences between the North and the South on that issue. *Uncle Tom's Cabin* had appeared in eleven French editions in its first year of publication. French papers had reported John Brown's raid and extensively covered his trial and execution. Victor Hugo had taken particular interest in Brown and submitted a petition calling on President James Buchanan to grant executive clemency to Brown; that petition was widely publicized in France and signed by many notables.[11] During the summer of 1860, Paris newspapers continued their coverage of the slavery issue as it emerged in the debate over the admission of Kansas as a state,[12] slavery's importance in the production of cotton,[13] and the role of cotton in diplomacy.[14]

For French newspapers the issue of slavery became particularly important in 1860. In that tumultuous presidential election year, political activities elicited enough attention so that an interested and intelligent Frenchman could have acquired a good knowledge of American government through careful examination of French newspapers. *Revue des deux mondes* penned an especially perceptive view of American government. That Orleanist organ, which advocated an orderly, constitutional government, was particularly concerned with restraints on unbridled democracy. The American constitution, emphasized the *Revue*, was designed to "give a rein" to pure democracy. Without an effective sharing of powers, thus limiting and controlling power, there would be no point of stability for the state, there would be no security for the citizens, and there would be no point of correction for the inconvenience of a purely democratic state. The members of the constitutional convention of 1787 accepted a social democratic state but rejected the policy of the "radical school," which the *Revue* defined as the government acting on the basis of a simple counting of individual wishes. Rather, the constitution of the United States was very different, with limitations or controls on the popular will. The state legislatures, not the people, chose the members of the Senate, and an electoral college, not the people, chose the president. Other breaks applied to the popular will had been loosened since the presidency of Thomas Jefferson, and "the despotism of the multitude would today be insupportable in America," claimed the *Revue*, except for two circumstances: the gigantic extent of American territory, and the division of the country into distinct states. Federalism had saved democracy in the American republic just as "the republic was lost in France the day when the party of the one and indivisible carried the day."[15]

French newspapers also described the American process for choosing a President, including explanations of party nominating conventions and the electoral college. One Liberal newspaper observed that the American system prevented truly outstanding men from being elected president; the failed presidential ambitions of Henry Clay, Daniel Webster, and John C. Calhoun provided evidence for that assertion. By elevating mediocrities to the presidency, claimed the *Presse*, the American system unfortunately undermined the basis of good government, which was the selection of the most worthy leaders. Rather than giving expression to the wishes of the people, the American political system put candidates at the disposition of adroit and intriguing politicians.[16] In a similar vein the Conservative *Constitutionnel* noted that political leaders in America did not belong to the elite of the country, as was true in Europe. The elite did not wish to descend to the political arena, which explained some of the excesses and regrettable scenes of American politics. On the other hand, the *Constitutionnel* pointed out that the political and social organization of the United States offered opportunity for the most obscure and worthy to rise. That was certainly true of Abraham Lincoln and Stephen Douglas, both of whom began life with rude apprenticeships. Douglas was one of the most remarkable men in public life, remarked the *Constitutionnel*, and he had been a teacher.[17]

According to a leading Liberal newspaper, the Republican convention in May, 1860, provided evidence that Americans did not select the most able men for president. The delegates bypassed William Seward, perhaps the most eminent statesman in America, because of fear of compromising the success of the political campaign. Seward had provoked ardent enmity among slavery partisans; it was also necessary to confess that superior talents always excite envy and jealousy, remarked *Siècle*.[18]

The successful Republican candidate, Abraham Lincoln, attracted much attention in the French press and was the subject of several biographical sketches. Born of very poor parents in Kentucky, he received only a limited education. He moved with his family to Indiana and later as an adolescent established himself in Illinois. He worked on a farm, became a *garçon de taverne*, and a clerk in a store. Ambitious and hard-working, he entered a law office, studied, and became a lawyer. He was elected to the Illinois legislature four times and once to Congress. In 1858 he ran for the United States Senate against the incumbent Stephen Douglas, actively debated with Douglas, and lost only because of a gerrymandered Illinois legislature.

Lincoln was "an American in all meaning of the word, a truly self-made man." Blessed with the gifts of an orator, his ardent and passionate eloquence pleased the popular masses. A devoted defender of the cause of free labor, he had long fought against "the retrograde and despotic efforts of the Southern oligarchy." Six feet, three inches tall and slender, Lincoln possessed prominent cheekbones, sad eyes, brown hair, and an expression of kindly candor spread throughout all his traits. He loved to tell stories and anecdotes. At first glance he appeared unpolished, but he was enlivened in conversation and his expression was agreeable. "The man of genius telegraphs his thought not only by words but also by physiognomy," explained one French newspaper. "Otherwise, how would Lincoln have made the conquest of his wife?"[19]

Not neglecting Democratic activities, French newspapers carefully reported the sharp differences between the Northern and Southern factions during the Democratic conventions of 1860 and the subsequent nominations by the divided wings of that party. The Northern Democrats selected Stephen Douglas as their Presidential candidate, while the Southern Democrats chose John C. Breckinridge. The French press paid little attention to the Constitutional Union party and its nominee, William Bell.

French newspapers repeatedly informed their readers of the major issue in the campaign, which they agreed was the question of slavery in the territories. Republicans claimed federal power to intervene in the territories to prohibit slavery. Southern Democrats also invoked federal power but for the protection of slavery. Northern Democrats opposed any federal intervention in the territories; rather, they would let the inhabitants of the territories decide the question of slavery. The Liberal *Presse* perceived Republicans as disguised abolitionists, Southern Democrats as confessed *esclavagistes*, and Northern Democrats as affecting neutrality on the issue. The Republican doctrine, claimed *Presse*, was "the most liberal in its goal but the most dictatorial in its means." The Southern Democratic doctrine was "most conformist to the letter of the constitution and would be the most impartial if it was a question of property other than a human being." *Presse* argued that the Northern Democratic doctrine was "the most expeditious" since it placed discussion of slavery outside of Congress, a doctrine that was consistent with a constitution which restrained as much as possible the power of the central government.[20]

The *Constitutionnel*, a leading supporter of the regime of Napoleon III, was much more sympathetic toward the Republicans. The Conservative newspaper not only predicted a Republican victory, but also solidly supported that party. The *Constitutionnel* repeatedly emphasized that the moderate Republican platform envisioned only diminishing the curse of slavery; far from proposing its abolition, the platform consented to its toleration as an indispensable evil. Thus Republicans would simply block its expansion, a very different approach from a program like John Brown's. Adversaries claimed that the Republicans were enemies of the Republic, and that their triumph would necessarily entail the rupture of the Republic. Would it not be better, queried the Conservative newspaper, to acknowledge the moderation of Republican views rather than exaggerate them?

The *Constitutionnel* interpreted the Democratic positions on slavery much less sympathetically. While the Democrats differed in principle—Southern Democrats insisted on federal protection of slavery in the territories while Northern Democrats would let settlers in the territories decide the issue— they did not differ in practice, because pro-slavery advocates would come into new territories (as in Kansas) and vote. Thus, concluded the *Constitutionnel*, "the goal of the Northern and Southern Democrats is the same; only their means differ. There is much candor among one group and more skillful hypocrisy among the other." Still, the disagreement was so strong that, if prolonged, it would lead to the triumph of the Republicans.[21]

The division among the Democrats led many French newspapers to predict a Republican victory. In southern France in July, 1860, the *Écho des Bouches-du-Rhône*, a newspaper housed at Aix-en-Provence, claimed that the person with the best chance of winning the presidency was "the honorable sénateur Lincoln."[22] Without confusing the role of Abraham Lincoln, the Liberal *Presse* repeatedly predicted a Republican victory because of divisions among the Democrats.[23]

Thus the French press not only anticipated the Republican triumph in 1860; French newspapers, almost without exception, also welcomed the outcome. The Liberal *Siècle* exuberantly rejoiced in the election of the party called the "black Republicans," the party that placed men above things and natural law above convention, and that considered slavery the most revolting of abuses. *Siècle* was particularly pleased that the election of the new president coincided with Italy's achievement of independence.[24]

In a much more restrained manner, the Orleanist *Revue des deux mondes* applauded the success of the Republican party, which it attributed to "immoral calculations" of the Democratic party. Those calculations tied its fate to the cause of slavery. As the party of slavery, intoned that circumspect review, the Democratic party "has not retreated before any excess, any corruption, and it falls today under a moral reaction which avenges the honor of the United States."[25] The Orleanist *Journal des débats* also focused on the slavery issue, explaining Lincoln's victory in terms of Northern indignation over Southern encroachments and disregard for such solemn agreements as the Missouri Compromise.[26]

The Governmental *Constitutionnel*, likewise pleased with Lincoln's victory, was careful to point out that it did not signify immediate emancipation; at the most it represented a reaction against the encroachments of the extreme slavery advocates. "It announces," asserted the *Constitutionnel*, "that a line of demarcation will be again maintained between the states afflicted with that scourge and the free states." The election meant that the slave trade would not be reopened and voters had rejected the doctrine that the American constitution made the entire republic a land of slavery.[27] Another conservative journal, *Pays*, agreed that "the abolition of slavery is a noble cause to defend and bring to a triumphant conclusion."[28]

While Frenchmen were aware that Southerners had threatened secession if Lincoln won the presidential canvas, after the election French newspapers paid little heed to such dire pronouncements. "Do not attach too much importance to the threats of disunion proffered by certain Southern states," reported the *Constitutionnel* reassuringly, adding that "we wish sincerely that it [the American Union] will emerge healthy and safe from the present crisis."[29] The Liberal *Presse* reported that the separatist movement had made no progress.[30] The Orleanist *Journal des débats* explained in a patronizing manner that "The English shout very loudly; the Americans, their cousins, shout even more loudly," but the Americans do not fight. Even though Americans had threatened dissolution at every presidential election in which there were important questions, the *Journal* predicted that "the Union endures always, and we believe that it will still resist this new threat."[31]

The Orleanist *Revue des deux mondes* was particularly emphatic in minimizing the threat of Southern secession. While Douglas received the fewest number of electoral votes, he still largely attained what he desired, according to the *Revue*'s analysis. In the free states Douglas had more votes than the combined total of Bell, the Constitutional Union candidate, and Breckinridge, the Southern Democratic candidate; indeed, Douglas had four times the votes of Breckinridge. In the states of the center, except for Missouri, Douglas lagged behind Bell but far outpolled Breckinridge. In the extreme South, Douglas obtained respectable minorities. "Even in defeat," claimed the Orleanist review, "Douglas had the consolation of having demonstrated the weakness" of the Southern Democrats. "That demonstration," continued *Revue*, "is the most important fact of the election of 1860, because it dissipates all fears" of Southern secession. How could there be a Southern confederation without Virginia, Tennessee, Kentucky, and Missouri? "The electoral campaign of 1860 will thus have the excellent result of ending the threats and fears of separation," concluded the *Revue des deux mondes*.[32]

The threats of separation were all too genuine, however, with the secession of South Carolina in December, 1860, followed by five other Southern states in January and February of 1861. After having been mistaken about the likelihood of secession, French newspapers now had to formulate explanations for the growing crisis in America and to speculate on the future of the New World Republic.

During the long interregnum between the election in November, 1860, and the inauguration of Abraham Lincoln in March, 1861, one Parisian newspaper, however, did not have to explain away its previous views about America. The Legitimist *Monde* repeatedly and consistently had pointed to perceived flaws in American behavior and explained the American crisis as the inevitable consequence of the evils of democracy. Eighty years before, noted the *Monde* in January, 1861, the republican tree was planted; now its spoiled fruits had fallen, and its roots were rotten. The paper saw little chance of maintaining the republic intact, since "Interest and self-love united will be recalcitrant to the voice of conciliation." The Clerical journal sarcastically observed that what was "most edifying" in the situation was the separation of the South with ardent, slaveholding liberals crying "*Vive la liberté*!"[33]

Unlike the *Monde*, which saw the American crisis arising from fundamental flaws in democracy, most French newspapers in the early months of 1861 blamed the South for the secession crisis and emphasized the role of slavery in fomenting the crisis. As a group, French journalists clearly viewed economic differences as of only secondary importance. The Governmental *Constitutionnel* explained that over time the South had become attached to slavery while the North was becoming more and more abolitionist. "From these two opposed movements," judged the *Constitutionnel*, "is born the present situation in the United States."[34] To safeguard "that dear 'peculiar institution' . . . the South proclaims itself rebellious against the federal constitution," charged the *Constitutionnel*, and slavery was "the principal cause of the catastrophe."[35]

One provincial Conservative newspaper flatly stated that the South was wrong. Southerners complained about the tariffs, but what they really wanted was to renew the slave trade and extend slavery into Mexico and Cuba. The North had its faults, also, but they were the vices of its virtues, of exuberance, the vices of a young nation.[36]

Another pro-Governmental journal, *Pays*, was less flattering to the North. That newspaper in February, 1861, printed three articles by Paul Pecquet du Bellet, a Louisianan living in Paris, which accused the North of giving the Constitution an abolitionist interpretation. The North, he said, wished to dominate the South, free the slaves, and introduce immigrant workers. While the North was motivated by material considerations, the South wished separation and coexistence. The South, concluded Bellet, was right, and the North was wrong.[37] Within a few months, these views regarding the causes of sectional differences became the standard position of journalistic supporters of the regime of Napoleon III.

Orleanist journals gave short shrift to an economic interpretation of the sectional difficulties. The tariff, claimed the *Journal des débats*, was not a major issue; slavery was the real issue. The newspaper also implied that lack of statesmanship contributed to the crisis. In a typical Orleanist view, the *Journal* lamented the absence of truly superior statesmen. "Where is the influential man," queried the Orleanist journal, "before whom small jealousies and small interests would give way with respect?"[38] Such a view is also consistent with the "needless war" theory of American Civil War historiography, which sees a lack of statesmanship as one reason for the conflict.

Liberal newspapers in early 1861 pointed to slavery as a major reason for the American crisis. *Siècle*, the leading Liberal journal, emphasized slavery as the key issue in its discussion of American events in the early months of 1861.[39] Likewise, the Liberal *Opinion nationale* featured the slavery issue.[40] The *Presse* found an irreconcilable "incompatibility of convictions and interests . . . between the free and industrial states of the North and the slave and agricultural states of the South." Every compromise would be "only a truce or a shameful capitulation," concluded the Liberal journal.[41]

If French newspapers substantially agreed about the causes of the crisis, most—but not all—also agreed that the crisis would lead to the breakup of the American Union. The *Constitutionnel* regretfully concluded that the election of the Republican candidate had pushed antagonism between the sections to extreme limits. It was "thus unfortunately probable," concluded the *Constitutionnel*, "that we will see consummated the scission of the great American republic."[42]

Liberal newspapers conspicuously disagreed about the prospects for the American Union. The *Presse* believed that hope of reconciliation between the sections had vanished, and the Union ought to be "regarded as irremediably lost."[43] Likewise, the Republican *Sémaphore de Marseille* argued that with a separate Southern government already set up, a permanent union between slave and free states was impossible, and it was best for the states attached to the North to adopt a policy of gradual emancipation.[44] The *Opinion nationale*, on the other hand, did not expect Northern acquiescence in Southern secession; rather, it foresaw an inevitable war. The newspaper cited Thomas Jefferson's view that the United States would never allow the occupation of New Orleans by a foreign power.[45] A Dijon Liberal organ also believed that a pacific solution was no longer possible.[46]

Orleanist journals were pessimistic about the prospects for the Union. The *Revue des deux mondes*, a consistent supporter of American constitutionalism and democracy, could not understand why the slave states would secede on the ground that Northerners refused to extradite fugitive slaves, as if their return would be more assured after the breaking of federal ties. Nevertheless, reported the *Revue*, political letters from the United States gave no hope of conciliation between the sections, while commercial letters stated that when the planters and the abolitionists had lost much money, they would quickly find a compromise.[47] A month later, the *Revue* was even more pessimistic, reporting that "nothing seems to be able to stop the separatist movement."[48] The *Revue* took the occasion to deliver a sad eulogy for American democracy. "We wish to hope yet," forlornly wrote the editor of that review,

> that the Union will escape the dissolution which threatens it; but if the ties are broken, . . . that beautiful political machine will not have lasted more than a century. . . . What does it matter? The grand ideal of political liberty and of individual energy in a great state once achieved, humanity can hope for the later and more durable success of that grand enterprise.[49]

A Conservative provincial newspaper showed less sensitivity. "The Union is dying; the Union is dead," exulted a La Rochelle journal.[50] If that was true—and most French newspapers in early 1861 believed that it was—what were the consequences for Europe and France? What posture should they assume if the disruption of the American Union led to war?

A Conservative provincial editor argued that slavery was a hideous institution; as a result, Europe would not support the South. While the British were worried about the possible loss of cotton, the provincial newspaper implied that the French should not be alarmed.[51] A number of provincial newspapers, however, were clearly concerned about the economic impact of an American Civil War. A Dijon newspaper reported that "All our great manufacturers are in a state of anxiety"; already business had fallen drastically in the Charente, whose brandies found an important market in the United States.[52] A Marseille newspaper was also troubled because a "useless war" would be deadly to America and "very prejudicial to the commercial nations of the old world." Nevertheless, even in that situation France should limit itself to conciliation and neutrality, the newspaper counseled; no doubt it would be a long time before the government would face the necessity of recognition.[53]

Likewise, the Parisian Governmental organ the *Constitutionnel* confined itself to hand wringing over the American situation. Viewing secession as a tragedy, a "catastrophe," the newspaper said France should take pride in its role in the American revolution and also should take pride in American progress. Now France could only express regret. "Far from encouraging the separatist views," asserted the Imperial journal, "France would see with pleasure smoothing the differences which have been raised between the North and the South of the great republic."[54]

A fellow Conservative journal, *Pays*, did not lament the breakup of the American republic; rather, it relished the economic opportunity that the breakup created for France. Recognition of the South, said the *Pays* in February, 1861, would open the door to free trade, free exchanges with French industry and agriculture, and would also strengthen links of race and culture.[55] Likewise, the Liberal *Presse* did not see separation as a "danger." If the two confederations became an established fact, French recognition would simply reflect the present law of nations. France must not forget that at the "head" of the new confederation was Louisiana, "a province French in language and manners." (Conservative

Southern defenders were to make this point repeatedly during the Civil War.) North America was big enough for two powers; "a courageous resignation" to the divorce was the best policy for the North.[56]

Whatever their political persuasion, French newspapers eagerly looked forward to Abraham Lincoln's inauguration on March 4; many printed the entire text of the inaugural address. The reaction of *Constitutionnel* to Lincoln's address was particularly significant. Up to this time, the Conservative newspaper had supported the antislavery movement and advocated preservation of the American republic. With its report of Lincoln's address, the newspaper showed that it had completely changed its position regarding the American crisis. The newspaper carried an extensive report by its Washington correspondent, who related that the crisis in American would result in a "*guerre civile*." The correspondent's dire prediction was based on his belief that the American Union, as then constituted, would not endure but rather would be replaced by a loose alliance of nations. Consistent with that belief, the correspondent found Lincoln's words "cold like steel and a sentence of death, so cold that the speaker attempted to warm them by a peroration full of biblical poetry, . . . [referring] to mystic cords touched by angels." Lincoln's program was strictly constitutional, the correspondent conceded, with formal recognition of both the just and the unjust rights of the slave states. Lincoln did not, however, recognize the accomplished fact: the state of discontent that had already separated seven states and minute by minute was eroding the ties of affection retained by several more. As a statement of law, Lincoln's speech was passable; as a political measure, it was "deplorable." The American press correctly understood that Lincoln's intention was not to make a threat, yet what could have been more threatening than his decision to collect revenues in a country that did not recognize his authority? Essentially, the correspondent was claiming, Lincoln's goal of preserving the Union was wrong when separation had already occurred.[57]

The other Imperial newspapers were even more pessimistic about the future of the American republic. The *Patrie* reported that disunion was the probable outcome, with republics in the center, West, and Pacific, as well as North and South. The *Pays* claimed that Lincoln's statements revealed a "vagueness of ideas, hesitation, mistrust of himself."[58]

If the Governmental press at Paris was unanimously negative about Lincoln's approach, the Governmental press in the provinces was less united. In the southern part of France the *Ami de l'ordre* agreed with the Conservative Parisian journals. If Lincoln limited himself to affirming the Union and defending federal properties, claimed the Conservative editor, then one could say "End of the Union."[59] Other provincial governmental journals were more positive regarding Lincoln's statement. A thoughtful editor in the Loire valley believed that if Lincoln had made his conciliatory proposals earlier (especially on the subject of slavery), then there would have been no problem. In his inaugural, Lincoln showed excellent intentions and a lively desire to arrive at a settlement between the North and the South. Nevertheless, complained the editor, "one searched vainly for indications of steps to be followed if the separatist states repulse all attempts at conciliation."[60] One La Rochelle newspaper, officially pro-Governmental, sharply disagreed withe the Parisian pro-Governmental journals. While Lincoln was conciliatory toward the South, Lincoln also firmly asserted the right of the government to execute the laws and equally as firmly denied the right of secession. After those statements, "the die is cast." Without question the mass of the population in the North and West was singularly excited against the South, related that Conservative newspaper, and Lincoln had become "the organ of national sentiment."[61]

Nor was the Liberal press of one mind regarding Lincoln's inauguration. The *Presse* reported that the speech lent itself to a "on the one hand, on the other hand" interpretation; occupy and possess federal properties but not repossess federal properties. His first acts were as indecisive as his words. Lincoln had two problems: to maintain the Union and circumscribe slavery. Maintenance of the Union, claimed the *Presse*, was a capital interest for the equilibrium of the maritime world and for human liberty, of which America had been "the most magnificent temple." That was why, continued the Liberal newspaper, "we would have applauded the policy which would have been able to conciliate those two grand moral and material interests."[62] *Siècle* was much more flattering in its report on Lincoln's inauguration, noting particularly that Stephen Douglas praised the inaugural address. *Opinion nationale*, which consistently supported the North during the Civil War, was the most positive in its analysis of Lincoln's inauguration. Lincoln had no desire or right to interfere with slavery where it existed, but to break the compact forming the Union required the consent of all the parties. To allow separation, asserted the Republican organ, would provide a precedent for other secessions.[63]

Orleanist reaction to Lincoln's inauguration was generally positive. The provincial Orleanist newspaper *Progrès* of Lyons noted that Lincoln accepted the law regarding fugitive slaves and was willing to guarantee slavery, but he also held to a firm determination to maintain the Union. Sadly, the *Progrès* concluded that it looked like war.[64] Another Orleanist journal reported Lincoln's resolve to defend national property, collect the revenues, and execute the law.[65] The *Revue des deux mondes* reported the peaceful inauguration of Lincoln despite threats. It attributed the weak beginning of the Lincoln administration to Buchanan's legacy of a Washington government stricken with paralysis.[66]

The principal Legitimist organ, *Monde*, simply printed the text of Lincoln's inaugural without comment. On the very day of Lincoln's inauguration, however, it claimed that the famous American government was falling "like a theater decoration." That republic would no longer serve as an argument against Catholic peoples and Catholic doctrines. "Our free thinkers and Anglophiles," rejoiced the clerical journal, "have one less arm."[67]

The new administration scarcely had time to perfect a policy, much less think about these varied French reactions. An immediate crisis arose at Ft. Sumter in Charleston. One of the very few federal installations in a seceded state still under Washington's control, Sumter was an important symbol. Meekly surrendering the fort to Confederate forces would imply recognition of the Confederacy. On the other hand, if Washington vigorously reinforced Sumter, the Confederacy could cry out against Northern aggression. With the garrison on the verge of surrender because of lack of provisions, Lincoln took the limited step of sending food only—and that only after explicit communication to South Carolina officials. Unwilling to tolerate what they considered a foreign presence within their territory, Confederate officials ordered an artillery bombardment against the Union garrison, a bombardment that led to its surrender on April 12, 1861.

While American historians have strenuously debated responsibility for the attack on Sumter,[68] French newspapers, whatever their political persuasion, showed surprising agreement on the consequences of the bombardment of Sumter. The attack and Lincoln's subsequent call for 75,000 troops to put down the insurrection meant that a "collision . . . seems inevitable." The attack on Sumter put all of the responsibility on the South for having begun the war, stated a Governmental provincial newspaper.[69] With the attack on Sumter, there was no other alternative than to reduce the South by force or let the new confederation organize freely, concluded a Conservative Loire journal.[70] The Conservative *Courrier de La Rochelle* agreed that hostilities had decidedly begun at Sumter; the "evil, we believe, is now without remedy, and there remains now the hope that the war will end as soon as possible."[71] The Orleanist *Journal des débats* saw no great military significance in the fall of Fort Sumter, but the political consequence was grave, since it diminished the possibility of conciliation.[72]

With the outbreak of the Civil War, European governments were forced to grapple with the diplomatic consequences of the hostilities. The British responded with a declaration of neutrality on May 14, a proclamation that deeply angered and offended the Northern public and Washington officials, who were fearful that the proclamation was but a precursor to formal recognition of the Southern Confederacy. The American minister to Great Britain, Charles Francis Adams, charged that British recognition of Southern belligerency was an unwarranted interference in an America domestic matter. The official view of the Washington administration was that the South was still an integral part of the United States. As a result, Washington held that the Confederates were simply rebels and not entitled to the status of belligerency. When the French made a similar declaration a month later on June 10, American public opinion was much less aroused, and Washington's official reaction also was more restrained. Of course, Abraham Lincoln, by his proclamation of April 19 blockading Southern ports, implicitly recognized Southern belligerency, since a blockade is an act of war. In addition, Northern practice during the Civil War was to treat Southerners as legitimate soldiers and sailors, not as outlaws and pirates. In short, Washington for all practical purposes accorded the South belligerent status, though denying that status in principle.[73]

French newspapers made little comment about the British and French proclamations of neutrality. One provincial newspaper observed that the declarations had aroused lively emotions in New York.[74] The Progressive *Opinion nationale* claimed that while the British and French had resolved to observe a strict neutrality, their approaches were essentially different. The French declaration employed "friendly terms" and was marked by a "more conciliatory spirit" than the British declaration.[75] The *Presse* claimed that the Americans could not complain that the recognition of belligerency was premature, since the United States had promptly recognized the independence of Texas and Hungary.[76] Most French newspapers, however, simply reported the French action, some with the comment that the French government was resolved to maintain a strict neutrality.[77]

By the time of the declarations of neutrality French newspapers were exhibiting definite patterns in their stances toward the Civil War. These patterns were closely correlated with French political affiliations. As Liberal Catholic Augustin Cochin explained, since America was "the only powerful republic founded in modern times, monarchists will not speak well of it, republicans dare not speak ill of it.[78] Although there were exceptions—sometimes assessment of events modified views, and provincial newspapers were less ideologically pure than Parisian journals—nevertheless political ideology provides the most useful framework for analyzing French journalistic opinions about the Civil War.

Without doubt the most ideological and consistent newspapers were those of Legitimist-Catholic persuasion. They were scathing in their denunciation of American democracy. "The folly of this century," devoutly observed *Monde*, was to "banish God from the affairs of the world." The United States, like the French Republic, placed itself under the Supreme Being, but human reason had not produced a brilliant specimen in the United States. Only religion, warned the Clerical journal, "cements the social edifice and protects against the injuries of time and interior corruption." Thus in France the work of Clovis and of William and his Normans had endured and was as solid as ever, while the United States was crumbling. Another reason for American weakness was that the pretended political society in America was only a commercial society. It was perishing because of a dispute among business associates, "a dispute born of a question of interest." Not slavery, but greed, brought on the contest between the North and the South, and within a few days it would be necessary to liquidate "la société Washington, Franklin, et Ci. . . ."[79]

A Liberal Catholic journal, on the other hand, had a very different perspective on the American situation. That journal found all the wrong on one side—the South, which made compromise difficult.[80]

Religious principles led one provincial Catholic newspaper to a similar conclusion. The *Ami du peuple* saw the cause of the war as a conflict between Southern support for the institution of slavery and opposition by Northern abolitionists, who helped slaves escape. The election of Lincoln, who was antislavery, precipitated a crisis; in vain did reasonable men in the North and South seek to prevent the explosion. The editor had made his choice between the two parties: "slavery," he wrote, was

> an odious institution, anti-Christian, which God reproves and conscience condemns; it is why we make our vows for the triumph of the American North. A Southern victory would maintain slavery and extend it, while a Northern victory would mean the fall of slavery.

A few months later the editor reiterated his position, once more buttressed by religious values. He favored a Northern triumph because of the slavery issue. "Servitude is heathen," he claimed, "but liberty comes from the sky; it is a fruit of the Gospel."[81]

One of the most interesting features of Civil War attitudes was the dramatic change in 1861 by Parisian Conservative newspapers. Early in the year, Conservative journals were critical of Southern separatists. "Whereas the North," related the *Constitutionnel* in January, 1861,

> has shown itself conciliatory and moderate in its victory, the South has hastened to act with heated reply following its defeat. . . . After having pursued constantly an aggressive policy, it declares itself menaced before being attacked, and separates itself from the Union, which has not committed any crime against it by electing constitutionally a President representing the sentiments of an immense majority.[82]

The *Constitutionnel* explained that the antislavery movement developed in the North, while Southerners came to view slavery as "a divine institution, the most admirable system of work and the sign of the highest civilization." Those opposing movements gave birth to the present situation in the United States.[83]

By May, 1861, the three Parisian Governmental newspapers, *Patrie, Pays*, and *Constitutionnel* had completely reversed their stance from support of the North to support of the South. In May, the *Constitutionnel* claimed that the war had no *raison d'être*. Since the abolitionists were few in number, it was not a question of liberty for the slaves. Nor was it a question of liberty for the inhabitants of the North. "A separation of states has taken place," continued the *Constitutionnel*, and it made no difference

> whether it be based upon a true or false interpretation of the federal compact. . . . It is incontestable . . . that governments depend only upon the consent of the governed. By what right, today, does the North desire to impose its government upon the South which does not desire it?[84]

Later the *Constitutionnel* more systematically explained the reasons for the Civil War. The people of the North and South differed in basic ideas and development. Moreover, the founding fathers sowed the seeds of discord by permitting slavery and by trying to create a nation from sovereign states. In addition, the people of the North knew Southerners believed that the election of Lincoln justified secession, but they persisted in electing Lincoln, thus rejecting compromise.[85]

The dramatic switch in the Imperial Parisian newspapers, or the semi-official press, raised obvious questions about the attitude of the French government. The American minister in Paris, William L. Dayton, specifically asked about a *Patrie* article that linked French recognition of the Kingdom of Italy with eventual recognition of the South. Even more disturbing was the reprinting of the article by the *Moniteur*, the official French organ. Antoine Thouvenel, French foreign minister, replied that *Patrie* had ceased being a semi-official newspaper ten days previously and did not reflect the government's views; reprinting of the article by *Moniteur* was an error which occurred during the absence of an official charged with scrutiny of the press. "The French government," added Thouvenel, "has no sympathy whatever with the seceding States of the South. It has no idea of recognizing them as an independent power."[86] Despite Thouvenel's statement, the Emperor Napoleon III clearly had changed his views regarding the crisis in America. In January, 1861, he conveyed sincere regrets about American misfortunes; in May, 1861, he confided to the British minister to France that he could not forget "the overbearing insolence" of the American government, and that he hoped Britain would join him in siding with the South.[87]

A Conservative provincial journal found numerous reasons to support the South. The (La Rochelle) *Charente-Inférieure* charged that Northerners were not truly negrophiles. Among those people, "who flatter themselves as being the most Christian of the earth, in all public places, even in the churches, a black is parked as an inconvenient beast." What use was there for liberty when it was not accompanied by equality (as in France)? Further, the Confederates were grandchildren of French grandparents, while Northerners were descended from Anglo-Saxons. The North was anti-free exchange, while the South favored freedom of commerce. The South asked for separation because its tendencies, its tastes, and its principles were opposed to those of the North. The fusion of two races into a single people would be henceforth impossible and, stated the Conservative newspaper, "we would be less surprised to see one day Jefferson David [*sic*], or Beauregard, or some other, found a dynasty as emperor of the South than to see the Confederates sheltered again under the Stars and Stripes."[88]

Another Conservative provincial journal supported the South for economic reasons. As the Cherbourg journal explained, Southern commerce was then going through New York; it should go directly to Europe, to Brest, Cherbourg, or Le Havre. Could the British and French governments pass up the opportunities of the cotton harvest in October? Since the South had also created a government, the opportune moment would come to recognize the South. "It seems to us difficult to find," claimed the *Vigie de Cherbourg*, "a better solution for European interests."[89]

In the latter half of 1861, Liberal Parisian newspapers did not take a common stance on the American question. They were most nearly in agreement on the causes of the war, which they attributed to slavery—with qualification. As the Orleanist *Temps* explained, slavery was "in question" in the United States, but the abolition of slavery was not in question. While slavery was "at the essence of the war" because it created two hostile interests, abolition was not the cause of the war because abolitionists had never been but a weak minority in the North. But if slavery was neither the cause nor the goal of the war could not abolition be the result or consequence? Probably not, the *Temps* sadly concluded. If the North won (not very probable), the North would not complicate the task of pacification by abolition. If the South won, no doubt it would keep its property. The most humane wish, concluded the *Temps*, was that the Southern states themselves would decide to abolish slavery if they became independent.[90]

The Liberal *Presse* took a similar position. The Republican party, it noted, did support the abolition of slavery but, rather, "resistance to the extension of slavery." The Democratic party was an instrument of the Southern oligarchy; the latter wished to extend slavery over all of the republic.[91] The *Presse* became increasingly impatient when Lincoln would not turn the war into an anti-slavery crusade. The North had two choices: 1) an amicable separation or 2) abolition, which would give the war a moral goal; peace or liberty for all.[92]

A much less flattering view of the war was expressed by the *Courrier du dimanche*, when it claimed that slavery was not the cause of the war, since the cause could be found entirely in tariffs. "The South," explained the Orleanist journal, "which has no manufacturers, does not like tariffs, which protect Northern industry; there is the whole quarrel."[93] The *Revue des deux mondes* held a very different view of the conflict. "Our regret," wrote the editor of that Orleanist review, Eugène Forcade, was not primarily over any disturbance to the balance of power as a consequence of the disruption of the Union. Rather, lamented Forcade,

> our regret is more disinterested. The American government has been among the governments of the modern world which has in the highest degree this character of being a creation of the human reason.[94]

Whatever their views of the causes of the war, in mid-1861 many Liberal organs, including the *Revue des deux mondes*, were convinced that the North could not win, could not subjugate the South. "The Union is dissolved," claimed the *Courrier du dimanche*. "Twenty victories by the men of the North could not reform the work of Washington, of Jefferson, and of Franklin. It is a frightful misfortune, which all the friends of liberty ought to deplore, but it is a misfortune without remedy."[95] The Liberal Catholic *Correspondant* was even more pessimistic. That journal, which throughout the Civil War was consistently outspoken in its praise of American institutions, believed that slavery would not survive the conflict, but the future of democracy was less certain. Indeed, feared *Correspondant,* it was more likely that America would follow the European model than Europe follow the American example.[96]

Thus, by the summer of 1861, the most consistent views emanated from the Legitimist-Clerical *Monde*. Anti-democratic and unsympathetic toward the North, that newspaper attributed the cause of the war to flaws inherent in democracy and to Yankee greed. The *Monde* clearly hoped for and expected a Southern victory.

By mid-1861, the Imperial newspapers had done a complete flip-flop. Early in the year they expressed sympathy for preservation of the Union and blamed sectional difficulties on the slave issue. By midyear they explained the war in terms of economic aggression by the North and viewed sympathetically Southern aspirations for independence.

The Progressive and Orleanist newspapers viewed American democracy sympathetically and generally blamed slavery as the cause of the conflict. By mid-1861, however, they were badly divided about whether the North would be successful in preserving the American Union. Most of them sadly conceded that the North should acquiesce in peaceful separation.

NOTES

1. Gaillardet, *Presse*, August, 18, 1860.
2. Texier, *Siècle*, July 15, 1860.
3. *Ibid.*
4. Gaillardet, *Presse*, September 4, 1860.
5. Martin, *Constitutionnel*, July 28, 1860.
6. Durand Echeverria, "L'Amérique devant l'opinion française, 1734–1870: Question de méthode et d'interprétation," *Revue d'histoire moderne et contemporaine*, 9 (1962), 61.
7. Martin, *Constitutionnel*, July 7, 1861.
8. M. F. Belly, "La Question du l'Isthme Américain," *Revue des deux mondes*, July 15, 1860, 344.
9. Henry Moreau, *Correspondant*, 54, October, 1861, 330, 332. Moreau was reviewing a biography of George Washington and Thomas Jefferson by Cornelius de Witt; in that review, Moreau contrasted the wise, moderate views of Washington with those of the ultra-democratic followers of Jefferson.
10. Slavery was abolished in France as a result of the revolution in 1789; slavery in the colonies was abolished in 1848. Augustin Cochin, *Abolition de l'esclavage* (1861), treated abolition in France, Britain, and Latin America. Reviewed by H. Wallon, *Correspondant*, 55, November, 1861, 451–74.
11. Seymour Drescher, "British Way, French Way: Opinion Building and Revolution in the Second French Slave Emancipation," *American Historical Review*, 96 (June, 1991), 709–34; Seymour Drescher, "Servile Insurrection and John Brown's Body in Europe," *Journal of American History*, 80 (September, 1993), 499–524; George Gavronsky, *The French Liberal Opposition and the American Civil War* (New York, Humanities Press, 1968), pp. 41, 43–44; *Revue des deux mondes*, December 31, 1859, cited in Louis M. Sears, " Neglected Critic of our Civil War," in *Mississippi Valley Historical Review*, I (1915), 533. The reviewer of Harriet Beecher Stowe's novel, *The Pearl of Orr's Island*, reported that hundreds of thousands had read *Uncle Tom* and that Stowe played a role in the unleashing of the Civil War; Cucheval-Clarigny, "Une Famille Américaine," *Revue des deux mondes*, December 1, 1861, 638.

12. "Correspondance particulière" from New York, *Siècle*, June 18, 1860.

13. Baudrillart, *Journal des débats*, June 16, 1860.

14. Martin, *Constitutionnel*, July 28, 1861.

15. Cornelius de Witt, "Thomas Jefferson: sa vie et sa correspondance," *Revue des deux mondes*, September 1, 1860, 105–107.

16. Gaillardet, *Presse*, July 26, 1860.

17. Martin, *Constitutionnel*, September 19, 1860.

18. "Correspondance particulière," New York, May 19, 1860, *Siècle*, June 4, 1860.

19. This description of Lincoln is derived from Gaillardet, *Presse*, July 31, 1860; Martin, *Constitutionnel*, September 19, 1860; and Cucheval-Clarigny, "Les Partis et l'élection présidentielle aux États-Unis," *Revue des deux mondes*, December 1, 1860, 676–81.

20. Gaillardet, *Presse*, July 29, 1860.

21. Martin, *Constitutionnel*, September 1, 1860.

22. Makaire, (Aix-en-Provence) *Écho des Bouches-du-Rhône*, July 8, 1860.

23. Gaillardet, *Presse*, September 4, October 4, 1860.

24. Commitaire, *Siècle*, November 24, 1860.

25. Forcade, *Revue des deux mondes*, November 30, 1860, 771.

26. Léo, *Journal des débats*, December 4, 1860, cited in West, *French Opinion*, p. 22.

27. Martin, *Constitutionnel*, November 22, 1860.

28. Esparbié, *Pays*, November 22, 1860, quoted in West, *French Opinion*, p. 10.

29. Martin, *Constitutionnel*, November 21, 1860.

30. Nefftzer, *Presse*, November 27, 1860.

31. Lemoinne, *Journal des débats*, December 7, 1860.

32. Cucheval-Clarigny, "Les Partis et l'élection présidentielle aux Etats-Unis," in *Revue des deux mondes*, December 1, 1860, 689–90.

A Liberal Catholic, warmly sympathetic to American democracy, reported that Europeans were astonished when the crisis burst in America. Its causes were understood only by a small number of persons who knew America. With rare exceptions, the hypothesis of a war between the North and the South only met incredulous responses. Henry Moreau, *Correspondant*, 54, October, 1861, 315.

33. Coquille, *Monde*, January 8, 1861.

34. Martin, *Constitutionnel*, January 24, 28, 1861.

35. *Ibid.*, January 10, 1861.

36. Filingre, (Vesoul) *Journal de la Haute-Saône*, January 30, 1861.

37. *Pays*, February 9, 15, 21, 1861, cited in Gavronsky, *French Liberal Opposition*, pp. 55–56.

At Bellet's request, the chief editor of *Pays* "generously extended to the South the free use of his columns to vindicate the character of the Confederate States of America." Paul Pecquet du Bellet, *The Diplomacy of the Confederate Cabinet of Richmond and its Agents Abroad* (Tuscaloosa, AL, University of Alabama Press, 1963), p. 29. Shortly after the war, Pequet wrote his narrative of his experiences in Paris. He was sharply critical of Confederate agents in Europe and the Jefferson Davis administration in general.

38. Camus, *Journal des débats*, February 14, 1861, quoted in West, *French Opinion*, p. 36.

39. See, for example, Jordan, *Siècle*, January 11, 1861, and "Correspondance particulière" from New York, *Siècle*, January 30, 1861, February 15, 1861.

40. Malespine, *Opinion nationale*, January 1, February 7, 1861.

41. Gaillardet, *Presse*, February 25, 1861.

42. Martin, *Constitutionnel*, January 20, 1861.
43. Gaillardet, *Presse*, February 2, 1861.
44. Carle, *Sémaphore de Marseille*, February 26, 1861.
45. Malespine, *Opinion nationale*, February 7, 1861.
46. Vincent, (Dijon) *Journal de la Côte-d'Or*, January 12, 1861.
47. Forcade, *Revue des deux mondes*, January 15, 1861, p. 498.
48. *Ibid.*, February 1, 1861, p. 752.
49. *Ibid.*, p. 754.
50. The quotation is from a New York dispatch of January 30, 1861; (La Rochelle) *Charente-Inférieure*, February 17, 1861.
51. Filingre, (Vesoul) *Journal de la Haute-Saône*, January 30, 1861.
52. Vincent, (Dijon), *Journal de la Côte-d'Or*, February 19, 1861.
53. Carle, *Sémaphore de Marseille*, February 2, 1861.
54. Martin, *Constitutionnel*, February 2, 1861.
55. Quoted in Donaldson Jordan and Edwin Pratt, *Europe and the American Civil War* (Boston, Houghton Mifflin, 1931), p. 224.
56. Gaillardet, *Presse*, February 25, 1861.
57. Edward Amun, "the American correspondent," March 4, 1861, *Constitutionnel*, March 26, 1861.
58. Watteville, *Patrie*, March 25, 1861, and Boulie, *Pays*., March 26, 1861, cited in West, *French Opinion*, pp. 21, 35–36.
59. Barbaroux, (Digne) *Ami de l'ordre*, March 21, 1861.
60. Gaches, (Saint-Étienne) *Mémorial de la Loire*, March 20, 1861.
61. P. L., *Courrier de La Rochelle*, March 20, 1861.
62. Gaillardet, *Presse*, March 26, 1861.
63. Malespine, *Opinion nationale*, March 21, 1861.
64. Chanoine, *Progrès*, March 19, 21, 1861.
65. Vincent, (Dijon) *Journal de la Côte-d'Or*, March 21, 1861.
66. Forcade, *Revue des deux mondes*, April 1, 1861, pp. 757, 758.
67. Coquille, *Monde*, March 4, 1861.
68. For a good brief discussion of Lincoln and the Fort Sumter supply question, see James M. McPherson, *Battle Cry of Freedom* (New York, Oxford University Press, 1988), pp. 264–73. See, also, Richard N. Current, *Lincoln and the First Shot* (Philadelphia, Lippincott, 1963).
69. Bayvet, (La Rochelle) *Charente-Inférieure*, June 2, 5, 1861.
70. Gaches, (Saint-Étienne) *Mémorial de la Loire*, April 27, 1861.
71. Siret, *Courrier de La Rochelle*, April 27, 1861.
72. Alloury, *Journal des débats*, April 27, 1861, cited in West, *French Opinion*, p. 19.
73. For an extended discussion of this issue, see Lynn M. Case and Warren F. Spencer, *The United States and France: Civil War Diplomacy* (Philadelphia, University of Pennsylvania Press, 1970), pp. 45–76.
74. Dufour, (Bourg-en-Bresse) *Courrier de l'Ain*, June 13, 1861.
75. Malespine, *Opinion nationale*, June 17, 1861.
76. Gaillardet, *Presse*, June 20, 1861.
77. For example, see Sauter, (Colmar) *Journal du Haut-Rhin*, June 16, 1861.
78. Augustin Cochin, *The Results of Slavery*, trans. Mary L. Booth (Boston, n.p., 1863), p. 1, cited in Charles and Anne Marie Poinsatte, "Augustin Cochin's *L'Abolition de l'esclavage* and the Emancipation Proclamation," in *Review of Politics*, 46 (July, 1984), 412.
79. Coquille, *Monde*, September 1, 1861.

80. Douhaire, *Correspondant*, 43, July, 1861, 630.

81. Cumot, (Angers) *Ami du peuple*, May 4, September 21, 1861.

82. Martin, *Constitutionnel*, January 10, 1861.

83. *Ibid.*, January 28, 1861.

84. Gaulhiac, *Constitutionnel*, May 16, 1861 quoted in West, *French Opinion*, pp. 28–29.

85. Gaillardet, *Constitutionnel*, November 19, 1861, cited in West, *French Opinion*, pp. 29–30.

86. The *Patrie* article appeared June 14, 1861; discussion of this incident is based upon Case and Spencer, *Civil War Diplomacy*, pp. 62–63. Liberal *Presse* did not approve of the *Patrie* article. It was not a good idea, warned *Presse*, to offend Americans; Gaillardet, *Presse*, June 20, 1861.

87. Henry Blumenthal, *A Reappraisal of Franco-American Relations: 1830–1871,* (Chapel Hill, University of North Carolina Press, 1959), p. 143.

88. "X," (La Rochelle) *Charente-Inférieure*, August 11, 1861.

89. Prévost, *Vigie de Cherbourg*, June, 6, 1861.

90. Scherer, *Temps*, October 19, 1861.

91. Juif, *Presse*, October 27, 1861.

92. Gaillardet, *Presse*, August 6, 1861.

93. Assollant, *Courrier du dimanche*, August 11, 1861.

94. *Revue des deux mondes*, May 14, 1861, 505, quoted in Sears, "A Neglected Critic of our Civil War," p. 535.

95. Assollant, *Courrier du dimanche*, July 14, 1861.

96. Cochin, *Correspondant*, 43, July, 1861, 605.

Chapter 3

The *Trent* Affair

> Let us occupy ourselves one last time about MM Mason and Slidell to announce that they are on route to Europe. At the moment when their mission begins, their importance ceases.
>
> Mahias, *Presse*, January 17, 1862

A diplomatic firestorm erupted when a boarding party from the Union warship *San Jacinto* forcibly removed two Confederate commissioners from the deck of the British merchant ship *Trent*. The incident attracted much attention because strong feelings on both sides could have led to war between Britain and the North. Although the affair directly involved only London and Washington, the French took a lively interest in the matter and the French foreign minister, Antoine Thouvenel, sent an important diplomatic note to Washington urging the release of the commissioners. French newspapers differed sharply on various issues regarding the seizure of Mason and Slidell by Northern forces.

In March, 1861, before the firing on Ft. Sumter, Confederate President Jefferson Davis appointed William Yancey, Pierre Rost, and Dudley Mann as roving Confederate commissioners to Europe. When they failed in the summer of 1861 to obtain French and British recognition of Southern independence, Davis in August of that same year appointed James M. Mason, of Virginia, as commissioner to Great Britain and John Slidell, of Louisiana, as commissioner to France. The Confederate government publicly announced the mission some six weeks before the two men ran the blockade in front of Charleston during the night of October 11–12. Arriving in Havana on October 22, the two men made no secret of their presence in that Cuban city. A Union warship, the *San Jacinto*, was also at Havana at the same time. The two Confederate commissioners left Havana on November 7 aboard a British vessel, the *Trent*, and the following day, November 8, the *San Jacinto*, Charles Wilkes commanding, stopped the *Trent*. Acting without authorization from Washington authorities, Wilkes ordered a boarding party to remove the two emissaries and their secretaries from the English vessel, and subsequently Wilkes took the Confederates to Boston as prisoners.[1]

The British public was outraged over the insult to the British flag, and the British government peremptorily demanded that Washington officials release the commissioners and apologize for the action. British officials dispatched their demands on the first of December; there then followed a ten-day period for the note to cross the Atlantic. Meanwhile, Northerners jubilantly celebrated Wilkes' aggressive initiative; numerous public actions, including a resolution of praise by the House of Representatives, provided ample evidence that people in the North were delighted with Wilkes' seizure of the Confederate commissioners. Well aware of the outraged reaction of the British government to Wilkes' action and the enthusiastic approval of American public opinion, Washington officials faced a difficult choice. In the end sanity won. The American Secretary of State, the able William Seward, realized that Wilkes' seizure of the commissioners rested on shaky legal ground; indeed, Wilkes' action bore an uncanny resemblance to previous British practices against which America had lodged bitter protests. In addition, if their seizure resulted in a war with Great Britain, the commissioners would have achieved far more than they could have accomplished through normal diplomatic channels. Perhaps, also, a note from Antoine Thouvenel, French foreign minister, which arrived in Washington before the final decision was made, played an influential role. Thouvenel argued that America should pursue its traditional policy of supporting neutral rights on the high seas. During crucial cabinet meetings, Seward's views prevailed, and Washington decided to release the commissioners. Since Washington officials had not authorized Wilkes' actions, Seward found a graceful way to release the commissioners. Seward first congratulated the British on accepting American views on neutral rights. He ordered the release of the commissioners for procedural reasons: Wilkes himself should not have made the decision to seize the commissioners. Rather, he should have taken the ship and commissioners to port; there an appropriate court could have ruled that the commissioners were contraband of war and consequently ordered their incarceration.

From the very beginning of the *Trent* affair Frenchmen realized the importance of Wilkes' action. In Paris "at the moment of going to press" the *Temps* hastily reported "news of the highest gravity," the removal of Slidell and Mason from a British ship.[2] In the Loire valley and other localities, residents quickly learned of great excitement and anger in Britain.[3]

French newspapers discussed in much detail the many issues in the affair. Typically, French newspapers made a distinction between Wilkes' searching of the British ship on the high seas and the actual seizure of the commissioners. French newspapers agreed that Union officials had the legal right to visit and search the British ship. Even the Republican *Presse*, which was sharply critical of the seizure of the commissioners, readily conceded that there was a right of search.[4] The British themselves, noted a Republican provincial newspaper, had introduced the right of visit in maritime law, even exercising the right of visit against French sailors.[5]

On the question of the removal of the Confederate commissioners, French newspapers overwhelmingly agreed that Wilkes acted improperly. Some Parisian newspapers were caustically critical of the American action. The *Pays*, an Imperial newspaper, argued that since Mason and Slidell were on an English ship, they were on British territory and hence not subject to seizure. Nor could Washington claim them because they belonged to a nation at war; such an action would implicitly admit the legal existence of the Confederacy. If Washington claimed that they were rebels, then Washington should extradite them, which would require a court judgment.[6] The Progressive *Presse* was even more harsh in denouncing "that flagrant violation of the rights of man and direct insult to England." The North might try to justify the seizure of the agents either as enemy agents or as contraband of war, but neither claim, asserted the *Presse*, had merit.[7] It was impossible, added the *Presse*, not to admire the public spirit which burst from one end of England to the other.[8] The Legitimist *Monde* sharply denounced the action as a "*faute grave*" and an "insult against the British flag." Wondering what motivated Washington, the *Monde* speculated that it was more than irritation against British recognition of belligerency. Since the beginning of the war, Washington had sought to engage Europe in the quarrel, and, no doubt, Washington now hoped to find allies against Britain.[9] The Orleanist *Revue des deux mondes* was also critical of the American action. The British, thought the *Revue*, were absolutely correct, and it was probable that the United States government could not give satisfaction because of American public opinion. In the past Britain had endured insults because of cotton; the *Revue*'s editor hoped that Britain would also be moderate on this occasion.[10]

It was not only Orleanist friends of America who became despondent over the affair. Louis Garnier-Pagès, one of five Republican members of the *Corps législatif*, was a "stalwart friend of the Union cause," reported the American consul at Paris, "partly because of his aversion to slavery, partly because of his aversion to the Imperial government, . . . and partly because he believed that the future of republicanism in Europe depended upon the success of republicanism in America." Yet he became convinced that disunion was inevitable because he despaired of a peaceful resolution of the *Trent* affair.[11]

Journalists in the provinces were also doubtful that the affair could be resolved peacefully. The outrage inflicted on the British flag, reported a provincial newspaper, inflamed that island nation to the point of seizing the occasion to make the United States pay for their past insolences.[12] Another Conservative provincial journal was even more scathing. Washington premeditated the seizure to prevent by all means, "legal or violent," the passage of the Confederate commissioners to Europe. The Union consul at Havana advised the United States of their arrival and succeeded in having the *San Jacinto*, Wilkes' warship, sent to that port. As a result, the commissioners were accosted, violated, and seized in an outrageous manner with an unequaled insolence. Seward and Lincoln deserved all of the odium and responsibility for the incident. The rights of all neutrals were involved; the premeditated affront against England was "an injurious challenge carried to Europe."[13]

Many newspapers which readily agreed that Wilkes acted improperly nevertheless viewed the American government in a more friendly fashion. The Imperial *Constitutionnel* candidly stated that the United States was wrong but also clearly hoped that Washington would repair the mistake. The pro-Governmental journal balanced its criticism of America by criticizing Britain for threatening force.[14] The Republican *Siècle* extensively discussed the topic, regretfully concluding that Wilkes was wrong. Obviously, the newspaper hoped that Washington officials would disavow the commander and return the prisoners. The Liberal journal was hopeful for a peaceful solution: Anglo-Saxons, it observed, were like wolves; they did not eat each other.[15] The Orleanist *Temps* evenhandedly noted that public opinion in New York was the exact mirror of public opinion in London—both experienced the same thoughtless explosion. American legal experts diametrically opposed English experts. Perhaps, however, "The good practical sense of the two countries will surmount . . . the sad inspirations of anger and pride," hoped the *Temps*.[16]

The defenders of American actions were lonely, but there were a few. The officially Governmental but politically maverick *Courrier de La Rochelle* claimed that the United States was right. American newspapers had shown that the *Trent* had erred either in shipping Confederate dispatches or in inscribing Mason and Slidell on its books as commissioners of the separatist states. Admitting that most French newspapers were severely critical of the American action, the provincial newspaper nevertheless noted that Britain had introduced the right of visit and applied maritime law with extreme vigor.[17] What Wilkes had done, the La Rochelle newspaper pointedly observed, "the English had done not once but one hundred times in 1812."[18] Likewise, the Legitimist *Monde* argued that the Americans had followed the laws of war while the British were concerned about cotton. "The right of national defense," asserted the very conservative journal, "is assuredly superior to the conveniences of commerce."[19]

French newspapers were much more evenly divided on the question of responsibility for the action. As suggested above, those journalists most critical of American seizure of the commissioners tended to explain the incident in terms of premeditation by Washington officials. Those who wrote with sorrow about the incident, notably the *Journal des débats*, doubted that Wilkes acted on orders of his government.[20] As one editor observed, the disavowal of Wilkes was not too much of a sacrifice if Wilkes acted on his own; the editor was clearly hinting that it was in American interest to repudiate the ardent naval officer.[21]

Whatever role the American government might have played, it was fortunate, according to one Legitimist provincial newspaper, that the effort in 1857 to lay an Atlantic cable had not been a success. With the instantaneous transmission of information and existing emotion, there would have been war. Without the cable, messages took a month to go from Europe to America and back;

during that time, the Legitimist provincial editor hoped, reason would prevail.[22] Indeed, a simple perusal of French newspaper reporting about the *Trent* affair clearly shows the effect of time and distance. Frenchmen read about the British note demanding release of the commissioners; ten days elapsed while that note crossed the Atlantic; after its arrival in Washington, American officials examined the British note and formulated a reply; and finally it took ten more days for the American note to reach Europe. Frenchmen in early December, 1861, realized that they had to wait a month for events to unfold, events that were important to them because the *Trent* affair could well have led to war between America and Britain.

Fully aware of the disastrous consequences of such a war, the French government took an active interest in the quarrel.[23] French officials very quickly informed London of their belief that the American action was wrong, and later Thouvenel, the French foreign minister, sent a note to the United States explaining French official views. Thouvenel argued that if Washington considered Mason and Slidell as enemies, then the British flag protected them, as the United States had agreed in a treaty with France. Nor could Washington, Thouvenel reasoned, consider the two men as contraband, because treaties made special provision for persons. Further, the *Trent* was plying between neutral ports; hence, the British flag covered both persons and goods, including dispatches carried by the commissioners. If Washington considered the two men as rebels, then they had a very clear right of asylum on board a British ship.[24]

Case and Spencer asserted that Thouvenel's note was influential in persuading Abraham Lincoln to accept William Seward's recommendation to release the two commissioners. Thouvenel's note, they reasoned, provided conclusive evidence that Washington could not expect support from European powers. The note also dashed Lincoln's plan to propose arbitration as a face-saving measure, since France was the most obvious choice as an arbitrator, and the French had clearly made up their mind on the matter.[25]

When the text of Thouvenel's note was made public about December 23, 1861, the French press expressed almost unanimous support. Thouvenel's message enunciated "the same principles which we have supported in our columns," reported the Liberal *Presse*.[26] The notably Republican and pro-Union *Siècle* was pleased that Thouvenel supported the French doctrine of the inviolability of a neutral flag. The newspaper hoped that from the dispute would come a more explicit recognition of neutral rights. The *Siècle*, which had repeatedly urged French mediation of the dispute, had only one regret about Thouvenel's note: France's position was so clear that the French government could not offer its good offices or become an arbitrator.[27] The Legitimist *Ami du peuple* was one of the few French journals to express reservations about the note. The staunchly antislavery religious journal, which saw slavery as the only important issue in the Civil War, resolutely opposed any measure that could increase the hopes of the slaveholders.[28]

If the French press overwhelmingly supported Thouvenel's note and hoped that it would bring about a peaceful resolution of the dispute, nevertheless, fears still remained that the *Trent* affair would lead to a war between London and Washington. French newspapers were sharply divided on the role their country should play in such an eventuality. This division, unlike other Civil War issues, did not follow ideological lines.

Those who believed that France should support Britain included some Conservatives and also the often maverick Republican *Presse*. The *Presse* argued that France had the option of playing either of two roles in the event of war between London and Washington: common action with England or an absolute neutrality. While the writer for that Republican newspaper loved liberty in America, in America he also found egotism and an absolute indifference for all causes. Besides, the question of rights on the sea was important; France, he concluded, ought to join England in the war.[29] The Governmental *Constitutionnel* favored the British, and, charged some of its critics, actually advocated going to war on their side.[30] The Governmental *Patrie* also favored entry in the war with the British.[31]

Far more newspapers, however, urged French neutrality if the *Trent* affair led to war between Britain and the United States. One provincial Conservative journalist from La Rochelle argued that the British desired to have a war with the United States and were utilizing the occasion as an excuse to bring about hostilities. While the *Trent* affair was political in appearance, it was mercantile in reality. British prime minister Palmerston was angry more because of the cotton shortage in Manchester than because Mason and Slidell could not walk in Regent's Park or Piccadilly. Would not the claimed insult to the *Trent* be forgotten if President Lincoln allowed cotton to be transported to British ports? Further, queried the skeptical French journalist, did the manufacturing interests and political sensibilities of Britain touch Frenchmen to the point of associating in an enterprise debatable from the point of view of law?[32]

A journalist writing in another La Rochelle newspaper wondered whether it was wise to encourage England in its eternal pretensions to supremacy. The British had used the right of visit against French sailors. The *Courrier de La Rochelle* further saw England expecting France to become an auxiliary for those who sought a pretext against the republic of Washington and Franklin. As for us, continued the *Courrier*, we would remain faithful to our sympathies for the cause of the American union. The most simple good sense would be for France not to encourage England to seize the pretext, which it had sought, to annihilate the fleet of the United States. That fleet could become a powerful auxiliary for the French fleet.[33]

The Clerical *Ami du peuple* strongly urged "the most strict neutrality" because of numerous material reasons. In a war with the United States Britain would destroy the American fleet, a fleet that could provide a counter to the enormous preponderance of the British naval power. If France joined Britain, France would also be supporting slavery in the South. On the other hand, if France went to war against Britain, that would be deadly for French commercial and other interests.[34] Thus, because of ideology, economic interest, and *raison d'état* France should stay neutral.

The Governmental *Avenir*, of Blois, also believed that France should maintain strict neutrality. Wilkes was wrong, but if reparation was to be gained through war, Britain had no need of French ships or troops. All of those in France who understood the mission of America, who had seen a violent but incontestable step toward a more advanced civilization, had made vows for the success of General George McClellan. At the moment when the cause of slavery was compromised, France should not unite with Britain to make more irremediable the fall of the republic whose alliance was an integral part of French political interests. Neutrality satisfied French interests and sympathies. The British would raise the blockade, thus satisfying French interests.[35] France should stay neutral, agreed Quimper's Conservative *Impartial du Finistère*. England was more concerned about cotton; the English navy had done far worse many times. Nothing obliged France to leave its role as observer.[36]

The Orleanist *Courrier du dimanche* argued that France should not join in a war with Britain over freedom of the seas because that would deprive France of its only ally to maintain freedom of the seas. Nor should France recognize the South; such a step would be incompatible with the idea of liberty and progress. In any event the *Courrier* did not expect war because a democratic government, which did not have the "pride of certain ancient monarchies, will experience no difficulty in repairing an involuntary wrong."[37]

The Legitimist *Monde* even suggested the possibility of intervention on the American side. Louis XVI, after all, had helped the United States in order to weaken Britain. Further, France was the natural defender of secondary maritime powers; it was not in French interests to see America defeated by the British. Hence, good sense dictated that French neutrality should be conditional and armed; it could happen that France one day would be forced to intervene, almost certainly if the war were prolonged. When it was a question of the dissolution of an empire of 30 million, which was important to French commerce, would Frenchmen see themselves impassive "on the ruins of the same people who owe us their existence?" If the North and the South separated of their own will, France would accept that; but it was not a matter of indifference if the British intervened on the side of the South. France could not let Britain "confiscate" the South.[38] (It will be remembered that the *Monde* was one of the few French newspapers that defended the actions of the Captain Wilkes.)

In an extended analysis of Civil War issues related to the *Trent* affair, the Liberal Catholic *Correspondant* argued that France should not join Britain in any war with the United States but, rather, assume the glorious role of mediator. By implication, the *Correspondant* was arguing that it was in French interest to see the United States survive.

The Liberal Catholic journal began its analysis with an economic argument, noting that the United States was the best commercial client of France, more important for the goods it bought from France than the cotton it furnished. The *Correspondant* also argued for the preservation of the American republic on political grounds which could have appealed even to conservatives. Those who were opposed to American institutions and saw in their failure the collapse of a revolutionary establishment ought not forget that the South rebelled in the name of revolution; the pretended right to separate reversed a regular election because it was not pleasing; it also changed the flag and territory of the *patrie*. Nor was the South justified by reasons of justice and humanity. The South had no right of secession; the South could not justify secession to defend slavery, since neither the president nor Congress had the constitutional right to abolish slavery.

French national interests, urged the *Correspondant*, demanded a united, powerful America. If the United States fell, England would no longer have a counterweight; in case of war, Britain would perform acts far worse than that which presently excited them. Britain also, claimed the *Correspondant*, had vastly different interests than France. Cotton excited Britain, but there was then no famine and the British had taken steps to assure a supply in the future. The real passion for Britain in the *Trent* affair was revenge against a rival, to destroy a national, commercial, maritime power. The existence of America was "as odious to England as it ought to be dear to us."

Assuredly, admitted the *Correspondant*, the capture of the Confederate commissioners was wrong, though there were extenuating circumstances. The right of visit was not contested; nor was the right to lead a suspected ship to port contested. Wilkes was, however, wrong to make himself judge, and to seize Mason and Slidell instead of seizing the ship.

In this situation France should play a glorious role and mediate between England and the United States. "Mediation would be glorious, neutrality would be useful, while cooperation with England would be madness," concluded the *Correspondant*.[39]

A provincial editor conveniently summarized the attitudes of Parisian newspapers about the French role if war erupted between Britain and the United States. Favoring neutrality were the Orleanist *Journal des débats* and *Temps*, the Imperial *Constitutionnel*, and the Republican *Opinion nationale* and *Siècle*. The Republican *Presse* and the Imperial *Patrie* thought France ought to join Britain.[40] On this issue political ideology clearly did not play a determining role.

With evident relief French newspapers published news of the pacific resolution of the *Trent* affair. While over and over again they repeated a statement attributed to Abraham Lincoln that he could not have two wars at the same time and therefore was releasing the two commissioners, French newspapers also found other explanations for resolution of the dispute.

French public opinion, reported a Conservative provincial newspaper, everywhere "pronounces itself in favor of the wisdom which the federal government has demonstrated in difficult circumstances."[41] A Republican provincial journal toasted "Honor to the government of the United States! Honor also to American public opinion! To recognize the necessities of a situation, to conform to it with a manly resignation, is a proof of wisdom which is not yet common among governments and peoples." While the satisfaction of the moment was for England, reported the provincial journal, "the true triumph is clearly for the United States and for the cause of liberty of the seas."[42] In returning the commissioners, America assured the triumph of principles that it had always supported against the British.[43] The American response, full of good will and skill, added a Chalon newspaper, promoted the civilized principles that France defended; to the great satisfaction of the maritime world, the American response also tied Britain to those principles for the future. Henceforth, "the neutral flag covers merchandise and persons vis-à-vis the belligerents." If the *Trent* affair had been troubling, it at least had served to inaugurate a grand principle.[44] The Liberal *Correspondant* rejoiced that the old maxim—"when the people are king, the rabble is the queen"—was not true. President Lincoln and Secretary of State Seward solved that perilous incident with as much moderation as sagacity.[45]

A few French newspapers voiced skepticism about American motivation in settling the *Trent* affair. The Legitimist *Monde* briefly observed that in the presence of European diplomacy, which pronounced itself in so categoric a fashion, Lincoln had no choice but to retreat. On the other hand, there was no real solution, since other questions could also arise.[46] A provincial Legitimist journal cynically noted that Lincoln's explanation that he could not have two wars at the same time permitted appreciation of the true character of the American concession. "We were right to predict since the origin of the crisis," concluded the skeptical editor, "that Jonathan and John Bull, merchants above all, would at the end exchange only *balles de coton*."[47] The *Presse* was scathing: the settlement was a "profound disappointment." Seward had sacrificed all principles of maritime law; his position was "the absolute negation of the doctrines and conclusions of M. Thouvenel."[48]

Such views were not typical, however, since French reaction to the American action was almost overwhelmingly positive. Some Frenchmen did explain the successful settlement, however, in terms of the tact and wisdom displayed by the British, which made it easy for the Americans to release the commissioners.

Many more Frenchmen pointed with pride to Thouvenel's role. His circular, wrote an otherwise unhappy *Presse*, deserves "for the greatest part, the honor for the pacific conclusion" of the affair.[49] A good part of the "remarkable result" was because of Thouvenel's "wise and energetic dispatch," agreed a Governmental provincial newspaper.[50]

Throughout the affair, French newspapers with Gallic slyness had pointed out the irony of Britain supporting rights of merchant ships under a neutral flag. It was surprising, reported one thoughtful provincial editor, that Britain was so pleased with the settlement of the affair, since the British seemed happy with the prospect of war when the news first broke. While Britain had gained a point in the settlement of the affair that perhaps satisfied British pride, the United States had achieved a more serious success. America, observed the editor, had led Britain to undertake the defense of the rights of neutrals that it had so often violated and which the United States had so often defended.[51]

NOTES

1. This paragraph is based on Lynn M. Case and Warren F. Spencer, *The United States and France: Civil War Diplomacy* (Philadelphia, University of Pennsylvania Press, 1970), pp. 190–92. Case and Spencer hypothesized that Confederate officials set "a trap deliberately to force England into war against the North by exposing this new mission to the possibility of Federal capture on a neutral British ship"; *ibid.*, p. 190. Gordon H. Warren, *Fountain of Discontent: The Trent Affair and Freedom of the Seas* (Boston, Northeastern University Press1981), p. viii, said that Case and Spencer presented a "superb history of the French side of the crisis . . . marred only by its curious acceptance of the old conspiracy theory that Captain Charles Wilkes connived with Mason and Slidell in the capture." Daniel Carroll, *Henri Mercier and the American Civil War* (Princeton, N. J., Princeton University Press, 1971), pp. 99–100, supported "the Case thesis that the South set up Mason and Slidell."

The literature on the *Trent* affair is extensive; for treatment of the affair from various perspectives, see in addition to the above titles, Norman B. Ferris, *The Trent Affair: A Diplomat Crisis* (Knoxville, University of Tennessee Press, 1977); John M. Taylor, *William Henry Seward: Lincoln's Right Hand* (New York, Harper Collins, 1991); David Crook, *The North, the South, and the Powers, 1861–1865* (New York, John Wiley, 1974); Ephraim D. Adams, *Great Britain and the American Civil War* (2 vols., New York, Longmans, Green and Co., 1925).

2. "Bulletin du jour," *Temps*, November 28, 1861.

3. Poitevin, (Blois) *Avenir*, December 1, 1861.

4. Labiche, *Presse*, December 2, 1861.

5. Siret, *Courrier de La Rochelle*, December 7, 1861.

6. Lomon, *Pays*, December 6, 1861, cited in W. Reed West, *Contemporary French Opinion on the American Civil War* (Baltimore, Johns Hopkins University Press, 1924), p. 44.

7. Labiche, *Presse*, December 2, 1861.

8. Mahias, *Presse*, December 1, 1861.

9. Chantrel, *Monde*, November 30, 1861.

10. Forcade, *Revue des deux mondes*, January 1, 1862, 245.

11. John Bigelow, *Retrospections of an Active Life* (5 vols., New York, 1909), I, 385.

12. Martin, (Châlons) *Journal de la Marne*, December 4, 1861.

13. Glorieux, *Vigie de Cherbourg*, December 1, 8, 1861.

14. Gaillardet, *Constitutionnel*, November 29, 1861; Limayrac, *Constitutionnel*, November 30, 1861, cited in West, *French Opinion*, p. 41.

15. Jourdan, *Siècle*, December 2, 1861.

16. Hébrard, *Temps*, December 8, 12, 1861.

17. Ferrier, *Courrier de La Rochelle*, December 4, 1861.

18. *Ibid.*, December 18, 1861.

19. Coquille, *Monde*, January 6, 1862. This statement represents a change in position, because on November 30, 1861, *Monde* had sharply criticized the American action; see *supra*, p. 47.

20. Alloury, *Journal des débats*, December 1, 1861, cited in West, *French Opinion*, p. 46.

21. Filingre, (Vesoul) *Journal de la Haute-Saône*, December 7, 1861.

22. Cumot, (Angers) *Ami du peuple*, December 12, 1861.

23. Ferris, *Trent Affair*, p. 80, related suspicions of British officials that French concern in the matter was not disinterested; they attributed French activity to a desire for war between the North and Britain so that the blockade would be lifted.

24. For a copy of Thouvenel's note, see Case and Spencer, *Civil War Diplomacy*, pp. 202–204. Case and Spencer contended that maintaining the entente with Britain and "earning diplomatic capital" were "probably the chief factors in the French decision" to support London. The French also saw an opportunity to reaffirm their liberal position on neutral rights. Carroll, *Henri Mercier*, p. 106. Ephraim D. Adams, *Great Britain and the American Civil War* (2 vols., London, Longmans, Green, and Co., 1925), I, 234–35, hinted that Thouvenel's note was a reflection on former British practices and that one reason for European support of Great Britain in the *Trent* crisis was "to tie her to a limitation of belligerent maritime power."

25. Case and Spencer, *Civil War Diplomacy*, pp. 227–28. Historians of the *Trent* affair do not agree about the influence of Thouvenel's note on American officials. Ferris, *Trent Affair*, p. 182, asserted that two Cabinet members, who were initially opposed to releasing the commissioners, were "greatly shaken" upon learning of European (including French) feelings on the *Trent* question. Ferris also asserted, however (p. 245), that Case and Spencer gave the French note "undue weight." Ferris doubted that "the decision of the cabinet would have been different had Thouvenel's note never arrived." According to Carroll, *Henri Mercier*, p. 111, Thouvenel's "note had much to do with changing the president's mind on a very crucial point—the possibility of arbitrating the dispute." Marvin Zahniser, *Uncertain Friendship: American-French Diplomatic Relationships Through the Cold War* (New York, Wiley, 1975), p. 139, considered Thouvenel's "note so sensible, logical, and tactful that it became much easier than expected for the Union government to release the prisoners." Warren, *Fountain of Discontent*, p. 182, said that the Cabinet realized that it could not count on French support in a war with Britain. While Thouvenel's note was not the only factor in cabinet considerations," related Warren, it helped demolish "hope that Anglo-French rivalry would be America's gain in the present crisis." Howard Jones, *Union in Peril: The Crisis over British Intervention in the Civil War* (Chapel Hill, University of North Carolina Press, 1992), did not mention Thouvenel's note, nor did Glyndon van Deusen, *William Henry Seward* (New York, 1967). Brian Jenkins, *Britain and the War for the Union* (2 vols., Montreal, McGill-Queens University Press, 1974, 1980), I, 227, reported that Thouvenel's dispatch was read to Seward, so that the cabinet realized that France would be strongly tempted to join Britain in case of war with America.

26. Mahias, *Presse*, December 24, 25, 1861.

27. Bernard, *Siècle*, January 3, 1862, cited in West, *French Opinion*, pp. 52–53.

28. Cumot, (Angers) *Ami du peuple*, December 28, 1861.

29. Peyrat, *Presse*, December 7, 1861.

30. Cumot, (Angers) *Ami du peuple*, December 24, 1861.

31. Poitevin, (Blois) *Avenir*, December 12, 1861.

32. Bayvet, (La Rochelle) *Charente-Inférieure*, December 31, 1861.

33. Siret, *Courrier de La Rochelle*, December 7, 1861.

34. Cumot, (Angers) *Ami du peuple*, December 14, 1861.

35. Poitevin, (Blois) *Avenir*, December 12, 1861.

36. Bayvet, (Quimper) *Impartial du Finistère*, December 7, 1861.

37. Horn, *Courrier du dimanche*, January 5, 1862.

38. Fontaines, *Monde*, January 5, 1862; Coquille, *ibid.*, January 7, 1862.

39. Douhaire, *Correspondant*, 54, December, 1861, 734–39.

40. Dufour, (Bourg-en-Bresse) *Courrier de l'Ain*, December 10, 1861.

41. Fonville, (Maçon) *Journal de Saône-et-Loire*, January 1, 1862.

42. *Journal de Beaune*, January 11, 1862, quoting Nefftzer, *Temps*, n.d.

43. Ferrier, *Courrier de La Rochelle*, January 11, 1862.

44. Sordet, (Chalon) *Courrier de Saône-et-Loire*, January 11, 1862.

45. Douhaire, *Correspondant*, 55, January, 1862, 168.

46. Coquille, *Monde*, January 10, 11, 1862.

47. La Porte, (Le Mans) *Chronique de l'ouest*, January 10, 1862.

48. Labiche, *Presse*, January 19, 1862.

49. Mahias, *Presse*, January 10, 1862.

50. Fissot, (Grenoble) *Courrier de l'Isère*, January 14, 1862. The French minister to the United States, Henri Mercier, thought that Seward deserved credit for helping to keep the peace; Seward's quick publication of Thouvenel's dispatch showed that France had helped him greatly; Carroll; *Henri Mercier*, p. 117.

51. Gaches, *Journal de Saint-Étienne*, January 12, 19, 1862.

Chapter 4

Changing Military Fortunes and Emancipation

It is not the first time, that after a battle both sides sing the **Te Deum**.
Lapierre, (Évreux) *Courrier de l'Eure,* October 11, 1862

The North and the South are neither able to invade or to dominate the other. What they ought to do is conciliate each other while separating.
Sordet, (Chalon) *Courrier de Saône-et-Loire*, October 8, 1862

[According to Abraham Lincoln] No person will have slaves, except ourselves and our friends.
Conil, (Saintes) *Courrier des deux Charentes*, January 25, 1863

From a French point of view, 1862 was the most important year in the Civil War. The *Trent* crisis (Chapter 3), resolved by Washington in January, 1862, was one of the most serious international crises of the war. In the spring and early summer of 1862, while General George McClellan was waging his Peninsular campaign and seemed on the verge of capturing Richmond, many Frenchmen confidently expected an early end to the war. Such hopes were dashed when General Robert E. Lee drove McClellan away from the gates of Richmond in the Seven Days' campaign and later launched a counter invasion of the North, which culminated in the battle of Antietam. Many Frenchmen replaced expectations of a Northern triumph with a belief that neither side could achieve victory. After these stirring military events, Lincoln issued the preliminary Emancipation Proclamation. In this chapter we describe French attitudes toward military events of 1862 and Lincoln's Emancipation Proclamations. The cotton *crise* (Chapter 5), exacerbated by the shortage of Southern cotton, led to dire economic consequences by the end of 1862. The *crise* and changing military fortunes led Napoleon III to offer mediation in October, 1862 (Chapter 6), a measure many Conservative newspapers had advocated for several months. Thus the two factors of crucial importance in determining French attitudes toward the

Civil war—political ideology and assessment of military actions—as well as domestic consequences and the slavery issue influenced French opinion about the Civil War in the pivotal year of 1862.

French newspapers exhibited a wide range of views regarding military events in 1862. An analysis of attitudes must take into account the varying military fortunes of the North and South as well as the political orientation of French newspapers. In addition, the Parisian and provincial presses exhibited some striking differences.

The most consistent and clear-cut patterns appeared in the Parisian newspapers, whose attitudes toward the varying military fortunes largely followed ideological fault lines. The Conservative newspapers, *Pays*, *Patrie*, and *Constitutionnel*, were staunchly and consistently pro-South in their interpretation of military events.[1] They minimized the importance of Union successes early in the year. In April, 1862, Union forces captured New Orleans, the principal Southern port, an event that one Conservative journal characterized as insignificant from a commercial point of view. Since Texas offered other ports which were not blockaded, claimed the *Pays*, the capture of New Orleans was not even a "secondary event."[2] While the *Pays* grudgingly admitted that the North could gain victories, nevertheless, it claimed that Southern will was undiminished. Even if a Northern conquest was possible, there would be more problems, and the establishment of a true union would be more difficult. The only solution, concluded the *Pays,* was "an honorable compromise."[3] Early in the year the *Pays* claimed that Northern victories would not lead to significant results; later in the year, the Conservative organ cited Southern victories to justify French recognition of Southern independence.[4]

Nor did military events in 1862 change the position of the *Monde*, the principal Parisian Legitimist organ. A consistent supporter of the Southern right to secede, the *Monde* cited evidence of fierce Southern determination in the first half of 1862 as evidence that the war would last indefinitely. In the latter part of 1862 the *Monde* could envision only an indefinite prolongation of the war and total exhaustion of the "former" United States if the North persisted in its efforts to maintain the Union.[5]

Republican and Orleanist Parisian newspapers took a different view of military events in America. In the early part of the year hopes were high. Expecting decisive military results in the year, as "the grand American drama approaches its *dénouement*," the Orleanist *Revue* asserted that "all presages a Northern victory."[6] Later the *Revue* explicitly linked ideology and Federal military success when it claimed that North America had "already done enough [militarily] to justify the sympathies which it has inspired . . . in French liberalism."[7] In April, the Orleanist *Courrier du dimanche* looked forward to the day when "the cause of liberty and of emancipation will triumph definitively."[8] During McClellan's Peninsular campaign, the *Temps* reported that the antislavery cause had not only the sympathy of the French public but also its confidence.[9]

Even after McClellan's withdrawal from the Peninsula, the Republican *Presse* asserted that "the North wishes to maintain the Union, and it is going to maintain it."[10] The *Revue des deux mondes* also maintained a stiff upper lip. While deploring the recent military events in America and admitting that "no doubt" the government at Washington had made errors, the Orleanist semi-monthly still firmly believed in August that such faults inevitably accompanied the state of liberty, and that the American cause was worthy of the interest of liberals throughout the world.[11] Continued Union setbacks in the fall of 1862 severely shook the *Revue's* confidence, however, and with a heavy heart it admitted late in the year that the South manifestly had "military superiority over the North." With more resources but the disadvantages of liberty, the North needed superior leadership. Would the North produce a Cromwell, speculated Forcade, the editor of the review.[12]

Provincial newspapers did not follow the consistent ideological furrows of their counterparts in Paris. Often they acknowledged that they could not discern clear patterns in American military operations because the news from America was so confusing. "We give up trying to find the truth in the midst of the obscurities and contradictions which characterize the news from America," confessed one editor.[13] In addition, sighed another, sometimes the North had victory; sometimes the South had victory. In the middle of these conflicts *sans cesse* it was impossible to foresee the end of such a state of things.[14]

Some provincial Conservative newspapers, however, did have very clear and sharply focused reactions to events in America. Files for the critical year, 1862, at the Versailles annex to the Bibliothèque Nationale are sufficiently complete to determine the attitudes of twenty-seven Conservative provincial newspapers toward the Civil War. Of these, four were consistently pro-North, thirteen were consistently pro-South, while ten switched their views in the course of the year.

The four Conservative newspapers consistently sympathetic with the Northern cause were particularly confident of a Northern victory early in the year. "The affairs of America march rapidly toward a satisfactory solution," claimed the Boulogne *Impartial*; that journal hoped that the separatists would give up their "miserable pretensions" in a short time.[15] The news from America was favorable to the North, and a decisive combat was imminent. "If it leads, as one hopes," explained a Government Verdun newspaper, "to the submission of several insurgent provinces, it will be a great step towards the arrangement proposed with so much sagacity and wisdom by President Lincoln."[16] In October the (Privas) *Écho de l'Ardèche* reported calmness in America in the face of disappointments, a serenity because "the force" was in the American nation, not in the government.[17]

A far larger number of provincial Conservative journals, thirteen, were consistently—even scathingly—anti-North throughout 1862. One of the more outspoken, the (Chalon) *Courrier de Saône-et-Loire*, cited the dissolution of the American republic in 1861 as one of two major world events in that year. That "model republic," formerly so vaunted by certain parties in Europe, "a true spoiled infant, capricious and turbulent, from which Europe has suffered for a long time

. . . is on the point of falling into dissolution," rejoiced that Conservative newspaper.[18] After Lee turned back McClellan's advance on Richmond, a Marseille editor claimed that discouragement had seized the spirits in the North, while the Confederates kept all of their energy. Even the people on the streets lost enthusiasm, as had the soldiers of fortune from Ireland, Germany, and Norway, who marched in the hope of sharing the lands of the planters.[19]

While the reference to greedy soldiers of fortune suggests a deliberate effort to use dispatches to influence attitudes, there is persuasive evidence that in fact military events in America influenced French attitudes. Because of the gloomy news for Federal arms in the fall of 1862, claimed one Conservative journal, "the cause of the North loses numerous adherents each day in France."[20] The *Journal de Saint-Étienne*, sympathetic to the North at the beginning of the war, became disgusted in September as "battles continue and nothing is decided." The old Union is dead, concluded that newspaper.[21] Likewise the (Le Puy) *Moniteur de la Haute-Loire* lamented that the reverses of the Union were "distressing for all friends of progress and of civilization. But is one able to struggle against the force of things?" While it had formerly supported the North when Federal forces seemed about to win, by the fall of 1862, the newspaper believed that events had created two nations in America.[22] The Governmental (Évreux) *Courrier de l'Eure*, which early in the year had sympathetically reported news for the North, likewise concluded in October that the situation had created the desire, "or better, the need of terminating the struggle by an amiable arrangement."[23] The (Cahors) *Courrier de Lot* reported in July that abolition was the goal of the war; in which case the North played the honorable role of champion of liberty, while the South played the role of champion of slavery. "Sympathies ought to be declared for the first, while disfavor ought to weigh on the second," claimed the Governmental newspaper. In November, the same newspaper charged that the meaning of the quarrel in America escaped "the most clairvoyant."[24] The Imperial (Montauban) *Courrier de Tarn-et-Garonne* would have been the first to have been happy if the North had won the war, but by September believed that divisions in the North combined with skill in the South had nullified Northern material advantages.[25]

One provincial editor carefully explained how he ultimately arrived at a pro-Southern position. He first noted that the European press was divided: some newspapers, "carried away by their sympathies for the customs and republican doctrines of the North, have embraced its cause blindly; others, preferring the aristocratic allures of the South" have supported the South despite slavery. We favored the North, reported the editor, when it seemed about to win, but events have shown us wrong, since the South had mounted a resistance that presaged "a war without end and without result." One should not argue with facts. Events in America had created two nations that henceforth would be separated, concluded the editor.[26] Thus one editor explicitly recognized the roles of ideology and battlefield results in determining sympathies in the Civil War.

Unfortunately, the Versailles annex has very few files of Republican or Orleanist journals for 1862. The one Orleanist journal provides almost no clues on its attitude toward the Civil War. Of the four provincial Republican newspapers only the well-known (Nantes) *Phare de la Loire*, the outspoken and most often quoted Republican provincial journal, was consistently and unabashedly pro-North. The (Marseille) *Sémaphore* in early 1861 said that the North should accept separation; later in the war, however, the Marseille newspaper was clearly pro-North.[27] Files for the other two provincial Republican newspapers do not provide sufficient evidence to ascertain their sympathies in the Civil War.[28]

The six provincial Legitimist newspapers with files for 1862 at the Versailles annex took a variety of approaches. Two of them had so few comments that their attitudes were indiscernible. Another was concerned about America falling into barbarity and hoped for mediation.[29] Three Legitimist newspapers, however, took very distinctive points of view. The (Pau) *Mémorial des Pyrénées* claimed that while France was more sympathetic toward the South, it was even more interested in peace than in seeing one side or the other win. Between "adversaries as irreconcilable" it was only possible to have a separation more or less amiable or a war of extermination. After so much bloodshed and hatred, reestablishment of the old Union was impossible. In September the newspaper reported that Confederate victories had produced a lively sensation. The Clerical newspaper's notably hard-headed conclusion: "it is not the success of such or such a party which has our sympathies; it is the chances that these victories would finally be able to give to the reestablishment of peace."[30] The (Bordeaux) *Guienne* took an equally realistic approach: while it complained of racism in America, it regretted Northern defeats since the United States was the enemy of Britain and hence the ally of France.[31]

Another Clerical editor, the provincial Clerical editor most frequently quoted by the Paris press, took a very different position. "We are assuredly not the enthusiastic admirers of America of the North," wrote the editor of (Angers) *Ami du peuple*, and

> we know everything that one can say against these republicans who push to the most absurd fanaticism the pride of blood and prejudice of color; but it suffices that the cause of the South is the cause of slavery that our wishes have been and continue to be for the triumph of the states over which Mr. Lincoln presides.

After reporting both the defeat of McClellan at the Seven Days' Battle and his statement that he would still take Richmond, the editor reminded his readers that "whoever knows the perseverance and tenacity [of the people of the North] is able to affirm that bad fortune increases their tenacity and energy, far from discouraging them." While the North had suffered a grave defeat, it was redoubling its efforts. The editor continued to favor the North and did not doubt their victory. The editor hoped that the war would end soon, in part because he believed slavery would not survive the war. The editor did not care about other issues: let the South separate; let monarchy replace the republic. The only important issue to him was slavery.[32]

Thus French newspapers took cognizance of the dramatic reversal in Union military fortunes in the course of 1862, and some provincial newspapers changed their stance toward the war as a result. French newspapers also took cognizance of the slavery issue; there is no evidence, however, that any newspapers changed their views of the Civil War as a result of the dramatic developments regarding slavery. A review of the slavery issue in the Civil War will put in perspective French views regarding Abraham Lincoln's preliminary Emancipation Proclamation, issued after the Battle of Antietam in September, and the final proclamation on January 1, 1863.[33]

The first point to be noted is that French Liberals wrote several tracts trying to persuade the French public to react against slavery. Agénor de Gasparin, who was a Liberal Protestant and author of *Un grand peuple qui se relève* (1861), passionately supported the antislavery cause. Eugène Pelletan, one of the few Liberal members of the Legislative Assembly, authored the *Adresse au roi coton* (1863), which blamed slavery as the principal cause of the war. The Liberal Catholic Augustin Cochin, editor of the *Correspondant*, penned *L'Abolition de l'esclavage* (1859), while the noted champion of American democracy, Edouard Laboulaye, wrote various works on slavery and the constitution.[34]

Certainly French journalists were aware of the importance of the slavery issue in America. Indeed, almost all French newspapers during the early stages of the secession crisis assumed that slavery was the principal issue. A common interpretation of secession was that the election of an antislavery, Republican president threatened the existence of slavery. Faced with this revolutionary movement from the North, Southerners then seceded to protect what they viewed as a vital institution. French newspapers described other differences between the sections, but in 1860 and 1861 agreed that slavery was the most significant issue. French newspapers also were aware that Abraham Lincoln was no abolitionist, that is, one who favored immediate steps for the abolition of slavery. French newspapers explained that Lincoln had publicly pledged not to interfere with the institution of slavery in states where it then existed; rather, he called for prohibiting the extension of slavery into new territories. In addition, French journalistic treatment of these issues clearly shows that Frenchmen were strongly opposed to slavery, and appalled that such an institution could exist in the 1860s.[35]

A very few provincial Clerical newspapers continued to identify slavery as *the* issue in the war. One Clerical editor, previously cited, did not care which of the two contending parties won or lost, or whether America became a republic or a monarchy, because the question of slavery was of overriding importance. Since the North was antislavery, a Northern victory would necessarily result in the abolition of slavery, and hence the paper favored a Northern victory. Expressing a similar view, a provincial Conservative journal reasoned that a Northern victory was of secondary importance; abolition was of primary importance. If it was impossible to save the Union, one should not despair of abolition.[36]

For many French newspapers, however, by the latter half of 1861 slavery was no longer the universally accepted explanation of the cause of the Civil War or the determinant of attitudes toward the war. Rather, the issue of slavery became a political fault line that divided French newspapers, with Liberal supporters of the North emphasizing the importance of the slavery issue and Conservative Southern supporters denying that it was the major issue in the conflict. Thus for French newspapers the slavery issue became a debating device and a political litmus test of attitudes toward the warring American sections.

The major Parisian Liberal journals, whether they were Republican or Orleanist, throughout the war emphasized the importance of the slavery issue. To the Orleanist *Temps*, slavery was "at the essence of the war" because it created two hostile interests.[37] The Republican *Presse* agreed. "Fundamentally," it claimed, "the cause of the war arose from concerns of slaveholders, motivated by the constant progression of abolitionist ideas."[38]

Edouard Laboulaye, noted Liberal writer and outspoken admirer of American political institutions, expressed concern in 1862 that "the South has many friends in France, and slavery has found more favor than we would have imagined. . . . The North has gathered, however, a host of defenders who have not abandoned the old and glorious traditions of France." Laboulaye was tying the slavery issue to France's historic role during the American Revolution.[39]

As the quotation from Laboulaye suggests, Frenchmen did differ upon the slavery question. Indeed, slavery was the subject of much bickering among rival newspapers. The *Temps* became involved in a typical quarrel regarding the slavery question with the Imperial *Patrie* when the latter complained that the North did not act energetically enough against slavery. The *Temps* replied that everyone had a right to reproach the North for its shilly-shallying on the issue—except defenders of the South, such as the *Patrie*. Slavery, explained the *Temps*, was the cause of the conflict, but until Lincoln's election, the South controlled the country and hence there was no way to strike at slavery. Unfortunately, the North found itself in a no-win situation. If the North was moderate, the *Patrie* said it was not doing enough; but when John C. Fremont announced his program for the abolition of slavery, the *Constitutionnel* spoke of barbarity.[40]

Nor were Liberal journalists slow in taunting Conservative colleagues, repeatedly labeling them as "*esclavagistes*," meaning supporters of slavery. Liberal newspapers particularly relished the opportunity to report Southern justifications of slavery. A famous speech of Alexander Stephens, the Confederate vice president, gave Liberal newspapers a golden opportunity. In his speech Stephens noted that Thomas Jefferson and a majority of statesmen at the time held that slavery was a violation of the laws of nature. Not so, said Stephens; Jefferson was wrong, and the new Confederate government was based on exactly contrary ideas. Its cornerstone ("*pierre d'angle*") was slavery, and the Confederacy was based on the great truth that the Negro was not the equal of the white, and slavery was his natural and moral condition.[41] Liberal newspapers made frequent references to Stephens's speech by writing of slavery as the *pierre d'angle* or *pierre angulaire* of the Confederacy.

In view of the overwhelming French opposition to slavery, French supporters of the Confederacy sought to minimize the importance of the slave question. They denied that the Civil War was a crusade to abolish slavery.[42] As evidence of that assertion, they quoted statements of Abraham Lincoln, including his letter to Horace Greeley, in which he explained that thc goal of the war was not to abolish slavery but rather to preserve the Union.[43] If slavery did not bring about the Civil War, then why did the war occur? Conservative journals saw base motives at work. The "only" reason for the conflict, wrote the *Pays*, was economic interest, as represented in the Morrill Tariff.[44] The war, agreed the *Patrie*, was "born by a question of tariff, encouraged by material ambitions, [and] pursued with the aid of frantic speculators."[45] Both Imperial and Clerical journals also viewed the war as an ethnic-religious conflict, in which Protestant, Anglo-Saxon Northerners sought to oppress Catholic, French-descended Southerners.[46]

The greedy, aggressive Yankees, in the view of Conservatives, far from being supporters of black rights, were instead guilty of racism. Northerners hated blacks and discriminated against them in cities like New York. What was the value of liberty when there was no equality, demanded one Conservative provincial newspaper. The United States, charged that journal, carried high the standard of democratic principles, but on one side of the standard was the word "*liberté*," while on the other side was the word "Humbug"![47]

Government newspapers also attempted to put their pro-Southern views in harmony with French antislavery sentiment by arguing that Southern efforts to free the slaves had been frustrated by Northern opposition. Hence, they concluded, the best way to free the slaves was to bring about Southern independence.[48]

The most outspoken, provincial Republican newspaper, the (Nantes) *Phare de la Loire*, sought to summarize the controversy over slavery from its Liberal perspective. The newspaper observed that Frenchmen who were pro-South had claimed that the question of slavery was "for nothing" in the American Civil War. Not daring to brave overwhelming French antislavery opinion, defenders of the South had made "every effort to reduce the American conflict to the most miserable proportions: mercantile rivalries were everything; principles, nothing; . . . the citizens of the North [were prejudiced] against the men of color." Contrary to such "rationalizations," the *Phare de la Loire* was willing to "render to President Jefferson Davis and to the newspapers of the South, the justice which is due to them. They have never dissimulated the real cause of the insurrection." While pro-Southern European newspapers denied that slavery was an issue in the war, the president of the Southern Confederacy and Southern newspapers declared openly that the goal in the war was to save "the peculiar institution which is the arch saint of the South."

In its assessment of the Northern position on the slavery question the *Phare* was equally candid and realistic. The provincial Republican journal confessed that the "sole goal" of the Federal government was "to reconstitute the Union." The abolitionists had been a little timid and willing to compromise for the sake of the Republic. The *Phare* also admitted that Abraham Lincoln at first did not wish to make any attempt to free the blacks, but the Liberal newspaper predicted that very likely a crisis would change public opinion and bring about a remedy from which "timid spirits would retreat during peace." As a matter of fact, the *Phare* claimed that the abolitionists had gained much ground since the beginning of the war.[49]

It is fair to conclude that by 1862 both pro-North and pro-South journalists sought to utilize the slavery issue to secure support from antislavery Frenchmen. Conservatives complained that Progressives talked about slavery "*sans cesse*." Progressive newspapers habitually utilized the word "*esclavagistes*" in referring to their pro-Southern counterparts, implying that they supported slavery. On the other hand, Conservatives repeatedly charged that Northerners were guilty of hypocrisy on the race issue, talking of emancipation while practicing the most blatant discrimination. The Conservative claim that the best way to achieve emancipation was through a Southern victory suggests that Conservatives also were trying to secure the support of antislavery elements in France.

With the French press polarized on the slavery issue, it is not surprising that Abraham Lincoln's attack on slavery in the Emancipation Proclamations, the preliminary proclamation of September, 1862, and the final one on New Year's Day, 1863, elicited strong reactions in the French press. Lincoln's program freed slaves behind enemy lines only. The American President deliberately did not try to emancipate slaves behind Northern lines because he justified his action on the ground of military necessity; he could not claim any military advantage in freeing slaves behind Northern lines, while freeing slaves behind enemy lines theoretically could weaken his military foes.

Lincoln's emancipation program provoked an almost unanimous negative reaction among Government newspapers. Despite the lament of one editor that "God knows what will be the consequence of that measure,"[50] Conservative journals vied with each other suggesting dire consequences. One editor believed that the proclamation was simply an appeal for servile insurrection in the vain hope of drowning the rebellion in floods of blood.[51] French concern about servile insurrection was common throughout the Civil War, and arose from slave rebellions in Roman history and in Santo Domingo.[52]

Conservatives also perceived inconsistencies and contradictions in Lincoln's program. Although Lincoln's professed goal was restoration of the Union, one provincial newspaper claimed that Lincoln's actions would redouble the ardor and animosity that existed between the sections ("oil thrown on the fire"); they would scarcely encourage slaveholders to return to the Union.[53] Another Conservative editor saw "a singular opposition of ideas" with the president saying that the war would be continued with the goal of reestablishing the constitutional relationship between the North and the South, but that the slaves in the rebellious states would be freed. By engendering hostility between the sections, claimed the provincial newspaper, Lincoln was not encouraging the reestablishment of the American Union.[54]

The Conservative *Pays* saw other inconsistencies. No longer could one argue that the North was against slavery, since slavery was banned in the South and welcomed in the North. Indeed, there was a bonus to the faithful of the North.[55] The proclamation reaffirmed the constitutional legitimacy of slavery, added a provincial journal, and "proved" that the North was not thinking about abolishing slavery, but rather used slavery as a "means of punishment and vengeance."[56] The proclamation, agreed another Conservative organ, was "*une absurdité.*" The only logical and sincere step was to destroy slavery where the Federal government exercised authority. "Mr. Lincoln, on the contrary," acidly observed the newspaper, "wishes to abolish slavery where he is not able to achieve it and to save it where he would be able to abolish it.[57]

More charitably, one Conservative provincial newspaper explained that while Lincoln proclaimed abolition "*in partibus infidelium*," the proclamation would not produce decisive results. On the other hand, it would not be sterile or lead to catastrophe. No doubt Northern generals would free slaves locally as they invaded the South; no one hoped that there would be a servile war.[58]

Liberal newspapers were less charitable in commenting about Lincoln's preliminary proclamation. The *Temps* criticized Lincoln's hesitation in acting against slavery and further deplored justifying emancipation as a wartime expedient rather than as an act of principle. While taking an equally doctrinaire—or principled—approach, the Republican *Siècle* asserted that

> in the interest of immortal principle and of individual liberty, and perhaps in that of the United States itself, it would have been better that, since the beginning of the war, the North would have clearly and in an indelible manner declared slavery abolished. That would have been more grandiose and more decisive. All spirits, or philosophers or Christians would have immediately rallied to the cause of the North, which would have been that of humanity.[59]

After Lincoln issued his final Emancipation Proclamation in January, 1863, Conservative newspapers continued their drumfire of opposition against the measure. One newspaper claimed that it would be ineffective, since the proclamation concerned only slaves in the separatist states where Federal authority was "unknown."[60] Another paper attacked the speed of emancipation. Take men after long servitude, who have suffered, who were bitter, 99 out of 100 of whom had no moral or intellectual education—to free suddenly such men would bring on horrors. "That violent country that one calls America," caustically observed the Conservative journal, was giving to the world such a "terrible spectacle." Slavery was odious, but there were worse evils. The British example of gradual emancipation was much better.[61] Emancipation might excite a servile insurrection within the Southern states, which would recall the horrors of Santo Domingo. It could lead to a "fratricidal war," darkly predicted one provincial journal, which would cover the American soil "with blood and ruins."[62] One Conservative journal skeptically observed that the slaves would only be able to profit from emancipation if they could escape from their masters. But would Union states welcome the proclamation? The antipathy of whites against blacks was well known; perhaps that would lead some governors to oppose the measure.[63] In a surprising twist, a few Conservative provincial newspapers used kind words in writing about the proclamation. One spoke of the proclamation as a powerful blow against the cause of the South and its partisans.[64] Another noted that Lincoln not only recommended that blacks abstain from violence except when necessary for personal defense, but also urged them to work for wages; Lincoln also said blacks would be received into the service of the United States as garrison troops for forts and as crews for ships.[65] This pro-Emancipation Conservative editor summarized the views of his many Conservative colleagues who were attacking Lincoln's Emancipation Proclamation. These newspapers accused him of promoting servile warfare. They also accused him of bad faith, of Machiavellian behavior, of a lying application of his principles. Lincoln's critics charged that he abolished slavery in dissident states but allowed it to exist in Union states. Thus, held the critics, Lincoln lacked sincerity and abolition of slavery was not his goal. He did not seek justice or victory for humanity, but rather "the ruin of the Southern states."

The pro-Emancipation Conservative editor did not agree with the views of his colleagues. To his mind the proclamation was not execrable; in addition, the editor perceived many extenuating circumstances in Lincoln's favor. Lincoln was fighting against those who denied *la patrie*, Southerners who without valid reasons sought to break up the Federal union. Lincoln was pursuing a legitimate goal—preservation of the Union. Was it a crime to be devoted to institutions he had taken an oath to defend? As for slavery, Lincoln had abolished that odious institution in principle, and its final suppression for the states behind Union lines was "only a question of time." Lincoln had already proposed compensated emancipation for slaves behind Union lines, offering indemnities to facilitate solution of the problem. Lincoln did not have the same obligations or necessity of sugarcoating measures against slavery in the seceded states. In striking against slavery behind enemy lines he was not contradicting previous policies or invoking servile warfare. Lincoln wished that the war would end quickly. It was to "hasten the end of the war," concluded the careful statement in defense of Lincoln, "that he proclaims the freeing of the slaves."[66]

Indeed, said the somewhat maverick Imperial *Courrier de La Rochelle*, Lincoln's proclamation deleted slavery from the Constitution of the United States. Conservatives and *esclavagistes* charged that "old Abraham has sold the skin of the bear before he killed it; they are wrong, he has struck slavery a death blow."[67] Yet the views of these two Government newspapers should be put in perspective; most of their peers did not approve of Lincoln's actions against slavery.

If most of the Conservative press was critical of the Emancipation Proclamation, so was much of the Parisian Liberal press—though for different reasons. The Progressive *Presse* complained that the declaration was "tardy." The paper also found fault with Secretary of State William Seward's explanation that the measure was a military act, a justification the *Presse* did not find satisfying; that newspaper would have preferred a moral act. Instead of acting on principle, the Union had placed a bomb among the population of the South.[68] Better abolition—the same day—in *all* of the states. Every half-measure was always a miscarriage, charged the *Presse*.[69] In October, 1862, the Republican *Siècle*, an outspoken champion of the Federal Union, also found fault with Lincoln's proclamation because it freed only those slaves behind Confederate lines. If Lincoln had abolished slavery completely, that would have been nobler and more decisive, and perhaps would have terminated the war.[70] In January, 1863, however, the *Siècle* muted its criticisms and said that the proclamation was "the most decisive measure which has been taken since the beginning of these sad hostilities."[71]

The outspoken Republican newspaper, the (Nantes) *Phare de la Loire*, agreed that the principle of emancipation suffered a grave blow because of the exception of the faithful states, but Washington marched no less firmly to "its goal by a detoured path." How could slavery subsist in the North after emancipation in the South? If Lincoln appeared inconsistent from the point of view of principle, nevertheless he was profoundly skillful because, in fact, "the proclamation opens a large path to absolute abolition of forced labor."[72]

Orleanist journals were more flattering in their reaction to Lincoln's program. "Finally," sighed the *Temps*, "President Lincoln has placed the dispute between the North and the South on its true ground." The *Temps* confessed that Lincoln took the decisive step late and only as a result of victories by Lee and Jackson. Thus emancipation was but a military expedient and not based on principle. As Lincoln said in his letter to Greeley, he would abolish slavery to save the Union. Still, such a step was logical and inevitable from Lincoln's desire not to extend slavery.[73] If Lincoln's final proclamation was "hardly able to have any immediate effect, . . . it is not less one of those words destined to resound in history, to become converted into action, and to become definitive. Slavery is not yet abolished in fact in the United States, but it is virtually, and it will not revive."[74] The *Revue des deux mondes* very carefully hoped that the Emancipation Proclamation was the beginning of the "definitive abolition of slavery." That was not what the Democratic party wished, and the proclamation had revived that party. Thus, wrote the knowledgeable editor of the *Revue*, one could see how delicate it was to touch slavery if one wished to maintain the union of parties in the North.[75]

Predictably, the Parisian Legitimist press was not happy with Lincoln's emancipation program. The Emancipation Proclamation provided further evidence to the *Monde*, the leading Parisian Legitimist journal, of poor Northern motivation. Far from condemning slavery, charged the *Monde*, the President "permits its maintenance" in states that would submit before January 1. Such a procedure, charged the *Monde*, was

> a singular manner of abolishing an institution which one disapproves, by making a kind of bonus of encouragement! Mr. Lincoln himself thus declares that slavery is not the cause of the war. It is not for the triumph of an idea that the states of the North struggle; there was first a struggle

> for supremacy; the South then raised itself as one man to maintain its independence.

According to the *Monde*, the proclamation also showed that the North despaired of winning by a regular war, and that the question of slavery was only a means of fighting a war.[76]

Thus, Abraham Lincoln's Emancipation Proclamation enjoyed a mixed reception among the French. Except for a few provincial journals, Conservative newspapers were scathing in their criticism. Parisian Republican journals were restrained in their support, much preferring that Lincoln would have freed all the slaves. Orleanist journals were more charitable, while the leading Parisian Legitimist journal was sharply critical.

The debate over emancipation coincided with extensive discussion of another issue, the cotton *crise*, which affected Frenchmen even more directly. Frenchmen realized that, because of the American Civil War, their economy had suffered devastating losses.

NOTES

1. Other newspapers routinely referred to those three publications as official or semi-official; their Southern sympathies were well known. A Clerical newspaper, for example, reported that it continued to favor the North and did not doubt their victory despite statements of the official journals, which were partisans of the South and slavery; Cumot, (Angers) *Ami du peuple*, July 26, 1862.
2. *Pays*, May 24, 1862.
3. Lomon, *Pays*, April 19, 1862.
4. Paul Pecquet du Bellet, *Pays*, September 11, 1862. This was the first in a series of three letters to the editor of the journal written by a Southern-born propagandist; the *Pays* published several of his defenses of the South.
5. Coquille, *Monde*, June 9-10, 1862; Chantrel, *ibid.*, November 15, 1862.
6. Forcade, *Revue des deux mondes*, 37, February 15, 1862, 1022; 38, March 1, 1862, 243.
7. Forcade, *Revue des deux mondes*, 38, April 1, 1862, 773.
8. Laurent-Lapp, *Courrier du dimanche*, April 27, 1862.
9. "Bulletin du jour," *Temps*, July 5, 1862.
10. Gaïffe, *Presse*, July 20, 1862. The *Temps* repeatedly discussed the Northern failure at Richmond but still retained confidence in a Northern victory; Grenier, *Temps*, July 17, 1862, and succeeding days.
11. Forcade, *Revue des deux mondes*, 40, August 1, 1862, p. 771.
12. *Ibid.*, 41, September 15, 1862, 482.
13. Gaches, *Journal de Saint-Étienne*, September 14, 1862.
14. Conantry, (Compiègne) *Écho de l'Oise*, February 25, 1862.
15. Petit, (Boulogne) *Impartial*, March 3, 1862.
16. Lallemant, *Courrier de Verdun*, April 18, 1862.
17. Roure, (Privas) *Écho de l'Ardèche*, October 2, 1862.
18. Bellomet, (Chalon) *Courrier de Saône-et-Loire*, January 1, 1862.
19. Bosq, (Marseille) *Nouvelliste*, August 1, 1862.
20. Dorcesse, (Soissons) *Argus Soissonnais*, October 9, 1862.

21. For example, Gaches, *Journal de Saint-Étienne*, March 30, 1862, September 14, 1862.

22. Perroud, (Le Puy) *Moniteur de la Haute-Loire*, September 18, November 15, 1862.

23. Lapierre, (Évreux) *Courrier de l'Eure*, October 7, 1862. This newspaper later became pro-North once again.

24. Verger, (Cahors) *Courrier du Lot*, July 22, 1862. Plantade, *ibid.*, November 19, 1862.

25. Havas, (Montauban) *Courrier de Tarn-et-Garonne*, September 30, 1862.

26. Perroud, (Le Puy) *Moniteur de la Haute-Loire*, November 15, 1862.

27. Carle, *Sémaphore de Marseille*, February 26, 1861.

28. The (Nancy) *Impartial* and the *Journal de Beaune* were the other Republican newspapers.

29. Domin, (Caen) *Ordre et la liberté*, September 25, 1862.

30. Capdevielle, (Pau) *Mémorial des Pyrénées*, July 24, July 31, September 18, 1862.

31. Batz-Trenquelléon, (Bordeaux) *Guienne*, July 23, 1862; Ribadieu, *ibid.*, September 16, 1862.

32. Cumot, (Angers) *Ami du peuple*, May 3, 1862.

33. France had abolished slavery within France itself in 1794 and in the colonies in 1848. Seymour Drescher, "British Way, French Way: Opinion Building and Revolution in the Second French Slave Emancipation," in *American Historical Review*, 96 (June, 1991), 709–34.

34. Barbara Karsky, "Les Libéraux français et l'émancipation des esclaves aux États-Unis," *Revue d'histoire moderne et contemporaine*, 21 (1974), 576–77.

Because of his *L'Abolition de l'esclavage*, Cochin received in 1862 one of the annual rewards of the French Academy. Cochin argued for abolition of slavery on moral or Christian principles and also for economic reasons. Charles and Anne Marie Poinsatte, "Augustin Cochin's *L'Abolition de l'esclavage* and the Emancipation Proclamation," in *Review of Politics*, 46 (1984), 410.

35. See, for example, Martin, Conservative *Constitutionnel*, January 10, 1862, and Forcade, Orleanist *Revue des deux mondes*, 31, February 1, 1861, 752.

36. Cumot, (Angers) *Ami du peuple*, May 3, 1862; Perroud, (Le Puy) *Moniteur de la Haute-Loire*, November 15, 1862.

37. Scherer, *Temps*, October 19, 1861.

38. Fargues, *Presse*, April 27, 1862.

39. John Bigelow was very impressed with Laboulaye's articles which appeared in *Journal des débats*, August 26, 27, 1862, and secured his permission to publish them in pamphlet form. He summarized Laboulaye's views as: first, the desire to perpetuate slavery was the cause of the revolt of the South; second, constitutionally, the South had no right of secession; third, the commercial interests of France (and the traditions of Louis XVI and Napoleon) counseled neutrality since the unity of the United States was necessary to balance British maritime power and guarantee freedom of the seas. John Bigelow, *Retrospections of an Active Life* (5 vols., New York, The Baker and Taylor Co., 1909–1913), I, 532–36.

40. *Temps*, July 26, 1862.

41. Duvernois, *Temps*, July 28, 1862, commented on the speech, which was printed in the Republican *Opinion nationale*, July 27, 1862.

42. Augustin Cochin observed that Southern sympathizers in England and France "continue to affirm that slavery is not the cause of the war;" this was, he observed, "a good way to prevent emancipation from being its consequence." *Journal des débats*, August 9, 1862, quoted in Charles and Anne Marie Poinsatte, "Augustin Cochin," p. 420.

43. For a typical expression of this idea, see Bosq, (Marseille) *Nouvelliste*, September 11, 1862.

44. Lomon, *Pays*, August 27, 1862; Melvil, *ibid.*, January 9, 1863.

45. Gullaud, *Patrie*, May 9, 1865.

46. Taconet, *Monde*, May 28, 1864.

47. "X," (La Rochelle) *Charente-Inférieure*, August 11, 1861. Justin Améro, *Correspondant*, 55, March, 1862, 528, lamented that "the unfortunate Negro is as strongly scorned in the North as mistreated in the South." A Liberal Catholic review, *Correspondant* was strongly antislavery and disappointed that the North was not fighting the war to end slavery.

48. Melvil, *Pays*, January 9, 1863.

49. Mangin, (Nantes) *Phare de la Loire*, October 15, 1862. The idea that Lincoln had been timid in striking at slavery was a common theme among Liberal journals. Only a crusade to end slavery would be a "legitimate cause for the war, which is only blasphemous if it is not a sacred war." Audoy, *Temps*, March 24, 1862, quoted in Karsky, "Les Libéraux français et l'émancipation des esclaves aux États-Unis," p. 584.

50. Fonville, (Maçon) *Journal de Saône-et-Loire*, October 8, 1862.

51. Gaches, *Journal de Saint-Étienne*, October 12, 1862.

52. Seymour Drescher, "Service Insurrection and John Brown's Body in Europe," *JAH*, 80 (September, 1993), 506.

53. (La Rochelle) *Charente-Inférieure*, October 9, 1862.

54. Céas, (Valence) *Courrier de la Drôme*, October 7, 1862.

55. *Pays*, October 7, 26, 1862.

56. Dorcesse, (Soissons) *Argus Soissonnais*, October 9, 1862.

57. Gaches, (Saint-Étienne) *Journal de Saint-Étienne*, October 12, 1862.

58. Filingre, (Vesoul) *Journal de la Haute-Saône*, October 11, 1862.

59. Grenier, *Temps*, October 9, 1862; Plée, *Siècle*, October 12, 1862, quoted in Karsky, "Les Libéraux français et l'émancipation des esclaves aux États-Unis," p. 586.

60. Normand, (Lyon) *Salut public*, January 16, 1863.

61. Vigeau, (Annecy) *Mont-Blanc*, January 18, 1863.

62. Sordet, (Chalon) *Courrier de Saône-et-Loire*, January 17, 31, 1863.

63. Conantry, (Compiègne) *Écho de l'Oise*, January 16, 1863.

64. Lapierre, (Évreux) *Courrier de l'Eure*, October 16, 1862.

65. Filingre, (Vesoul) *Journal de la Haute-Saône*, January 24, 1863.

66. *Ibid.* This Conservative journal was consistently pro-Union throughout 1862.

67. Bullier, *Courrier de La Rochelle*, January 17, 1863.

68. Regnault, *Presse*, October 6, 15, 1862.

69. Girardin, *Presse*, January 19, 1863.

70. Plée, *Siècle*, October 12, 1862, cited in West, *French Opinion*, p. 85.

71. Bédollière, *Siècle*, January 15, 1863.

72. Mangin, (Nantes) *Phare de la Loire*, October 8, 1862, January 14, 1863.

73. Grenier, *Temps*, October 9, 1862.

74. "Bulletin du jour," *Temps*, January 14, 1863.

75. Forcade, *Revue des deux mondes*, 42, November 1, 1862, 249.

76. Chantrel, *Monde*, October 6, 1862.

Chapter 5

The Cotton *Crise*

The war in the United States is a disaster for industrial and agricultural France. One follows its episodes with anxiety in the workshops, in the stores, at the shipyard where ships remain at anchor, at the vineyard where the *négociants* of New York or of Louisiana no longer visit.
Bayvet, (La Rochelle) *Charente-Inférieure*, August 10, 1862

Frenchmen were vitally interested in and affected by economic aspects of the sectional conflict in America. That interest became almost an obsession when, in part because of the Civil War, France faced "one of the worst economic depressions in her history."[1] It is not surprising that Conservatives and Liberals differed about economic aspects of the war, as they did on so many other issues. Conservatives typically emphasized the role of economic interest in causing the war and argued that an independent South would be commercially advantageous for France. They sought to alleviate economic distress arising from the war through intervention by the French government to end the conflict on the basis of Southern independence. Liberals, on the other hand, typically minimized the role of economic interest in explaining causes of the war; in addition, they argued that a united America was more economically desirable for France than two independent American countries. Liberals sought to alleviate economic suffering through organized charity rather than French intervention to end the war. Both groups did agree, however, that the war adversely affected the French economy, with the peak of distress and suffering occurring in late 1862 and early 1863.

Even before the firing on Fort Sumter, Frenchmen were suffering from the economic consequences of sectional differences between the North and the South. Describing conditions in the last quarter of 1860, French district attorneys reported that the unsettled state of American affairs had led to sharp reductions in the export of such luxury goods as carpets, silks, and velvets.[2] The Parisian newspaper,

Constitutionnel, on March 4, 1861, the day of the inauguration of Abraham Lincoln, featured a large advertisement for a distress sale of goods, a sale which occurred as a result of the crisis in the United States.

It was not only Parisian merchandisers who were concerned about possible conflict in America. Indeed, claimed a Liberal Marseille newspaper in February, 1861, a war would not only be deadly to America; it would also be very prejudicial to the commerce of Europe.[3] "All our big manufacturers are in a state of anxiety," added another provincial newspaper. Charente had already suffered serious losses in sales of its eaux-de-vie, which found an important market in the United States.[4] "If the United States does not produce cotton," warned an influential Orleanist organ, "the crisis would be terrible."[5]

Other Frenchmen, however, foresaw opportunities in the American conflict. Concerned about a shortage of cotton, the French government had developed a project to send Chinese to Algeria to raise cotton, reported a provincial newspaper in January, 1861. Within five years, the provincial newspaper hopefully forecast, France could largely supply its domestic needs. The newspaper also suggested that the program could employ French children on the project and at the same time provide them with religious training; the children would thus not only help the French economy, but they would, moreover, become "disciplined, moral, and hard-working."[6] The Conservative *Pays* in February, 1861, similarly took an optimistic view of the American crisis. In the event of reconciliation the *Pays* hoped that the tariff would be abolished; if the Union were not maintained, then the South would be open to free exchanges with French industry and agriculture.[7]

Still other Frenchmen who were opposed to both Southern slavery and Northern tariffs found it difficult to reconcile their conflicting values. The Liberal wryly observed that "commercial intolerance is preached in the free states and liberty of exchange in the slave states." In that mixed and contradictory situation, "the principles are on one side, and the interests are on the other."[8] One La Rochelle newspaper remarked that if conscientious Frenchmen had difficulty deciding between principle and interest, the British had no such problem. "In truth," acidly observed the provincial newspaper, "if the Pope possessed America and allowed the free export of cotton, England would become Catholic."[9]

After the firing on Fort Sumter and the commencement of large-scale military operations, "the alarm was great in the commercial and industrial world." As early as May, 1861, a Dijon newspaper claimed that both French and British manufacturers were suffering.[10] The *Temps* reported in September that English industry was particularly hard hit: industrialists had sharply lowered the price of products and had cut the wages of workers. Such measures, said the newspaper, were "grievous" if they were only provisional but "terrible if they have to have a long duration."[11]

For France the war initially had an adverse effect on its export industries. The war led to the "celebrated" Morrill tariff, enacted by the American Congress in 1861, which brought about changes of immense importance, according to one provincial newspaper.[12] "Poor La Rochelle" suffered from that act since cognac paid the same duty as did fine champagnes.[13] Ribbon producers in Saint-Étienne suffered incalculable losses by September because of the American *crise*.[14] The conflict would reduce the export of local fabrics, glove making, and leather industries, predicted another provincial journal.[15] Table 5.1 graphically demonstrates the sharp decline of certain traditional French exports to America.[16]

TABLE 5.1
FRENCH EXPORTS (IN FRANCS) OF SELECTED PRODUCTS TO AMERICA

	1859	1860	1861
Silk fabrics	136,000,000	103,000,000	25,000,000
Linen fabrics	28,000,000	34,000,000	10,000,000
Cotton fabrics	4,400,000		400,000
Wine	28,000,000	29,000,000	12,000,000

While French luxury industries were suffering by the end of 1861, a more important *crise* in the cotton industry loomed on the horizon. Typically, Liberal French newspapers in 1861 and early 1862 reported cotton shortages elsewhere, but warned that France would be affected in the future. Some Conservative newspapers simply ignored the problem. In May, 1861, one French newspaper noted a shortage of cotton in Catalonia, Spain, where the supplies were exhausted, or nearly so.[17] In the same month, another newspaper cited reports that the British, as well as the Spanish, were concerned about cotton.[18] Drawing on a statistical analysis of cotton stocks, a Liberal Marseille newspaper similarly reported shortages of cotton, especially in Britain. France had not been as badly impacted, since French imports had not been cut as sharply. There would, however, be a severe shortage in the future.[19] The *Temps*, a Parisian Orleanist newspaper and the most thorough chronicler of industrial activities, reported extensively on the cotton situation. British newspapers, it related in October, 1861, had been talking of the shortage of cotton for some time. The British had not been successful in getting cotton from India since the supply was limited and quality not as good as American cotton. The publicly available supply of cotton in Britain would be exhausted in December, claimed the *Temps*. In England, manufacturers were working part time; in France and on the continent, factories had not yet slowed down, but Europe would be seriously affected soon.[20] In January, 1862, the Orleanist *Revue des deux mondes* reassuringly reported that "the situation of the [French] cotton industry is certainly less deplorable than in England or in Massachusetts." Warehouses at Le Havre were more abundantly stocked than they were in 1859 and 1860, and several large establishments had a six-month supply of cotton. To justify its opposition against recognition of the South in the interest of the French cotton industry, the Liberal Catholic *Correspondant* reported in August, 1862, that up to that time the cotton industry, which was suffering so much in England, had not suffered a great deal in France.[21]

Despite indications of future difficulties, some French newspapers in 1861 continued to find glowing opportunities as a consequence of the American war.

Anticipating Southern independence, the Conservative *Vigie de Cherbourg* looked forward to the establishment of a direct line to New Orleans or other Southern ports for trade which at that time went through New York. The paper further expected that there would be an opportune moment to recognize the South; it would be difficult to "find in that question a better solution for European interests."[22] From La Rochelle, another French port, a Conservative editor painted an equally rosy picture if the South became independent. The South of the old Union, happy to exchange its cotton, its wood, and its wheat for the products of European industry, wished to lower the tariff on manufactured goods. That did not suit New York, which wanted above all to maintain the prosperity of its own factories. If the South triumphed, exulted the shipping port newspaper,

> we will have a people tied to France by sentiments of consanguinity and by mutual commercial interests. Very likely manufacturing cities of Germany and Italy would import their cottons from New Orleans by French ports in place of having them come from New York. We would be able to receive cottons in exchange for our eaux-de-vie, which would give a new activity in our relations with America.

The newspaper's view of a glowing future included recognition of the Confederacy, which would probably coincide with a new basin for La Rochelle capable of handling large ships.[23]

In the last months of 1861 the *Trent* affair clouded this happy scenario, with the threat of war between Britain and the United States. Such a war, warned one maritime provincial newspaper, would be a commercial disaster for France.[24] Indeed, several French newspapers described the *Trent* affair in economic terms, attributing British motives to a desire to break the blockade and secure cotton. The Clerical *Monde* suspected an even more far-reaching design: a scheme to "confiscate" the South. The South would be a fine market for the British; the South could become another Portugal, which, though never conquered by the British, was nevertheless Britain's best colony. That must not happen to the South, said the newspaper.[25] The pacific solution of the affair (described in Chapter 4) led one editor to offer congratulations in the interests of humanity and European commerce.[26]

Helpful as it was, the resolution of the *Trent* affair did not solve the severe problems that arose from the American Civil War. Several provincial newspapers deplored a contest that imposed so much suffering in Europe and in America.[27] In the first months of 1862 these problems principally affected Europe or Britain, according to French newspapers, which continued to minimize French distress. One provincial newspaper in a cotton-manufacturing area in February summarized reports of distress among English workers without mentioning the Civil War and without reference to distress among French workers.[28] In March another provincial paper spoke of a crisis that weighed heavily on all the manufacturing populations of England and on some of the great industrial centers of France.[29] It was only in the cotton-producing regions of Normandy that newspapers publicized special subscriptions to raise money for the poor and unemployed.[30]

By mid-year, 1862, a few newspapers did become more explicit about French difficulties. "Our industrial centers, our trading ports, our agriculture itself," reported a La Rochelle newspaper in June, "are grievously afflicted by the American war."[31] Still, as late as December, 1862, the editor of the *Revue des deux mondes* lamented that everyone knew only vaguely that there was distress among the workers in the cotton industry. While the press widely publicized hardship in Britain, among Frenchmen the practice was to "plug the ears and close the eyes" to distress at home. Forcade's bitter complaint that his fellow countrymen ignored the plight of the unemployed meant, he charged, that on one side was misery while on the other side was prosperity and opulence. Forcade's appeal to the daily press to help alleviate suffering had been heard by only a single newspaper in Paris, the *Temps*. Forcade explained that the press, under a monopoly regime, had adopted a habit of disinterest in internal affairs to the point of considering every initiative as sterile, if not perilous.[32]

Despite their reluctance to discuss distress at home, French newspapers eventually had to report the obvious: the American Civil War entailed disastrous consequences for French industries. Distress was particularly acute among manufacturers of cotton, the industry most seriously impacted by the American conflict. A brief description of the major characteristics of that industry will put the *crise* into perspective.

The most important French manufacturing activity, the cotton industry employed approximately 379,000 workers. Production was concentrated in three major areas. The most important, Normandy, with its center around Rouen, possessed some 2,500,000 spindles. The second region, the North of France, with major manufacturing establishments at Lille, among other cities, possessed some 1,500,000 spindles. The third region, Alsace and Lorraine, particularly represented at Nancy, Colmar, and Mulhouse, counted some 1,600,000 spindles.[33]

A critically important fact was French dependence on American cotton. In 1860, France imported 109,000 tons of cotton from America, that is, 92% of its cotton supply.[34] As a result of the Civil War, French imports of American cotton dropped to 295 tons in 1862, 254 tons in 1863, 900 tons in 1864, and 2,900 tons in 1865. Importations returned to a more normal 43,200 tons in 1866. Despite efforts to secure cotton elsewhere, total importation of cotton also dropped drastically during the Civil War, especially in 1862 and 1863. Table 5.2 shows imports with the years 1851–1853 as the standard (100) and other years in proportion.

Particularly noteworthy in the table is the "bowl" configuration of imports: abnormally large figures in 1861 and 1866 with sharply lower figures in between. Imports in 1861 reflected the record-breaking American cotton production in 1859 and 1860. As a result, the Northern blockade and the Southern embargo on the exporting of cotton did not have an immediate, adverse effect on the French cotton industry. Also noteworthy in the table is the sharp reduction of imports in 1862 and 1863. These figures are consistent with statements by knowledgeable observers that the cotton *crise* was at its peak in 1862 and 1863.

TABLE 5.2
INDEX OF TOTAL IMPORTATION OF COTTON INTO FRANCE[35]

1851–1853	100	1865	92
1861	164	1866	148
1862	40	1867	108
1863	64	1868	144
1864	84		

An even more sensitive indicator for distress in the industry than cotton imports was the price of American cotton at Le Havre, the major port for the industry. That figure reflected the supply of cotton, the prospects for peace, and speculation. The substantial cotton stocks in France at the beginning of the Civil War meant that cotton prices were comparatively low and stable in 1861. An index of cotton prices, using figures from January–June, 1861, as 100, reached 122 by December, 1861. In 1862, the price of cotton rose dramatically, with the index climbing to 150 in May, 1862, and 245 in September.

The sharp increase in 1862 reflected acceptance of reality. From the beginning of the war many Frenchmen believed that with the availability of transportation they would be able to import large quantities of American cotton. Only some time into the war did Frenchmen realize that it was not only the Federal blockade which prevented the importation of cotton; the Southern embargo on the export of cotton (in accordance with the King Cotton thesis) was perhaps even more effective in preventing the shipment of cotton to Europe in the early stages of the war. The capture of New Orleans in April, 1862, and the burning of stocks at that location by Confederates destroyed any French illusions that Southern cotton would readily be shipped if transportation were available. The dashing of such illusions and mixed battlefield results in 1862, which demonstrated that the war would be prolonged indefinitely, led to a period of intense speculation that culminated in higher prices in the fall of 1862.[36]

By February, 1863, the price index for cotton had dropped to 145, which can be attributed to mediation efforts of Napoleon III (discussed in Chapter 6). The dashing of hopes for peace and the seemingly endless war led to an increase to 190 in December, 1863. The price remained at approximately that same level through 1864. Finally the price began to drop in 1865: February, 160; March, 120; April, 105.

The problems in the cotton industry led to much discussion about the reasons for the *crise*. Typically Conservative newspapers explained the problems in terms of the Civil War. In particular, some Conservative newspapers blamed the blockade for the shortage of cotton, which led to high prices for the raw material, which in turn priced cotton fabrics out of the market and resulted in heavy unemployment and distress in the industry.[37]

Yet this was a misreading of the situation. The Union blockade alone did not lead to the cotton *crise* of 1862–1863. Indeed, suffering in the industry did not arise from any single cause. The *crise* can be understood in terms of multiple factors: the high price of cotton, a surplus of finished cotton goods in 1861, structural conditions within the industry, and problems related to wheat.

The high price of cotton, unquestionably a major element in the *crise,* cannot be explained in terms of a cotton famine, because there never was a famine. Early in the war, cotton was available from the bumper American crops of 1859 and 1860; later in the war, supplies arrived from other sources, such as India and Egypt. The stock of cotton at Liverpool at the end of 1862 was more than 400,000 bales, claimed the Liberal political leader Jules Ferry, and 2 million bales arrived during the year. In an extended analysis in January, 1863, of the available supply of cotton, the liberal *Temps* reported that more than 2.5 million bales of cotton was available while Europe normally used 4 million bales. Hence there should have been only a one-third reduction in work.[38] In January, 1863, the Clerical *Monde* cited a report that the supply of cotton was only 10% less than the previous year.[39]

The major force for high prices was not a famine but "fear of a shortage and especially speculation."[40] Profiteering was fueled by a perception that there would be a shortage. Such profiteering actually improved the bottom line for many French industrial establishments, who profited because their immense stocks of raw cotton in 1861 increased in value. While some industrialists turned their cotton raw material into fabrics at great profit, others sold their stores of raw material on the market at Le Havre rather than keep their factories operating.[41] That condition led the Liberal *Presse* to charge that the blockade brought enormous profits; manufacturers of Normandy, as well as the cotton lords of Lancashire, scathingly remarked that Paris newspaper, had "something on their conscience."[42]

The high price of cotton was not the only cause of the cotton *crise*; perhaps even more important was the surplus of finished cotton products in 1861. This surplus led to low prices for cotton products, prices so low that many producers could not make a profit, a situation that was aggravated by the ever-rising cost of raw cotton. In that situation many operators, particularly small concerns, were unwilling to buy the raw material at high prices for fear that the price of cotton might drop in the future.[43] Such conditions were particularly widespread in Normandy, where the industry produced modestly priced products with a low profit margin.

Thus cotton manufacturers suffered from the phenomenon of too much merchandise and not enough raw cotton; *ici, le trop plein; là, le trop peu* [here, too much; there, too little].[44] Only time would bring a solution to the problem. The *Revue des deux mondes* used a metaphor of two currents: when one current exhausted the supply of finished products and another current brought the raw cotton, there would be improvement in the economy; until then, there would be unemployment.[45]

Structural conditions within the cotton industry also played a role in the *crise.* Manufacturers of high-quality cotton products in Alsace, where the price of the finished products reflected labor costs that exceeded the cost of the raw material, suffered less from high prices for the raw material than did producers of low-quality cotton. Low-quality cotton products, which were characteristic of the industry in Normandy, were more seriously impacted because the cost of the raw material was a major element in the price of the finished product. In addition, small enterprises found it more difficult to survive in a turbulent era than did larger, well-established firms. It is not surprising that the cotton *crise* struck with particular ferocity in Normandy, where many of the establishments were small and produced low-quality cotton.[46]

A shortage of wheat also contributed to the *crise.* The poor French harvest in 1861 had several bad consequences, including larger wheat imports, disruption in the financial markets, and increases in the price of wheat and bread. Above all, higher prices for bread exhausted the resources of workers and resulted in decreased purchases of textiles. This series of events especially impacted the cotton industry in Normandy, which specialized in producing inexpensive fabrics for the working class. While the price of wheat dropped with an excellent harvest in 1862, the poor harvest of 1861 had already severely impacted the cotton industry.[47]

Thus the cotton *crise* was not the result of one single element. Frank Owsley explained the distress as a result of multiple reasons:

> overproduction; the partial loss of the American markets; the dearness of raw material; the competition of linen, wool, etc., with cotton goods; the fear of the markets being deluged with the great American surplus; and, finally, the scarcity of cotton resulting from the blockade and embargo.[48]

Notably absent from Owsley's list is the Cobden treaty of 1860, which had led to bitter complaints by French cotton producers. That treaty with Britain lowered tariff barriers, particularly French barriers against British textiles.[49] Long protected from their English rivals, some French cotton producers in "*une espèce de panique*," reduced wages drastically. While some journalists attributed problems in the cotton industry to the English treaty, the historian of the French textile industry, Claude Fohlen, believed that "the perturbation engendered by the treaty of commerce of 1860 was more psychological than real: no index reveals real trouble." After extensive examination of British-French imports and exports of cotton materials, Fohlen concluded that complaints by French producers were "only a cry of alarm on the part of industrialists too long accustomed to a protectionist regime."[50]

If the evil consequences of the commercial treaty with Britain were a myth, unemployment in the cotton industry was a reality. Unfortunately, it is difficult to state exactly how many cotton workers were unemployed since there was no agreement on the definition of a cotton worker or of an employed person. Many cotton operators were also farmers. How should such persons be classified? The other problem was the definition of unemployment; in Normandy, unemployed persons were those who worked less than two days per week. The standard for other regions of the country is not known. The uncertain state of statistics regarding employment clearly appears in figures for the department of Seine-Inférieure in Normandy. Certain estimates listed the number of unemployed at 118,000 in December, 1862, while another estimated at 81,000 the total number of cotton workers in the department.

Claude Fohlen, the historian of the industry, explained that only in Seine-Inférieure did authorities report unemployment numbers for 1862, but he maintained that an estimate of 96,679 unemployed was obviously exaggerated. Figures for France as a whole show the number of unemployed on April 15, 1863, as 223,336 (Seine-Inférieure 40,000) and 174,052 on February 23, 1864. Unemployment reached its maximum intensity, related Fohlen, during the winter of 1862–1863.[51]

With "frightful misery" among the working class,[52] Frenchmen debated what measures should be taken to relieve the distress. One possible solution was to end the war and lift the Union blockade. By the summer of 1862, Conservative newspapers were calling for French mediation to achieve those goals. The *Constitutionnel* justified mediation on the ground that it would promote the economic interests of France.[53] Others supported mediation for very general economic and non-economic reasons. "God grant, in the interest of commerce and of civilization," piously wished the *Journal du Lot*, "that the great powers intervene" and end the war in America.[54] With the worsening economic situation such cries for intervention reached a climax toward the end of 1862.

Liberal newspapers typically argued that intervention would not solve French economic woes. The *Courrier du dimanche* reasoned that economic problems in England and France were caused by the South, not by the North.[55] "[I]f we have need of cotton," added the *Presse*, "we also have need of wheat, and it is the North which produces wheat."[56] The *Siècle* also contended that French intervention either in the form of mediation or recognition of the South would mean war, and French industry would suffer a hundred times more than it did at that time.[57] Actually, argued the *Temps*, which made particular efforts to report the cotton *crise*, the interest of European manufacturers was "that the South be promptly and violently led back into the bosom of the Union."[58]

Thus Liberals and Conservatives differed on the wisdom of intervention as a device to relieve economic distress, as they did on so many other issues. Chapter 6 has an extended discussion of the issue of French intervention in the American conflict.

Rather than advocating intervention, Liberal journals typically promoted internal measures to alleviate economic problems arising from the war. One Orleanist newspaper urged the unemployed to accept their present distress as the work of Providence and join with their patrons in making the best of the situation. Follow the advice of John Bright, the English industrialist and statesman, urged the newspaper, and do not speak in favor of the South.[59] One provincial newspaper prominently featured the action of Manchester textile workers, who on January 1,

1863, voted their opposition to slavery and their support for Abraham Lincoln. Since Manchester was the place where workers suffered the most, it was impossible, said the newspaper, "not to admire . . . those men sacrificing their personal interests to their convictions, and wishing a continuation of a war which ruins them in order to bring about the abolition of slavery."[60] In October, 1862, a pro-Governmental newspaper pointedly expressed admiration for the attitude of the working class in Britain. While English workers were badly hurt by the American war, they still did not show sympathy for the slave states.[61] Such appeals for the French workers to show restraint in the face of suffering may have been effective. After the peak of suffering in the Seine-Inférieure had passed, a Rouen newspaper wrote of its population, one part "saintly resigned, the other nobly generous."[62] A student of nineteenth-century French labor concurred with that opinion. "The mass of the workers," he claimed,

> remained cold to pro-Confederate propaganda. Though they were without jobs or food, they did not call for intervention on the side of the South. Like the workers in England, they preferred to suffer rather than be allies of slave owners.

Unlike British workers, French workers did not demonstrate publicly on the issue because of political restrictions. Rather, they expressed their support for antislavery by remaining calm and avoiding any demonstration likely to disturb the peace.[63]

A modern scholar, however, has attacked what he calls the "myth" of French worker support for the North. While direct, first-hand evidence of worker attitudes is not available, Thomas A. Sancton cited indirect evidence to support his assertion. No working-class writer expressed "a single enthusiastic pro-North statement"; certain Parisian labor groups expressed no views on the Civil War when they had the means to do so; public opinion in distressed cotton manufacturing areas favored the South and sought French intervention to break the Union blockade. Sancton suggested that there was no major uprising by French workers because they believed that the emperor was doing all he could to relieve distress through relief efforts and intervention to end the war.[64]

Actually, relief efforts initially resulted not from programs by the emperor, but from activities by local authorities. At the end of 1861, the municipality of Rouen, Normandy, instituted a subscription that raised 250,000 francs to help the unemployed. In September, 1862, the first committee to aid the unemployed was organized in Flers, Normandy. In November, the Rouen Chamber of Commerce announced that 100,000 persons were unemployed in the department of Seine-Inférieure, and that the figure soon would be 150,000. A few days later, on November 13, 1862, civic leaders in that city organized the central Charity committee for the lower Seine. The committee raised 2 million francs by the end of December, 1862, and made distributions to the unemployed of one franc per head of family in the country and one and a half francs per head at Rouen and at Le Havre. The Rouen committee was transformed into a national Charitable committee in February, 1863, with subcommittees in each of the fourteen departments affected by the *crise*. The first general assembly of the national committee met in Rouen on April 15, 1863. That assembly distributed 660,000 francs at the rate of three francs per unemployed.

Meanwhile, the government was not inactive. In March, 1862, the government provided the minister of the interior with 2 million francs to subsidize public works and to fund charitable organizations in order to provide succor for the unemployed. The government provided additional funds in January, 1863, with grants of 5 million francs specifically designated for unemployed cotton workers. In May, 1863, the government added 1,200,000 francs for public works and charitable distribution. In addition, the government sponsored a national subscription for the unemployed, which combined the efforts of the national Committee and local committees. This national subscription raised more than 2,500,000 francs in February, 1863. The minister of the Interior distributed almost 600,000 francs in April and made another distribution of almost 500,000 francs in December, 1863. Several other distributions took place in 1864 and 1865, the last one in February, 1865.[65]

Many newspapers gave their support to such activities. Local committees, such as Le Comité Bienfaisance à Elbeuf, published appeals for funds since the cotton industry was in a "state of distress hitherto unknown," with the working class suffering from "frightful misery."[66] The Liberal *Temps* took national leadership in organizing support for the unemployed. Every French newspaper, it noted, had spoken of the distress of English workers; the same distress was felt in France; the Seine-Inférieure was the French Lancashire. The *Temps* applauded the work of the Rouen committee and helped to establish the national Committee to raise funds for the unemployed. Little communes, the *Temps* noted, had already exhausted their resources, and the newspaper appealed to all Frenchmen to help the unfortunates.[67] Other Liberal newspapers, in Paris and the provinces, actively supported these appeals.

Political controversy plagued even these efforts to help the distressed. The Liberal, anti-Clerical organ, *Siècle*, complained that people were not giving enough and cited figures from the Clerical *Monde* that 300,000 persons, without resources of work, needed at least 150,000 francs per day. But giving outside of the department of Seine-Inférieure had not exceeded 200,000. Was it more urgent to support cardinals in luxury in Rome? People in the country gave almost nothing; virtually all contributions had come from the cities. (The *Siècle's* none too subtle point: the country was Conservative, while Liberals were concentrated in the cities.)[68] The *Siècle* proudly reported that everyone at that newspaper had given once, and now all were offering a day's work. "We do not speak of the clergy," the *Siècle* acidly commented, "who know how to find 16 million for the needs of the Papal government."[69] The Liberal *Presse* and *Sémaphore de Marseille* likewise complained about stingy giving.[70] In a sharp rejoinder one provincial Conservative journal blamed the Liberal journals themselves for the poor giving. Some journalists, it charged, had encouraged the North to pursue an interminable war, and in the process discouraged readers and killed the subscription.[71]

Despite partisan bickering, by the end of 1863 the worst of the crisis had passed. One provincial newspaper even had reported the "end of the cotton *crise*" in April, 1863, with the news of the arrival of two ships laden with cotton.[72] In 1864 and 1865, the situation began to return to normal as France succeeded in securing alternate sources of cotton to replace cotton from America. In addition, the high price of cotton had also encouraged a shift to wool and linen. "In the rude school of necessity," claimed the *Revue des deux mondes*, "Europe has quickly learned to do without America."[73]

While it may have been politically convenient to blame suffering in the cotton industry on the Civil War, Blumenthal, in his study of Franco-American relations, asserted that those difficulties should not really be attributed to the conflict. Indeed, some large manufacturers argued that a sudden opening of cotton ports would have been a disaster, because French markets were gutted with goods that could be absorbed only with time. The war did, however, according to Blumenthal, have a detrimental effect on the French economy. The suspension of cotton exports meant that Americans did not have revenues to buy French products. In addition, financial exigencies brought on by the Civil War compelled the North to curtail its imports drastically. The result was that several French industries, such as silk and china, suffered a great deal. It was of little consolation to the workers in those industries that the linen, hemp, and wool industries prospered during the crisis. After citing those various cross-currents in the economy, Blumenthal concluded that even in the face of widespread suffering the French government could not justify intervention as a matter of "vital urgency."[74]

NOTES

1. Thomas A. Sancton, "The Myth of French Worker Support for the North in the American Civil War," *French Historical Studies*, 11 (1979), 58.

2. Lynn. M. Case, *French Opinion on the United States and Mexico, 1860-1867* (New York, 1936), pp. 10-11, cited in Case and Warren Spencer, *The United States and France: Civil War Diplomacy* (Philadelphia, University of Pennsylvania Press, 1970), p. 131.

3. Carle, *Sémaphore de Marseille*, February 26, 1861.

4. Vincent, (Dijon), *Journal de la Côte-d'Or*, February 19, 1861.

5. This warning may be found in John Ninet, "La Question du coton en Angleterre depuis la crise américaine,"*Revue des deux mondes*, March 1, 1861, 222.

6. Vincent, (Dijon) *Journal de la Côte-d'Or*, January 22, 1861.

7. Lauzières, *Pays*, February 28, 1861, cited in W. Reed West, *Contemporary French Opinion on the American Civil War* (Baltimore, Johns Hopkins University Press, 1924), p. 33.

8. Gaillardet, *Presse*, March 16, 1861.

9. Ferrier, *Courrier de La Rochelle*, April 10, 1861.

10. Justin Améro, *Correspondant*, 43, May, 1861, 110. Améro concluded, however, that the fears of a shortage of cotton were greatly exaggerated; with appropriate government response (seeking supplies elsewhere than America) commerce could be reassured;

Correspondant, 43, 135. Vincent, (Dijon) *Journal de la Côte-d'Or*, May 30, 1861.

11. "Bulletin du jour," *Temps*, September 21, 1861.

12. Barlatier, *Sémaphore de Marseille*, July 25, 1861.

13. "X," (La Rochelle) *Charente-Inférieure*, August 22, 1861.

14. Vincent, (Dijon) *Journal de la Côte-d'Or*, September 21, 1861.

15. Roret, (Chaumont) *Écho de la Haute-Marne*, May 7, 1861.

16. Conil, (Saintes) *Courrier des deux Charentes*, December 11, 1862. Same figures in Plantade, (Cahors), *Courrier du Lot*, December 20, 1862.

Claude Fohlen, "La Guerre de sécession et le commerce franco-américain," in *Revue d'histoire moderne et contemporaine*, 8 (1961), 259–64, argued that the war seriously interrupted French trade with America. Further, that trade was disrupted permanently because of tariffs and American industrialization.

17. Dufour, (Bourg-en-Bresse) *Courrier de l'Ain*, May 30, 1861.

18. Gaches, (Saint-Étienne) *Mémorial de la Loire*, May 30, 1861.

19. Barlatier, *Sémaphore de Marseille*, September 27–28, 1861.

20. Legaut, *Temps*, October 27, 1861.

21. Douhaire, *Correspondant*, August, 1862, p. 830. Earlier that same writer, Douhaire, *Correspondant*, 55, February, 1862, 408, claimed that industrial suffering in France and Britain occurred not because America did not send cotton, but rather because America no longer purchased European products.

22. Prévost, *Vigie de Cherbourg*, June 30, 1861.

23. "X," (La Rochelle) *Charente-Inférieure*, September 15, 1861.

24. Ferrier, *Courrier de La Rochelle*, January 11, 1862.

25. Coquille, *Monde*, January 7, 1862. This Clerical journal throughout the war expected a dissolution of the United States.

26. Bonnet, (Aurillac) *Moniteur du Cantal*, January 11, 1862.

27. Havas, (Montauban) *Courrier de Tarn-et-Garonne*, May 1, 1862.

28. (Yvetot) *Écho*, February 10, 1862.

29. Petit, (Boulogne) *Impartial*, March 7, 1862.

30. (Yvetot) *Écho*, March 10, 1862; the account simply listed the names of donors with the amounts given without mention of the Civil War. Petit, (Boulogne) *Impartial*, March 7, 1862, listed donors and amounts for workers who were unemployed in the Seine-Inférieure. Other newspapers also accepted donations, such as *Chronique de Rouen*, January 30, February 9, 1862.

31. Bayvet, (La Rochelle) *Charente-Inférieure*, June 19, 1862.

32. Forcade, *Revue des deux mondes*, 42, December 15, 1862, 42, 1005–11; 43, January 1, 1863, 228.

33. W. O. Henderson, "The Cotton Famine on the Continent, 1861–1865," *The Economic History Review*, IV (1933), 196. In an extended analysis of the cotton industry, region by region, Delaporte, *Pays*, January 25, 1863, concluded that there were 369,644 individuals working in the industry; 513,000 persons were involved if one counted members of families of those actually working in the industry.

For a history of the cotton industry, see Arthur L. Dunham, *The Anglo-French Treaty of Commerce of 1860 and the Progress of the Industrial Revolution in France* (Ann Arbor, University of Michigan Press, 1930), pp. 180–214, as well as the standard work by Claude Fohlen, *L'Industrie textile au temps du Second Empire* (Paris, Plon, 1956).

34. Fohlen, *L'Industrie textile*, p. 284.

35. *Ibid.*, p. 285.

36. Some Frenchmen were aware of Southern determination to prevent exporting of their cotton; see discussion of this point in Élisée Reclus, "Le Coton et la crise américaine," *Revue des deux mondes*, January 1, 1862, 183–84. "It is the North that one accuses, but it is the South which forbids its exportation"; Douhaire, *Correspondant*, 54, December, 1861, 735.

For Southern faith in the King Cotton theory, see Frank Owsley, *King Cotton Diplomacy* (Chicago, University of Chicago Press, 1959), ch. 1; for Southern efforts to prevent the exporting of cotton, see Owsley, ch. 2.

According to the historian of the French textile industry, the King Cotton theory did not work because Britain and France foresaw the crisis and made purchases in excess of normal needs from the abundant 1860 harvest; Southerners had overestimated the extent of social troubles among workers in the textile industry; and Southerners had underestimated the role of other producers. Claude Fohlen, "La Guerre de sécession et le commerce franco-américain," in *Revue d'histoire moderne et contemporaine*, 8 (1961), 264.

37. Delaporte, *Pays*, January 25, April 1, 1863. For typical statements about the deleterious effects of the Civil War on French industry, see Conil, (Saintes) *Courrier des deux Charentes*, February 26, 1863; Perroud, (Le Puy) *Moniteur de la Haute-Loire*, November 15, 1862.

38. Dollfus, *Temps*, January 29, 1863.

39. Chantrel, *Monde*, January 17, 1863.

40. Marcel Gillet, review of Claude Fohlen, *L'Industrie textile au temps du Second Empire* (Paris, 1956), in *Revue d'histoire moderne et contemporaine*, 3 (1956), 254.

41. Fohlen, *L'Industrie textile*, pp. 253, 301–303.

42. Foucou, *Presse*, November 20, 1862; Jules Ferry, January 12, 1863, *Presse*, cited in West, *French Opinion*, p. 61.

Resale of cotton belonging to manufacturers was an ordinary characteristic of the industry, conceded a le Havre newspaper, although not a daily occurrence. Mouttet, *Courrier du Havre*, January 23, 1863.

Claude Fohlen, "La Guerre de sécession et le commerce franco-américain," pp. 259–70.

43. Chantrel, *Monde*, January 17, 1863.

44. For an extended analysis with emphasis on particular difficulties in Normandy, see Dollfus, *Temps*, January 29, 1863.

45. Forcade, *Revue des deux mondes*, December 15, 1862.

A similar situation prevailed in Britain. Delaporte, *Pays*, April 1, 1863, described two theories for the problems of the British cotton industry. One theory held that excessive manufacture of cotton products in 1859 and 1860 led to a surplus of such goods; even if cotton were available from America, the surplus would still have weighed heavily, according to this theory. The other view attributed the *crise* exclusively to the high price of cotton either because of reduction of American exports or because of speculation. The *Pays* believed that "the two causes have acted simultaneously but to a degree which is impossible to determine." An Orleanist review supported the latter theory. For several years, related the *Revue des deux mondes*, England had suffered from a surplus of cotton. As a result of the "sudden shortage of cotton," the price of cotton went up and "enormous fortunes have been realized at Manchester and Liverpool." The stoppage of work in England was not so much from the shortage of cotton, but rather from its high price. If the prices of manufactured articles were in relation to the price of raw cotton, then manufacturers would not have hesitated to have resumed work. F. Verdeil, "La Disette du coton en Angleterre et les comités de prévoyance," *Revue des deux mondes*, January 1, 1863, 221, 225.

David P. Crook, *The North, the South, and the Powers* (New York, John Wiley,

1974), pp. 199–226, claimed that there was no real cotton famine; rather, the problem was overproduction. Speculators enjoyed a field day. See also, Eugene A. Brady, "A Reconsideration of the Lancashire 'Cotton Famine,'" *Agricultural History*, XXVII (October, 1963), 156–62.

46. Henry Sanford, American minister to Brussels, visited the cotton mills in Rouen, Normandy, and neighboring towns in the fall of 1862. He found that "the smaller mills had closed down, and the large number of handlooms were generally stopped, while large and better equipped establishments continued to work from half to full time." He believed that the use of handlooms, rather than modern machinery, and overproduction of previous years, rather than a shortage of cotton produced the textile crisis. Sanford to Seward, Paris, April 24, 1863, Seward Papers, cited in Blumenthal, *A Reappraisal of Franco-American Relations* (Chapel Hill, University of North Carolina Press, 1959), p. 155.

Flers, a village in Normandy, was particularly hard hit; in 1862, its business leaders gave five reasons for the crisis: 1) bad crops in France in 1861; 2) the American war with the doubling in price of cotton and loss of the American market; 3) the scarcity and rise in price of indigo; 4) the financial crisis with the restriction of credit; and 5) the Treaty of Commerce with Britain. Dunham, *Anglo-French Treaty of Commerce of 1860*, p. 196.

Blumenthal, *France and the United States*, pp. 98–99, emphasized that French manufacturers had an oversupply of cotton in 1861; with the exception of the year 1862, French manufacturers could purchase enough cotton. The depression occurred in the textile industry because of the obsolescence of French machinery and old-fashioned methods of production. The Cobden Treaty, 1860, which allowed importations from modern English textile factories, would have created a textile depression in France without a Civil War.

47. Fohlen, *L'Industrie textile*, pp. 287–89. For discussion of financial disruptions in Europe because of wheat imports from the United States in 1860, see Forcade, *Revue des deux mondes*, November 14, 1860, 496.

48. Frank Owsley, *King Cotton Diplomacy* (Chicago, University of Chicago Press, 1959), p.141.

49. Dunham, *The Anglo-French Treaty of Commerce of 1860*, pp. 79–102.

50. Fohlen, *L'Industrie textile*, pp. 289–93.

51. *Ibid.*, pp. 265–67. Fohlen based his figures on a number of contemporary sources. Unless otherwise noted, employment figures are derived from Fohlen's work.

52. (Yvetot) *Abeille Couchoise*, December 20, 1862.

53. Limayrac, *Constitutionnel*, May 8, 1862, cited in West, *French Opinion*, pp. 74–75.

54. *Pays*, June 10, 1862. Septavaux, (Tarbes) *Ère impériale*, June 12, 1862, called for mediation in the name of humanity and in the interests of civilization and human progress. For similar expressions of opinion, see, Coquille, *Monde*, June 9–10, 1862; Laytou, (Cahors) *Journal du Lot*, October 11, 1862.

55. Weiss, *Courrier du dimanche*, July 20, 1862.

56. Gaïffe, *Presse*, July 20, 1862.

57. Delord, *Siècle*, August 27, 1862, cited in West, *French Opinion*, p. 84.

58. Claude, *Temps*, October 2, 1862.

59. Léo, *Journal des débats*, December 26, 1862; cited in West, *French Opinion*, p. 93.

60. Roure, (Privas) *Écho de l'Ardèche*, January 5, 1863.

61. Huet, (Clermont) *Journal de Clermont*, October 30, 1862. Some modern scholars do not support the view that English workers unselfishly supported Northern efforts to free the slaves. Rather, Mary Ellison, *Support for Secession: Lancashire and the American Civil War* (Chicago, University of Chicago Press, 1965), and Norman Longmate, *The Hungry*

Mills: The Story of Lancashire Cotton Famine, 1861–1865 (London, 1978), argued that English cotton workers supported the South and favored British intervention to help secure Southern independence in order to bring the war to an end. Royden Harrison, *Before the Socialists* (Toronto and London, Routledge & K. Paul, 1965), p. 64, however, contended that from the end of 1862 there was "overwhelming evidence to support the view that the great majority of politically conscious [English] workmen were pro-Federal." Royden approvingly quoted Karl Marx, who argued that in the eighteenth century the American Revolution sounded the tocsin for the European middle class; in the nineteenth century the American Civil War sounded it for the European working class and gave an immense impetus to democratic government. Royden, *Before the Socialists*, p. 67.

62. Beuzeville, *Journal de Rouen*, May 9, 1863.

63. Samuel Bernstein, *Essays in Political and Intellectual History* (Freeport, Books for Libraries Press, 1969), p. 128. David I. Kulstein, "The Attitude of French Workers towards the Second Empire," in *French Historical Studies*, II (spring, 1962), 356–75, did not address the issue of worker attitudes toward the Civil War but noted that workers' presses and workers' organizations either did not exist or were closely controlled; the best sources for workers' views are reports of the *procureurs généraux*; workers generally supported the Second Empire until 1863, when social and economic discontent (in part arising from the cotton shortage) led to much worker opposition to the regime.

64. Sancton, "The Myth of French Worker Support for the North," especially pp. 67–79. Sancton claimed that those who argue French workers supported the North repeatedly cite as evidence the following statement by Forcade, *Revue des deux mondes*, February 1, 1863, 744–45. "While our government manifests not in its language, but in the significance of its acts, a certain partiality for the South, with the thought praiseworthy in itself of procuring as soon as possible elements of work for our workers, the attitude of the workers is completely different. If they were asked: 'Which do you prefer? the triumph of the South and the return of cotton with the maintenance of black slavery or the emancipation of the slaves with the continuation of unemployment and its miseries,' we are certain that they would respond: 'the misery for us a thousand times rather than to buy our well-being at the price of maintaining the servitude of four million souls.'"

Blumenthal, *France and the United States*, p. 84, stated that "French workers, like those of England, decided they would rather tighten their belts than lend support to the American slave owners." Blumenthal, however, did not cite any evidence for his statement. Donaldson Jordan and Edwin J. Pratt, *Europe and the American Civil War* (Boston, Houghton Mifflin, 1931), p. 229, claimed that "The working class, in France as in England, steadfastly upheld the Northern cause." Claude Fohlen noted the lack of social troubles among cotton workers as one reason for the failure of the King Cotton theory; "La Guerre de sécession et le commerce franco-américain," p. 264.

65. David H. Pinkney, "France and the Civil War," in Harold Hyman, ed., *Heard Round the World: The Impact Abroad of the Civil War* (New York, Knopf. 1969), pp. 132–34, is a good summary of private and public relief efforts. See, also, Fohlen, *L'Industrie textile*, pp. 268–76.

For the general topic of Napoleon and workers, see David I. Kulstein, *Napoleon III and the Working Class: A Study of Government Propaganda under the Second Empire* ([Sacramento], California State Colleges, 1969).

66. *Journal d'Elbeuf*, November 27, 30, December 7, 1862.

67. Nefftzer, *Temps*, December 3, 1862.

68. Bédollière, *Siècle*, January 6, 1863.

69. Havin, *Siècle*, January 10, 1863. After making a moving plea for Frenchmen to give generously to the suffering, Gaillard, Liberal Catholic *Correspondant*, January, 24, 1863, reacted angrily to a charge by *Siècle* that the lack of subscriptions to the distressed resulted from diversion of alms to Peter's Pence in order to keep the Pope in luxury.

70. Carle, *Sémaphore de Marseille*, January 11–12, 1863. Mahias, *Presse*, January 9, 1863.

71. Conil, (Saintes) *Courrier des deux Charentes*, January 15, 1863.

72. Valladier, (Toulouse) *Aigle Courrier du Midi*, April 30, 1863.

73. Louis Reybaud, "La Guerre d'Amérique et le marché du coton," *Revue des deux mondes*, March 1, 1865, p. 201.

74. Blumenthal, *Franco-American Relations*, p. 156.

Chapter 6

French Official Actions through Mediation

> Slavery is an indestructible cause of hatred between North and South. It also prevents European powers from giving the South the proofs of sympathy which it commands from the purely political point of view.
>
> Mouttet, (Le Havre) *Courrier du Havre*, January 30, 1863

> Fundamentally, in the present state of things, every attempt at conciliation coming from Europe can only be interpreted as a favorable step for the South.
>
> Massicault, (Bordeaux) *Gironde*, January 30, 1863

In the early stages of the Civil War, French newspapers of all political persuasions and the French government agreed on many aspects of that conflict. Both the French government and French newspapers regretted the Southern secession. French newspapers approved the government's proclamation of neutrality on June 10, 1861. French newspapers supported French foreign minister Antoine Thouvenel's diplomatic note on the *Trent* affair, which called for Washington to release the two Confederate commissioners. Finally, both French newspapers and the Imperial government were seriously disturbed at the economic consequences of the Civil War, which led to a loss of export markets and distress in the cotton industry. There were, however, sharp disagreements among French newspapers over diplomatic remedies for those problems.

The economic difficulties led the French government to focus much of its diplomacy on the blockade. At first it inquired about the legality of the Union blockade; but since these inquiries led to the conclusion that it was effective, the French government could not take legal action. French action against the blockade was also impractical because the British accepted its legality and effectiveness, and Napoleon III's policy was to cooperate with the British. Next the French government sought a relaxation of the blockade for a few ports in order that France could import some badly needed cotton. Early in 1862, American Secretary of

State William Seward opened Beaufort and Port Royal, in South Carolina, and New Orleans, each of which was under Union control. The French soon realized the hollowness of these concessions, however, since the Southern practice of embargoing the shipment of cotton prevented the export of any of that material to France.

In part as a consequence of the Southern embargo, French government officials seem to have concluded that the most direct way to secure cotton was to bring the war to an end. The timing of French mediation proposals to secure peace was related to the increasingly severe economic crisis in France by the end of 1862, which put Napoleon III under considerable political pressure to alleviate the distress. In addition, the military situation in America changed dramatically with the failure of Union General George McClellan's Peninsular campaign in the first half of 1862, Robert E. Lee's victory at Second Bull Run in August, and Lee's subsequent invasion of the North in September. As a result, the French government proposed mediation in October, 1862, and later in January, 1863, with the goal of ending the Civil War.[1]

Conservatives typically supported the mediation proposals as wise and useful to staunch the "needless effusion of blood" in America and to end European economic distress. Liberal supporters of the North usually maintained, on the contrary, that France should not intervene in the conflict, an action that would favor the South and not be acceptable to the North. Liberals further argued that the forcible return of the South to the Union was a better method for securing cotton.

Certain general considerations will help in understanding the debate over possible French intervention in the Civil War. Proposals for intervention ranged from mediation, to recognition of the South, to military alliance with the South. Seldom did any French newspaper advocate alliance with the South;[2] some Imperial journals advocated recognition of the South; many newspapers advocated mediation. The pattern was for Imperial and Clerical newspapers to support intervention, most typically in the form of mediation, while Progressive and Orleanist newspapers opposed intervention. In three stages in the Civil War—from the beginning of the war until the *Trent* affair; the *Trent* affair; from June until November, 1862—the press exhibited various patterns in discussing the wisdom of intervention.

In the first of these stages, from the firing on Fort Sumter to the *Trent* affair, French newspapers did not consistently follow the norm of Conservative newspapers favoring and Liberal newspapers opposing French intervention. The Orleanist *Journal des débats* in August, 1861, for example, believed that Europe would have to put an end to the war sooner or later.[3] A Liberal Marseille newspaper reported in September, 1861, that Lincoln had been unwise to spurn a Russian offer of mediation since the hazards of war were "so little favorable to his cause."[4]

At this time some Conservative newspapers also favored French intervention in the American conflict. Thus the *Patrie* in June, 1861, prophesied that the great European powers would recognize the Southern states.[5] A month later, a Conservative Cherbourg newspaper similarly predicted that the opportune moment would arise to recognize the South.[6] In September, 1861, a Saint-Étienne Conservative paper called for European intervention: the war was going poorly for the North, it threatened to last eternally, and it would cover America with blood to no one's profit.[7]

Opponents of French intervention during the early stages of the Civil War were far more numerous, however, and included Conservative as well as Liberal journals. The same Conservative Saint-Étienne editor cited above had reported rumors of French and British mediation in May; such mediation, he then claimed, would do no good.[8] The Orleanist *Temps* reported a movement in manufacturing centers of France and Britain to recognize the Confederate states because of the shortage of cotton. Simple recognition, however, would not help; Britain and France would have to force the raising of the blockade, which would be the equivalent of an act of war.[9] A provincial newspaper added that, by recognizing the South, Britain and France would make themselves accomplices of the Southern states, would accept responsibility for an equivocal cause, and would not contribute to the solution of the crisis.[10]

If there was no clear ideological cleavage in the stance of the press toward intervention in the early stages of the war, the *Trent* affair elicited surprising agreement about an appropriate role for France. Only two Parisian newspapers favored French participation as a British ally in the event of war between the North and Britain. The Liberal *Presse* argued that the question of rights on the sea was so important that France ought to join Britain in the war.[11] The Conservative *Patrie* agreed. The British were clearly right in their dispute with America, argued *Patrie*, and it would be difficult for France to remain indifferent in case of war.[12]

Other French newspapers counseled against such drastic action. Though critical of Wilkes' action, the Conservative *Constitutionnel* opposed French intervention, because, *Constitutionnel* pompously proclaimed, "The sword of Charlemagne and Napoleon leaves the scabbard only when the interest and glory of the French people are at stake."[13] While Legitimist newspapers expressed different nuances of opinion, all were agreed on the wisdom of neutrality. In particular, the *Monde* opposed joining with Britain in case of war with America. French interest, it claimed, lay in being the natural defenders of secondary maritime powers; it was not in France's interest to see America crushed by the British.[14] The most prominent provincial Clerical journal argued that France should maintain "the most strict neutrality." To permit the British to destroy a fleet that had served as a counterweight to Britain's naval preponderance was contrary to the policy of France. To wage war against Britain would be deadly for the French navy, commerce, and interest. To join Britain would also mean French support for slavery in the South.[15] Another Clerical journal contended that since the British were merely concerned about cotton, nothing obliged France to leave its role as an observer.[16]

With the exception of the *Presse*, all of the Paris Liberal journals favored neutrality. The *Journal des débats* said that France ought not join with Britain because that would deprive France of its only ally to maintain freedom of the seas. France ought not recognize the South either, because that would be incompatible with the idea of liberty and progress.[17] The *Revue des deux mondes* likewise advocated "strict" neutrality for France; indeed, the editor, E. Forcade, claimed that Frenchmen unanimously favored neutrality.[18]

Almost all provincial newspapers, whatever their political persuasion, advocated neutrality, though they assigned different reasons for their position. The Conservative (La Rochelle) *Charente-Inférieure* lectured its fellow journalists who supported Wilkes during the *Trent* crisis. In so doing they were forgetting that what today was an English interest might become a French interest tomorrow. The journal also lectured those who were interested in supporting the British. They should be concerned about French interests, which were to preserve neutrality but make its wishes known and insist on the rights of neutrals.[19]

A thoughtful Governmental provincial newspaper summarized the case against French intervention. "We should maintain strict neutrality," argued the journal. While Wilkes was wrong, England had no need of French assistance if reparation was necessary. All Frenchmen who understood the mission of America, who saw in the Civil War "a violent but incontestable step toward a civilization more advanced," realized that France should not unite with Britain to insure the fall of the republic when slavery was compromised. While an alliance with America was part of French political tradition, neutrality satisfied French interest and sympathies. Britain could raise the blockade, thus satisfying French material interests.[20]

The peaceful resolution of the *Trent* affair delighted Frenchmen, but fundamental problems arising from the American war still remained. The independence of the South, the clearing of the ports, the delivery of cotton to the market—where were they? Precisely where they were just before the seizure, grumbled one Conservative provincial newspaper.[21]

From the settlement of the *Trent* affair in January, 1862, until June of that year French newspapers occasionally considered steps to end the war or engaged in sporadic controversy about proposals for mediation. When the French minister to the United States, Henri Mercier, journeyed to Richmond in May, some newspapers speculated that his trip was related to French mediation.[22] The Liberal *Siècle* reported the Clerical *Union's* proposal in May of mediation on the basis of separation and abolition; the *Siècle* thought that was worthy of attention, but preferred mediation on the basis of union with abolition. French opinion would favor mediation that would lead to abolition, though the *Siècle* did not know the American reaction.[23]

The fitful attention by French newspapers to mediation during the first half of 1862 was related to military activities in America, where fortune generally favored the Union cause. Ulysses S. Grant achieved major victories in the West at Forts Henry and Donelson early in the year, and in the spring General George McClellan began his advance on Richmond. Such Union successes discouraged intervention proposals.

In the latter half of 1862, however, fortune did not shine on the Union cause. In the East, Robert E. Lee repulsed McClellan's advance on Richmond and subsequently seized the offensive against Northern forces. In the West, Union leaders frittered away the opportunities opened by Grant's advance, and, subsequently, in the fall Confederate General Braxton Bragg seized the initiative with an invasion of Northern-held territory. With these Confederate victories and increasing economic distress in France, it is not surprising that some French newspapers called for French intervention to end the war.

Beginning in the summer of 1862 and reaching a climax with Napoleon III's mediation proposal in October, Conservative newspapers clamorously called for French intervention in the American Civil War. The *Constitutionnel* initiated that campaign in June by recommending mediation to end the war. In a series of articles the Conservative newspaper struck on most of the themes that were to be cited repeatedly to justify mediation. The semi-official newspaper claimed that the North could not conquer the South, that neither party could end the war, and that peace could only come through mediation from the outside. The *Constitutionnel* also claimed that mediation was not only a means to bring about an end to slavery, but also a means to further the economic interests of France.[24]

Conservative Clerical newspapers emphasized the irreconcilability of the North and South. The *esclavagistes* and the Unionists were frenzied duelists "drunk with raging insanity," claimed one.[25] Another Clerical journal called for mediation as the "only solution of the American conflict." To reestablish the old union was "completely impossible after so much bloodshed and hatred."[26]

Conservative newspapers also justified mediation on military grounds. After news of the Confederate victory before Richmond, was there any need, queried one provincial newspaper, to demonstrate once more the impossibility of the North subduing the South and the necessity of an "intervention or a European mediation?"[27] A Legitimist paper in October claimed that the South was winning militarily and "undoubtedly" had installed a Southern confederacy.[28] Another provincial newspaper concluded that "the North and the South were not able to invade the other nor to dominate the other; an intervention by a third party was necessary to break the equilibrium which seems to be established."[29]

Conservative journals also cited idealistic reasons for their support of French intervention. One provincial journal, formerly supportive of the Federal cause, argued that mediation was "the best guarantor of abolition of slavery."[30] Another Conservative provincial journal claimed that in the name of humanity, interests of civilization, and human progress, the belligerent parties ought not reject mediation by Europe.[31]

Going beyond advocacy of mediation, the Conservative *Pays* in September published a series of three letters from a Southern-born sympathizer, Paul Pecquet du Bellet, arguing for French recognition of the South. The American

Union, he maintained, was established among sovereign states; hence, the Southern states had the right of secession. He pointed to other examples of separation, such as the Dutch states. Further, the South had established a formal government, and that government had shown its strength by defeating Union armies during the Peninsular campaign and at Manassas. Lincoln implicitly recognized the strength of the South by increasing the size of the Northern army.

In addition, Pecquet argued that recognition would encourage the Confederates and the Democrats, the party of peace in the North, while continued warfare would lead to much bloodshed. The United States could hardly complain about hasty recognition, since America had recognized Hungary prematurely during the latter's revolt in 1848. The great writer on international law, Vattel, said each country could protect its own interests, and Europe needed cotton.

Finally, Pecquet attacked the North and its leaders. Do not believe Lincoln, he warned: "he has deceived, he deceives, and he will deceive." The North pursues the Monroe Doctrine: it has excluded Europe from the New World but it will take over Mexico, Central America, and Canada. The North, he also charged, would exterminate blacks.[32]

A major justification for Conservative journals seeking intervention was the economic *crise* that ravaged France. Serving a maritime population, the (La Rochelle) *Charente-Inférieure* advocated mediation because industry, maritime commerce, and agricultural production suffered from the anarchic and violent situation of the United States. "Without adoring cotton, sugar, [and] coffee," wrote the port newspaper,

> we take them at their merit, so that we are not at all indifferent to sending by the ocean our silks, our wines, our articles of jewelry, of furniture, of fashion. The war is thus prejudicial materially, beyond that it shocks in us that sentiment of justice which does not admit that half of one nation might be oppressed or only mistreated by the other half. Such are the double reasons diplomats are authorized to obtain a truce first and an arbitrage later.[33]

Yet even some newspapers which favored the idea of French mediation in principle doubted that it would work in practice. The Conservative (Maçon) *Journal de Saône-et-Loire* believed that "without doubt mediation would be the best thing to do," but would the North and South submit their differences to arbitration? The newspaper was very doubtful.[34] The Governmental (Évreux) *Courrier de l'Eure* noted an article in the London *Times* calling for the French to mediate because American public opinion was too anti-British. But watch out!, cautioned the Conservative journal. It was questionable whether such a proposal would be acceptable to Americans; would France end up in war? The result might be that France would lose all influence in America.[35]

If some Conservative newspapers were not convinced that Americans would accept mediation, Progressive newspapers opposed mediation in principle. The Progressive *Presse* pointedly observed that mediation is proposed only between two recognized belligerent states. What would the Convention have said during the French Revolution if mediation had been suggested between it and the Vendée? What would France say if Alsace rebelled and Germany proposed mediation? The offer of mediation would place the combatants in a condition of moral equality, which the North would not accept.[36] The Orleanist *Journal des débats* would have welcomed mediation only if both the North and the South had sought it. Further, the *Journal* reasoned that mediation would lead to recognition of the South; hence mediation was only a first step toward intervention. If the intent of mediation was to favor the South and to lead to armed intervention in favor of the South, then the newspaper was opposed.[37]

Progressive newspapers also argued against European intervention on the economic grounds. When the South won battles, noted the Orleanist organ *Temps*, the price of cotton dropped. One reason for that phenomenon was "that public opinion in Europe has always counted and yet counts that some decisive advantages brought by the secessionists would lead to an intervention on the part of France and Britain." The *Temps* warned, however, that simple recognition would have no economic consequence, while armed intervention would make the crisis worse. Further, England did not want armed intervention, since the Civil War was aiding the British policy of promoting the British Indies and Indian cotton. While there was distress in England, charity prevented any danger to public order. In the long run, France and England would secure cotton elsewhere, so they would no longer be dependent on the South. The *Temps* also argued that slavery made the raising of cotton cheap in the South but ruined its production elsewhere; abolition in the South thus would result in cotton production elsewhere.[38] Finally, as for the plea of manufacturers that there was a need for cotton, there was also a need for wheat, and the North produced wheat, pointedly observed the *Presse*.[39]

The Liberal *Siècle*, with the largest circulation of any Parisian newspaper, spoke strongly against French interference. From a strictly legal point of view, conceded the *Siècle*, France might aid either the North or the South, but from a moral point of view France should not aid the cause of slavery. Recognition would not end the war, declared the Republican newspaper; nor would declaring the blockade ineffectual help French industry, for both of those actions would mean war, and, as a result, French industry would suffer a hundred times more difficulties than at present. Interest and honor, French principles and traditions, rather, called for an alliance with the North and would soon end the war. "But we do not," confessed the *Siècle*, "dare hope for such an event."[40]

Finally, a Conservative provincial newspaper was opposed to intervention because of the slavery question. Blood was running; humanity could order an end to the effusion of blood. But that was precisely the reason for the war: the tortures and the oppression by planters, who were more fierce than the Indians. If the powers that maintained ships to combat and annihilate the slave trade would intervene and recognize the Southern states, they could do so only by demanding the abolition of slavery, "precisely the cause of the present war." France had intervened in Italy, China, Syria, and "the regrettable expedition to Mexico" only for just causes. There was no way, claimed that Conservative newspaper, that France could instruct

> our sailors who pursue slave ships, our brave army whose constitution and life rest upon the equality so dear to Frenchmen, that you are going to throw the weight of your sword in order that the yoke . . . falls on the head of several millions of men, our brothers, children of the same God.[41]

Despite such opposition, the French government proposed joint mediation with Britain and Russia in October, 1862. The action by the French government is certainly understandable. The most important figure in French diplomacy, the Emperor Napoleon III, long before that date had come to favor the South. Historians have explained his pro-Southern stance in part because of his Mexican policy. Napoleon's plans for making an Austrian archduke the emperor of Mexico were well advanced, and he could expect opposition from Washington with its traditional policy of opposing European interference in the New World. Only with a divided United States could a French-supported puppet be possible in Mexico; indeed, the Southern Confederacy could support Napoleon's endeavors as *quid pro quo* for his aid in establishing Southern independence. Support for Southern nationalism was also consistent with Napoleon's belief in self-determination among European peoples. He had supported Italian and Rumanian attempts to create national states, and his use of plebiscites was also part of that pattern.

The timing of Napoleon's mediation efforts was related to French perception of the military situation in America. By November, 1862, many French people no longer had confident expectations of a Northern victory. Indeed, McClellan's defeat before Richmond and Lee's subsequent invasion of the North and defeat at Antietam in the fall convinced many Frenchmen that neither side could win. Napoleon's mediation proposal, based on the idea that neither side could triumph, implicitly reflected widely held views in France.[42]

The timing of the French mediation offer was also related to economic distress in the French cotton industry (see Chapter 5). That distress was particularly troubling for a political leader who had diligently sought to promote industrialization and prosperity in France. Ending hostilities and raising the blockade would relieve the crisis in French industry.

Finally, Napoleon was well aware of domestic political consideration when he made his mediation proposals. Case and Spencer saw a relationship between reports of deteriorating economic conditions in France and the pressure of public opinion, on the one hand, and the timing of the mediation proposal, on the other.[43] "One believes generally," reported the (Bourges) *Journal du Cher*, that the emperor made his proposal

> only from the point of view of his internal policy and . . . to demonstrate in the interests of French commerce, suffering as a consequence of the war in the United States and notably to the working population of our

> great industrial centers, that Emperor Napoleon had attempted all to have his offers of mediation prevail and that he would not be responsible for its lack of success.[44]

A Legitimist newspaper printed a report attributing the same reason for the French initiative: many factories were closed, and a great number of workers were without work. By publishing the mediation proposal, "the government has wished to prove to our working population that it had attempted to soften their suffering."[45]

Newspapers frequently reported rumors of European intervention throughout the summer and fall of 1862.[46] Rumor became fact on November 13, when the *Moniteur* published the official French mediation proposal. In a dispatch dated October 30, 1862, the French foreign minister, Drouyn de Lhuys, suggested that France, Britain, and Russia jointly propose a six-month truce to the two belligerents. Drouyn justified his proposal in terms of the suffering and prodigious shedding of blood in America, to which would soon be added the fears of servile warfare, a reference to the Emancipation Proclamation. The war had also brought suffering to the cotton industry of Europe. The military situation in America, claimed Drouyn, did not provide hope that one side or the other would soon achieve victory and thus bring about peace. In those circumstances, the emperor thought it wise to propose to Britain and Russia that the three powers approach both sides in America "for a six-month suspension of hostilities during which time any warlike act, direct or indirect, would temporarily cease on land and sea, and such a truce could be subsequently extended if necessary." Such action by the three powers would not imply any opinion on the causes of the war; their role would "consist solely in smoothing the way and of intervening only to the extent allowed by both parties." If the effort failed, it would have fulfilled a duty to humanity when passions made direct negotiations difficult.[47]

Reaction to the mediation proposal closely followed political lines. The overwhelming majority of Imperial French newspapers supported the mediation proposal. They gave various reasons for their support.

1) Mediation was in accord with French traditions of promoting peace and providing assistance. The *Pays* cited Louis XVI, Napoleon I, and Napoleon III as part of that tradition; in this case, it was simply trying to save America from ruin.[48] Whatever happened, claimed a provincial Imperial newspaper, it was a great honor that France was the first to take the initiative.[49]
2) Mediation could end a needless effusion of blood in America. Journalists repeatedly utilized the phrase "needless effusion of blood." Journalists also wrote frequently of a war without result and warned of the dangers of a servile revolution.[50]
3) Mediation leading to separation of the two sections was the best possible result for Americans, according to a provincial Imperial newspaper. Reconciliation for the two sections was impossible, since the South wanted independence and the North did not have enough power to bring about a reunion. Probably the North would win, predicted the paper, because the South lacked resources; but rather than a durable peace there would be perpetual internal struggles. That was why an amicable intervention before complete ruin was a work of

humanity and a wise policy.[51] Mediation could bring about an end to the war quicker than could fighting.[52] All thoughtful men in Europe considered the separation and autonomy of the Southern confederation as indubitable. "Such is the real sense, the effective significance" of Drouyn's proposal; no other meaning was possible.[53]

4) Mediation and the return of peace would help workers in diverse countries who were suffering from the war.[54] The proposal was in the interest of French commerce and "for the profit of humanity."[55] The (Saintes) *Courrier des deux Charentes* wanted "a solution as quickly as possible to that question which paralyzes the commerce and industry of France in general and the commerce and industry of our locality in particular."[56]

5) Mediation, claimed a Conservative provincial newspaper, found "a powerful echo in public opinion."[57] One paper predicted that "There will be only one voice in the French press for approving Drouyn's proposal.[58]

A few Governmental newspapers, however, expressed reservations. "The noble thought" that dictated Drouyn's circular would find an echo in generous hearts, but "I wonder," queried one journalist, "if the men of the North will accept an armistice by which the men of the South . . . will be able to procure money, munitions, thanks to immense quantities of goods which they will hasten to dispose of in Europe. What would the North thus gain from this mediation?"[59] Another Imperial provincial paper also was puzzled over the wisdom of mediation. From Europe it was difficult to determine what were the real feelings of the North and of the South. Did each hope for complete victory? Or were both discouraged, fatigued, and disposed to listen to European proposals? Europeans were completely ignorant of those matters.[60]

Legitimist newspapers had no difficulty in supporting the mediation proposal even in the face of the argument that successful mediation would mean Southern independence and a continuation of slavery. The *Monde* argued that slavery was not the cause of the war. Had not Lincoln promised protection of slavery if the Southern states came back? Maintenance of the Union, charged the Clerical newspaper, would only lead to the indefinite prolongation of the war and total exhaustion of the former United States.[61] A Caen Legitimist paper applauded the proposal for the usual reasons—effusion of blood, servile warfare, European consequences—but wondered about the reaction. Would Britain accept the proposal or accept the "shame" that would accompany a refusal.[62] Another provincial Legitimist newspaper thought that the proposal was good for "the irreconcilable factions of the former Union"; it could end a fatal crisis in America and also help many unhappy French workers.[63]

Taking a very different position than their Conservative colleagues, Progressive journalists opposed the mediation proposal. Commenting on rumors about the proposal, the *Presse* claimed that for an honorable peace there was only one condition: abolition of slavery.[64] While peace would be in the "general interest," France was still a country where "national honor has always spoken more highly than interest."[65] Was it equitable to treat on the same footing a recognized state and insurgents? Was the proposal impartial? What would the North gain?

Most important—not a word about slavery; if slavery continued, peace would be neither durable nor honorable. While it was unlikely that London and St. Petersburg would accept the proposal, the *Presse* concluded that the United States would not.[66]

The *Siècle* was likewise critical. Although initially favorable to the idea of mediation, the *Siècle* opposed the proposal upon learning that it involved a suspension of the blockade. Drawing upon the French Revolution analogy, the Liberal journal asked whether France would have accepted such a proposal when the Vendée revolted?[67] The Progressive *Sémaphore de Marseille* argued that the armistice of six months would only help the South by raising the blockade; at the end of six months the South would be in a better position to continue. Thus the proposal would help the South and impede the goal of putting an end to the war.[68]

Orleanist journals were equally critical. The *Temps* argued against the proposal on the grounds that there was no basis for mediation with both sides so determined; the proposal favored the South; and the proposal avoided "the great question of right, of justice, and of civilization which is the true interest and superior of the great American drama." The *Temps* also argued against the proposal because of *raison d'état*: "it is the permanent interest of France," emphasized the Orleanist journal, "that a great power continues to exist in America, and, by the sole fact of its presence in the world, serves as a counterweight against England and to guarantee freedom of the seas."[69] The *Revue des deux mondes* did not know how to hide its "profound chagrin" over Drouyn's mediation proposal. Although all people were saddened by the bloody conflict in America and by economic distress in France, the French proposal of an armistice nevertheless "could only be contrary to the government of the United States and favorable to the rebellion of the South."[70]

A provincial Republican newspaper also strongly opposed the mediation proposal. If French workers were distressed, should French vessels break the blockade to get cotton? Why should Europe be tributary to America for cotton when it could be cultivated elsewhere? The editor was also forced to respect the work of Washington, Lafayette, Rochambeau, and Louis XVI. On the other hand, what Jefferson Davis had done was not yet an accepted fact. Further, what would Frenchmen have said if the United States in 1795 had demanded that the revolutionaries should reconcile themselves with the *ancien régime*? Should the French revolutionaries have discontinued their struggle because America needed silks and wines? Not only had America stayed out of European affairs; in addition, Lincoln had the mantle of human liberty and Christian civilization.[71]

The British and Russians, of course, did not accept the French proposal. Tactfully, the British expressed doubt that Americans would accept the proposal and whether the goal could be obtained at that time. "The time was not right," "not yet," "too early," as many French newspapers paraphrased the British response. The Russians, likewise, did not accept the proposal.[72]

Governmental newspapers explained the British rejection in terms of ignoble motivation. The British were indifferent to suffering in Europe and awaited American extermination, asserted one provincial journal.[73] "Do we have to wait until India becomes the sole market to obtain cotton?" queried another.[74] Britain only acts for humanity when it is also in its own interests, claimed still another.[75] England needed cotton but was not unhappy to see the exhaustion of a power from which it had never retreated before. England remained deaf to the voice of humanity; let Americans perish, let workers of Lancashire perish provided that there would be in the world one less maritime power![76]

Although efforts to end the war through joint mediation did not succeed, France continued her search for an end to the American Civil War. French officials were encouraged in their pursuit of that goal by the increasing strength shown by anti-war Democrats in the November, 1862, elections in America and by continued Northern military failure, as shown by the replacement of General George McClellan and the subsequent defeat of his successor, General Ambrose Burnside, at Fredericksburg in December, 1862. "It is quite clear," however, wrote Daniel Carroll, that Emperor Napoleon III was "as interested in mollifying unemployed French workers as in shortening the American war." American minister to France Dayton also realized that the "first object [of the mediation proposal] was to operate at *home* to satisfy the manufacturers and workmen of France."[77]

On January 9, 1863, Drouyn made his second mediation attempt, a unilateral proposal that the Federal government enter into conversations with the Confederates at a neutral point. At the meeting the two parties could seek to determine whether their interests were irreconcilable. Such negotiations, Drouyn pointed out, did not necessarily imply the immediate cessation of hostilities and would occur under circumstances similar to the negotiations that ended the American Revolution.

Very different from the October proposal, the January note was "more like a friendly suggestion." Nevertheless, the second French mediation effort was no more successful than the first. American Secretary of State William Seward regarded the January proposal as a proposition for the American government to enter into diplomatic discussions with insurgents when it was engaged in suppressing an armed insurrection. Seward politely rejected the French initiative since there was no reason to expect that the insurgents would be willing to negotiate except on the basis of separation while the Union was determined to prevent separation. The Congress of the United States was the appropriate forum for discussion of peace between the insurgents and the people of the United States, concluded Seward.[78]

If Seward was not receptive, Imperial newspapers were effusive in their praise of the second French mediation proposal. They commented particularly on the "generous sentiments of humanity" and the "most sincere sympathy" for the United States embodied in the notes. Military events in America, "the terrible struggle which has devastated America" and covered American soil with blood and ruins, the balance of forces so that neither side could win, amply justified the Emperor's efforts to secure peace. Peace proposals in New York and a speech by the noted anti-war Democrat, Clement Vallandigham, provided evidence that the ground was well prepared in America. Finally, the suffering of the French laboring classes justified the action. Diplomacy, said one provincial newspaper, "has rarely spoken a language more noble, more humane, more in accord with general needs. May God wish that language might be understood. . . . But will it be heard?"[79]

The Clerical *Union* was also very pleased with the proposal. Drouyn phrased his message in the best possible way to assuage Northern sensibilities. There was no question of suspending hostilities, and conferees were to meet at a neutral point. The *Union* particularly liked the idea of France acting alone, which, it believed, had a better chance of success than joint action.[80]

Progressive newspapers reacted either cautiously or very negatively to the January proposal. After having criticized the previous proposal, the *Journal des débats* approved of the January suggestion. While it might not lead to peace, it was a great step toward respect of the right that the North represented.[81] The *Temps* praised the anticipated proposal both for its friendly tone but mainly because mediation had for its goal "reconciliation," which the Orleanist journal interpreted as meaning reconstitution of the Union. The *Temps* claimed that the language of the minister of foreign affairs would be much more sympathetic to the Federal cause than anyone had been able to forecast from the attitude of the official press.[82] When the proposal actually appeared, the *Temps* was more restrained. Though the overtures appeared more acceptable and much less contrary to the North than the first mediation proposal, nevertheless "we doubt that they might be accepted, or if they are accepted, that they would be followed by the desired effect." The North and the South were more irreconcilable than in 1861; the only solution seemed to be the full triumph of one of the two parties.[83] The *Revue des deux mondes* was more scathing. The French proposal was "sterile"; its only superfluous result was to show to the world France's desire for the reestablishment of peace in America. "We have also furnished Mr. Seward the occasion to ridicule us," charged the editor. In his reply to Drouyn's note, Seward asked France, in effect, to propose to the Southern states recognition of the Union as a preliminary and we will make peace. This experience "will cure, we hope," urged Forcade, "our taste for intervention in the American conflict."[84]

More than one Progressive newspaper was critical of the proposal because it did not address the slavery issue. The (Nantes) *Phare de la Loire* desired the end of the war, "but we wish more firmly yet the end of slavery and the reestablishment of the Union." The French minister of foreign affairs with regrettable care had avoided speaking of slavery, the real cause of the war.[85]

The Progressive (Bordeaux) *Gironde* even more bluntly denounced the armistice proposal. The Governmental press, it charged, had consistently exalted the Southern cause and publicized rumors of imminent intervention. This had encouraged the partisans of secession, who had based their calculations upon the influence of cotton in Europe. Britain, according to those calculations, could not live for three months without recognizing the South; the same was true for France. Not true, but the Government press had offered, under a thousand forms, sympathies and encouragements viewed as a prelude to a more evident and efficacious support. Suppress the hope of complicity in Europe, and the rebellion would never have been born; suppress the hope of complicity in Paris and London, and all the forces of resistance in the South would vanish. It was in that context that one should consider Drouyn's proposal, which could only encourage the South. "We have actively regretted," warned the *Gironde*, "a step whose effect seemed to us to lead to a result diametrically opposed to the noble goal dreamed by the minister." If one believed that the South would win, then recognize them and break the blockade. But France should also consider the question of slavery, and France should remember that Napoleon ceded Louisiana with the idea of creating a power as counterpoise to Britain.[86]

A provincial Orleanist newspaper also expressed reservations over the Drouyn proposal, though the dispatch was "irreproachable as to the spirit of propriety and moderation." It would be no more acceptable to Lincoln than the first, claimed the (Troyes) *Aube*. It seemed to say to William Seward that your Civil War had given birth to the cotton crise that weighed on all of Europe; it imposed rude sacrifices as much on the populations as on the governments of France and England. Hasten to put an end to the cause of so much misery in order to cast away all pretexts of discontent in Europe. Seward would see the proposal, claimed this skeptical newspaper, as encouraging the Confederacy.[87]

Other provincial newspapers, even those supportive of the emperor, expressed reservations. One Governmental provincial newspaper favored the French proposal but warned darkly about British motives. The secret desire of the British was the prolongation of the war and the ruin of the American navy, that redoubtable rival of the British navy. France should keep its eyes open that the British would not prevent or retard the triumph of French diplomacy. Admire the institutions of Britain if you wish, warned the newspaper, but do not forget that it was necessary to keep watch on the leopard.[88] Another Governmental newspaper warned that the British wished to kill American democracy, ruin a maritime rival, and reconquer industrial supremacy. They plotted to replace Southern cotton with Indian cotton. The ruin of the United States would only provoke "crocodile tears" from Britain.[89]

Thus the French proposals of mediation for the purpose of ending the Civil War evoked mixed reactions. Conservative newspapers typically praised the proposals, while Progressive newspapers expressed serious reservations. Many newspapers in both groups, however, also questioned whether the proposals would receive the necessary approval. As it turned out, Britain and Russia refused to join in the first, tri-partite, mediation proposal, and Washington rejected the second unilateral mediation proposal. It does seem likely, however, that Paris officials had expected these refusals. They had, after all, made the diplomatic initiatives largely for domestic political reasons, to show the French people their desire to alleviate economic difficulties arising from the Civil War. From that perspective, rejection of the French proposals was almost irrelevant.

NOTES

1. This summary of French policy follows the conclusions in Lynn Case and Warren Spencer, *The United States and France: Civil War Diplomacy* (Philadelphia, University of Pennsylvania Press, 1970), pp. 590–94. Marvin Zahniser, *Uncertain Friendship: American-French Diplomatic Relations through the Cold War* (New York, Wiley, 1975), pp. 142–43, emphasized Napoleon III's desire to help the Confederacy with positive steps.

2. Édouard Laboulaye, a prominent French professor, writer, and Union supporter, argued against French military intervention on the ground that it would be cheaper "to feed the laboring classes . . . game and champagne." Laboulaye, *Upon Whom Rests the Guilt of the War?* (New York, 1863), cited in Henry Blumenthal, *A Reappraisal of Franco-American Relations, 1830–1871* (Chapel Hill, University of North Carolina Press, 1959), pp. 136–37, 148–49.

3. Cited in Donaldson Jordan and Edwin J. Pratt, *Europe and the American Civil War* (Boston, Houghton Mifflin, 1931), p. 237.

4. Barlatier, *Sémaphore de Marseille*, September 27, 1861.

5. Bellet, *Patrie*, June 15, 1861, quoted in W. Reed West, *Contemporary French Opinion on the American Civil War* (Baltimore, Johns Hopkins University Press, 1924), p. 38. Disturbed at this report by a semi-official newspaper which he feared reflected official views, the American minister, William L. Dayton, complained to the French foreign affairs ministry. Thouvenel replied that the *Patrie* had ceased being a semi-official paper ten days before. The *Patrie* proposal attracted considerable attention, including reprinting in the official *Moniteur*. The Liberal *Presse* criticized the *Patrie* proposal on the ground that it was not a good idea to offend Americans. Gaillardet, *Presse*, June 20, 1861.

6. Prévost, *Vigie de Cherbourg*, July 7, 1861.

7. Gaches, *Journal de Saint-Étienne*, September 8, 1861.

8. Gaches, (Saint-Étienne) *Mémorial de la Loire*, May 15, 1861. Both the *Journal de Saint-Étienne* and the *Mémorial de la Loire* were based in Saint-Étienne. Ch. Gaches wrote articles for both.

9. Nefftzer, *Temps*, October 19, 1861.

10. Poitevin, (Blois) *Avenir*, October 20, 1861.

11. Peyrat, *Presse*, December 7, 1861.

12. Esparbié, *Patrie*, December 1, 1861, cited in West, *Contemporary Opinion*, p. 41. Provincial newspapers carefully reported the views of the Paris press, particularly on the *Trent* issue. See, for example, Dufour, *Courrier de l'Ain*, December 10, 1861.

13. Vitu, *Constitutionnel*, December 15, 1861, quoted in West, *French Opinion*, pp. 32, 43.

14. Fontaines, *Monde*, January 5, 1861.

15. Cumot, (Angers) *Ami du peuple*, December 7, 1861.

16. Bayvet, (Quimper) *Impartial de Finistère*, December 7, 1861.

17. Horn, *Journal des débats*, January 5, 1862.

18. Forcade, *Revue des deux mondes*, December 1, 1861, p. 757; December 15, 1861, p. 1017.

19. Bertrand, (La Rochelle) *Charente-Inférieure*, December 12, 1861.

20. Poitevin, (Blois) *Avenir*, December 1, 1861. The newspaper characterized as a "puerile calculation" the argument that French participation would allow France to stop the conflict when it became too prejudicial to America.

21. Bayvet, (La Rochelle) *Charente-Inférieure*, January 16, 1862.

22. Grandin, (Bourges) *Journal du Cher*, February 13, 1862; Pillon, (Limoges) *Courrier du Centre*, May 2, 6, 1862; Laytou, (Cahors) *Courrier du Lot*, April 28, 1862.

23. Delord, *Siècle*, May 5, 1862, cited in West, *French Opinion*, p. 74.

24. Limayrac, *Constitutionnel*, May 22, 1862, cited in West, *French Opinion*, pp. 74–75.

25. Barbaroux, (Digne) *Ami de l'ordre*, June 19, 1862.

26. Capdevielle, (Pau) *Mémorial des Pyrénées*, July 24, 1862.

27. Rolin, (Bar-le-Duc) *Écho de l'est*, July 16, 1862.

28. Barbaroux, (Digne) *Ami de l'ordre*, October 30, 1862.

29. Broise, *Journal d'Alençon*, October 2, 1862.

30. Laytou, (Cahors) *Journal du Lot*, June 22, 1862.

31. Septavaux, (Tarbes) *Ère impériale*, June 12, 1862.

32. Paul Pecquet du Bellet, *Pays*, September 11, 17, 1862. Another Conservative argued in August that the moment was propitious for mediation because for the next six months it would be too hot to fight. Bayvet, (La Rochelle) *Charente-Inférieure*, August 7, 1862.

33. Bayvet, (La Rochelle) *Charente-Inférieure*, October 30, 1862.

34. Fonville, (Maçon) *Journal de Saône-et-Loire*, June 11, 1862.

35. Lapierre, (Évreux) *Courrier de l'Eure*, June 14, 1862.

36. Regnault, *Presse*, June 13, 15, 1862.

37. Alloury, *Journal des débats*, June 9, 12, 15, 1862; cited in West, *French Opinion*, pp. 77–80.

38. Claude, *Temps*, October 2, 1862.

39. Gaïffe, *Presse*, July 20, 1862.

40. Bernard, *Siècle*, August 27, 1862, cited in West, *French Opinion*, p. 84.

41. (Périgueux) *Écho de Vesone*, August 9, 1862. Lacombe, "Le Mexique [et] la reconnaissance des États du Sud," *Correspondant*, November, 1862, 449–65, argued strongly against intervention (recognition) because of the slavery question. The author made frequent reference to the *pierre angulaire* Southern defense of slavery.

42. See Chapter 4 for the change of attitude among many Frenchmen over Northern prospects for victory. See Case and Spencer, *Civil War Diplomacy*, p. 352, for a discussion of Napoleon's reasons for proposing mediation.

43. Case and Spencer, *Civil War Diplomacy*, pp. 358–59. They particularly cite the reports of procureurs general, which both reflected public opinion and had much influence on the emperor.

44. Grandin, (Bourges) *Journal du Cher*, November 18, 1862. Clearly Napoleon was very interested in retaining popular support. Numerous works demonstrate his popularity among peasants, but he also was popular among workers. The latter, however, made a distinction between admiration for Napoleon personally and support for his ministers and his policies. Bernard Ménager, "Force et limites du bonapartisme populaire en milieu ouvrier sous le Second Empire" [force and limits of popular Bonapartism among workers in the Second Empire] in *Revue historique*, 265 (1981), 371–88.

45. "Correspondance particulière," (Bordeaux) *Guienne*, November 14, 1862. In a dispatch of November 14, 1862, the American minister in Paris, William Dayton, reported to Secretary of State Seward that in his judgment one of the purposes of the mediation proposal was "to satisfy the workmen and manufacturing interests of France that the Emperor has been, and is, anxious to do what he can to alleviate their distress." Quoted in Daniel Carroll, *Henri Mercier and the American Civil War* (Princeton, Princeton University Press, 1971), p. 241.

46. *Pays*, November 10, 1862, reported that France, Russia, and Britain were going to act together to end the war. That report was based on stories in British newspapers.

47. For a good discussion of the note, see Case and Spencer, *Civil War Diplomacy*, pp. 386–88.

48. Baralon, Germain, *Pays*, November 17, 22, 1862.

49. Septavaux, (Tarbes) *Ère impériale*, November 15, 1862.

50. Céas, (Valence) *Courrier de la Drôme*, November 15, 1862.

51. Massoubre, (Périgueux) *Écho de Vesone*, November 23, 1862.

52. Chuquet, (Bar-le-Duc) *Écho de l'est*, November 15, 1862.

53. Bayvet, (La Rochelle) *Charente-Inférieure*, November 23, 1862.

54. Baralon, Germain, *Pays*, November 16, 17, 22, 1862.

55. Roret, (Chaumont) *Écho de la Haute-Marne*, November 11, 1862.

56. Conil, (Saintes) *Courrier des deux Charentes*, November 16, 1862.

57. Filingre, *Journal de la Haute-Saône*, November 15, 1862.

58. Tierny, (Arras) *Courrier du Pas-de-Calais*, November 14, 1862.

59. Dorcesse, (Soissons) *Argus Soissonnais*, November 16, 1862.

60. Pouillard, (Charleville-Mézières) *Courrier des Ardennes*, November 15, 1862.

61. Chantrel, *Monde*, November 12, 14, 15, 1862.

62. Domin, (Caen) *Ordre et la liberté*, November 18, 1862.

63. Capdevielle, (Pau) *Mémorial des Pyrénées*, January 24, 1863.

64. Gaïffe, *Presse*, November 8, 1862.

65. Gaïffe, *ibid.*, November 10, 1862.

66. Gaïffe, *ibid.*, November 16, 1862.

67. Delord, *Siècle*, November 18, 1862; Plée, *Siècle*, November 19, 1862, cited in West, *French Opinion*, pp. 91–92.

68. Carle, *Sémaphore de Marseille*, November 14, 1862.

69. Hébrard, *Temps*, November 14, 15, 1862; Grenier, *ibid.*, November 16, 1862.

70. Forcade, *Revue des deux mondes*, November 15, 1862, pp. 485–93.

71. Ferrier, (Nancy) *Impartial de la Meurthe et des Vosges*, December 19, 1862.

72. Howard Jones, *Union in Peril: The Crisis over British Intervention in the Civil War* (Chapel Hill, University of North Carolina Press, 1992).

73. Roret, (Chaumont) *Écho de la Haute-Marne*, November 18, 1862.

74. Septavaux, (Tarbes) *Ère impériale*, November 15, 1862.

75. Filingre, (Vesoul) *Journal de la Haute-Saône*, November 15, 1862.

76. Chantrel, *Monde*, November 14, 1862. Ephraim Adams, *Great Britain and the American Civil War* (2 vols., London, Longmans, Green & Co., 1925), II, 66, attributed British refusal to the Russian rejection, a desire to maintain cabinet unity, and a belief that the North would not accept mediation. Public opinion "in the main heartily supported the Cabinet decision."

77. Daniel Carroll, *Henri Mercier*, pp. 261, 263.

78. Case and Spencer, *Civil War Diplomacy*, pp. 387–89, 396–97, summarized the French and American notes on the topic.

79. Cohen, (Maçon) *Journal de Saône-et-Loire*, January 31, 1863. For similar sentiments, see Lapierre, (Évreux) *Courrier de l'Eure*, January 29, 1863; Fissot, (Grenoble) *Courrier de l'Isère*, January 31, 1863; Duquesnel, (Saint-Malo) *Commerce Breton*, January 31, 1863.

80. Moreau, *Union*, January 30, 1863.

81. Weiss, *Journal des débats*, January 30, 1863, cited in West, *French Opinion*, p. 97.

82. Nefftzer, *Temps*, November 14, 1863.

83. Nefftzer, *ibid.*, January 29, 1863.

84. Forcade, *Revue des deux mondes*, March 1, 1863, p. 232.

85. Mangin, (Nantes) *Phare de la Loire,* January 28, 1863.
86. Lavertujon, (Bordeaux) *Gironde*, January 2, 1863.
87. Ferrier, (Troyes) *Aube*, January 30–31, 1863.
88. Dodivers, (Besançon) *Franche-Comté*, January 31, 1863.
89. Pierréal, (Saintes) *Courrier des deux Charentes*, January 25, 1863.

Chapter 7

1863 and 1864

> One feels a certain emotion, a certain astonishment mixed with terror and admiration, inspired by the immense efforts and the immense resources deployed by those two powerful belligerents that one believed so little apt in warfare. Everything is gigantic in those furious *mêlées* where armies of several hundred thousand men struggle hand-to-hand for entire weeks; on battlefields which cover areas more vast than our European countries; with rivers compared to which ours are only rivulets, where nature, itself wild and imposing, forms a background worthy of the events.
>
> Mille-Noé, *Sémaphore de Marseille*, January 23, 1863

> European opinion leaves the Federals and the Confederates to occupy itself with Poland.
>
> Bédollière, *Siècle*, March 16, 1863

French newspapers took a lively interest in the American Civil War in 1862, when the war disrupted the French economy. Especially during the latter half of 1862, Frenchmen vigorously debated possible French intervention in the conflict. During 1863 and 1864, however, French interest notably waned, and for some weeks even major Parisian newspapers scarcely mentioned the American Civil War. In part that lack of interest reflected preoccupation with stirring events in Europe; Liberals were particularly concerned about Polish efforts to secure independence. The lack of interest also reflected boredom and despair because of the interminable length of the American Civil War, whose battles led to slaughter but no discernable result.

Besides paying fitful attention to military operations, French newspapers intermittently commented on other aspects of the Civil War. They continued to debate the causes and goals of the war; they continued to disagree about French intervention in the conflict; they breathlessly reported the dramatic *Alabama*-

Kearsarge battle off Cherbourg; they drew varying conclusions about the presidential election in 1864. Since the views of the French press had long since become polarized along political fault lines, Liberals and Conservatives took sharply contrasting positions toward military, political, and diplomatic Civil War issues in 1863 and 1864.

MILITARY

Certain themes emerged clearly in French press discussion of military aspects of the Civil War. All shades of opinion in 1863 and 1864 agreed that the battles produced no military consequence except an appalling number of casualties. A shocked (Charleville-Mézières) *Courrier des Ardennes* wrote of "those frightful hecatombs of which America appears today to have the monopoly, bloody butcheries which do not find their compensation in any appreciable result."[1] Another Conservative provincial journal described Gettysburg as typical of the American war, "a bloody battle . . . without result."[2] The *Presse* agreed. "One of the most strange characteristics of the war," lamented the Liberal, pro-Northern newspaper,

> is that the most terrible battles of those great armies do not produce any perceptible result, do not discourage the defeated nor give superiority to the victors, do not make a step toward peace by a reunion or a definitive separation.

That was true, added the *Presse*, after the battles of Manassas, Antietam, Fredericksburg, Chancellorsville, and Gettysburg.[3] The scale of those bloody battles also impressed French journalists. Those bloody battles, reported a provincial Conservative newspaper, "which everywhere would decide the fate of nations, in America have only the result of increasing the effusion of blood in frightful proportions."[4]

If Liberal and Conservative newspapers agreed upon the huge scale of battles, the appalling number of casualties, and lack of results, they frequently differed along ideological lines about the significance of military events. Conservatives saw military events through a pro-Southern or anti-Northern prism. One Conservative newspaper, for example, claimed that Lincoln should view the disastrous Federal defeat at Fredericksburg as a means of ending the war.[5] A few months later, another Conservative newspaper reported that the war was going poorly for the North because of sickness and desertion, that its army had become indecisive, and that there were symptoms of fatigue and weakness everywhere.[6] While Gettysburg was a Northern success, conceded a Conservative newspaper, nevertheless that success was counterbalanced by internal differences in the North, such as the riots in New York. Besides, Lee's reverse at Gettysburg was limited to not being able to defeat the Union army, and the Southerners retired in good order.[7] The Clerical *Union* did not view Grant's victory at Chattanooga in November,

1863, as significant since Grant was not pursuing Confederate commander Braxton Bragg. So was Bragg beaten that badly?[8]

French Liberals were more positive about Union military operations in 1863. The Republican organ at Marseille claimed that the capture of Vicksburg and the Union victory at Gettysburg were of "capital importance."[9] A group of merchants in Bordeaux, whose trade with America was crippled as a result of the Civil War, at one point had wished "to see peace by *any means*," but in 1863, reported the American consul, "many *now* side with our Government because of *its success* at Gettysburg & Vicksburg."[10] Nevertheless, Liberal newspapers were restrained in their assessment of military operations. While agreeing that Union forces had achieved great victories, the Orleanist *Journal des débats* pointed to an inability of Northern generals to plan a campaign far in advance; Meade's victory at Gettysburg, added the pro-Northern newspaper, saved the capital but did not prevent a later return of the Confederate army.[11] "Unshakably attached" to the Northern cause, the Republican *Siècle*, believed that the North had all of the elements of victory but had yet to achieve coordination of those elements.[12] The Liberal *Courrier du dimanche* was even more somber. At the end of 1863, that paper feared that a Northern victory would result in less liberty in the North and a permanent army.[13]

Military events in 1864 furnished several occasions for Conservative newspapers to make negative comments about the Federal war machine. The appointment of Ulysses S. Grant as general in chief pleased Northern opinion, but now he faced the supreme test; he had never met an enemy as capable as Lee, gibed a Conservative newspaper.[14] Another saw scant hope for Grant since the operations of the Northern army were badly conceived, and the Confederates outnumbered the Union forces.[15] In May ,the Conservative *Moniteur* reported that Grant considered his position untenable with his supply lines too extended so that he could not support his army.[16] Grant was not doing well, reported a Conservative provincial newspaper. Somewhat gratuitously, the newspaper explained that Frenchmen were better warriors, while Americans loved gold.[17] Even if Richmond should fall, claimed the *Patrie*, the war would not be over; as evidence for that statement the *Patrie* argued that the captures of New Orleans and Chattanooga were not important either.[18]

During the summer of 1864 Conservative newspapers also viewed Sherman's operations negatively. After the capture of Atlanta, Sherman had to renounce pursuing Confederate commander John Hood. In addition, Sherman had to burn and evacuate Atlanta, claimed a Conservative newspaper, because he considered the defense of that place impossible.[19] The *Patrie* characterized Sherman's famous March to the Sea as demonstrating "more and more the character of a retreat." He had already lost half of his troops; the rest were "fatigued, demoralized and starving." Confederate leaders P. T. Beauregard, John Hood, Nathan B. Forrest, and John C. Breckinridge had acted with as much vigor as skill. Thus Sherman's March would likely become a new disaster for Union arms.[20]

Liberal newspapers in 1864 typically drew a more favorable, though restrained, view of Union military operations. The Orleanist *Revue des deux mondes* approvingly noted in June that Grant had shown "since the beginning of that [Wilderness] campaign a resolution and a persistence" not possessed by previous commanders.[21] The Liberal *Presse* regretted the losses in the Wilderness campaign—"they say Grant was a tanner who became a butcher"—but claimed that Grant was a great strategist who forced Lee to retreat.[22] At times, however, even Liberal newspapers despaired of a Union victory. Thus a discouraged Orleanist *Courrier du dimanche* in a lengthy commentary on the war in May, 1864, concluded that the North could not win.[23] After a long summer of fighting and maneuvering by Grant in the Richmond campaign and Sherman in the Atlanta campaign, the eminently judicious and level-headed *Revue des deux mondes* confessed in September that "the facts of war are always confused in America," and the editor experienced "a sort of repugnance" in deciphering the "contradictory vicissitudes of that interminable conflict." Still, the situation seemed favorable to the North. Grant's campaign, disastrously begun in Virginia, never ceased to threaten Richmond; Sherman was before Atlanta, and Farragut was forcing Mobile. In sum: the Federals were continually gaining territory while the Confederates were not gaining anything from the North.[24] By October the *Revue* was much more optimistic and saw the end of the war approaching, with the success of Sherman at Atlanta, Farragut at Mobile, and Philip Sheridan in his Shenandoah Valley campaign.[25]

CAUSES OF THE WAR

If Liberals and Conservatives had different interpretations of military events, in 1863 they differed even more profoundly on the causes of the Civil War and their appraisal of American—particularly Northern—society. Becoming more evident as the war progressed, the cleavage lines between Liberals and Conservatives were abundantly clear in 1863.

By that year debate on the causes of the Civil War followed fairly simplistic lines. Conservatives charged that the Northerners were the aggressors in the conflict and largely attributed their aggression to crass, economic motives. The question of slavery, declared the Conservative (Saint-Malo) *Commerce Breton*, was not the first cause of the war; the question of tariffs was "clearly more powerful. Material conflicts of interest dominated the situation."[26] The tariff was the "only cause of the war (and not slavery), as the liberal newspapers say," added the (Saintes) *Courrier des deux Charentes*.[27] Another Conservative provincial newspaper supported the South because the North, touched in their commercial interests, was the aggressor. Hypocritically utilizing the question of slavery as a pretext for their aggression, the North cited abolition as their goal, even though all of the acts of Lincoln had relegated slavery to a secondary role.[28] The Clerical *Monde* saw protective tariffs, which worked for the advantage of the North and ruined the South, as a major issue, but the *Monde* also claimed that the war arose because of oppression of the Franco-Spanish race in the South by the Anglo-Saxon race of the North.[29] Slavery, according to the *Monde*, was "the pretext, the occasion, and not the true cause of the war."[30] A Conservative provincial journal added that the public at first accepted the Liberal idea that the issue was slavery versus abolitionism, but opposing journals had brought about a "nearly general reversal of feeling."[31]

Liberal journals, on the other hand, defined the key issues as slavery and union. The Liberal *Siècle* saw the Northern cause as doubly sacred, first for abolition and second for the defense of the unity of the American confederation.[32] Why the war, inquired the Liberal *Presse*? One party wished to live separated, governing themselves in their own manner, forcing men of another race to work the land. The other group wished not to suffer separation and opposed using Negroes as instruments of labor, like horses.[33]

One Liberal Frenchmen who traveled extensively in the United States explicitly linked slavery, the war, and aristocracy. Conservatives contended, he wrote in 1864,

> that slavery is only a pretext for the ambitions of the North, that the overbearing attitude of the North and its tyrannical defiance of the Constitution are the real reasons that drove the desperate people of the South into rebellion. The Unionists are made to appear as alien despots while the Confederates are pictured as the true defenders of the nation and of liberty. This is not true. Abolition is not a mere excuse; nor was the Federal government the first to violate the law. The first breach of legality came rather from the Rebels: while calling themselves champions of the ravished Constitution they were the first to lay violent hands on it. The true causes of the war are slavery, the mutual hostility of the two rival societies, and, above all, the ambition of the Southerners, who arrogantly sought to perpetuate their dominance in spite of public opinion, and who raised the flag of revolt as soon as the presidency slipped out of their hands.
>
> All the while that slavery in the South, bound up as it was with the ownership of land, was giving birth to aristocratic vices that were eating out the heart of republican institutions, slavery in the North was unable to survive and grow. . . . The atmosphere of democracy was deadly to it.[34]

AMERICAN SOCIETY

Just as Liberals and Conservatives disagreed on the causes of the war, they likewise disagreed in their appraisals of American society. Conservatives saw an "unquiet" North with diverse interests, while the South possessed a unity of interests.[35] The North was in chaos, agreed a fellow Conservative provincial newspaper. Washington was "in the most complete disarray"; the North would be lucky to escape a military dictatorship. For that, however, it would need a victorious general, and the North could congratulate itself on its lack of such a general.[36]

Conservative journals saw Northern democracy as fatally flawed and doomed to degenerate into a dictatorship. One Conservative knew of two aristocracies in the North; one was an aristocracy of wealth. The other, the most terrible, comprised those "ultra puritan reverends," who had always led their numerous followers under a mantel of hypocrisy. They were responsible for blue laws, which condemned people to death for disobedience, for not worshiping the true god.[37] Another Conservative provincial newspaper charged that Lincoln already had committed despotic acts before which the Czar of Russia or the Sultan of Constantinople would have probably recoiled: he had suspended the writ of habeas corpus, practiced illegal imprisonment, interfered with slavery, and exorcised secession in West Virginia.[38] The Republican Congress was docile to the voice of its master and was as free as one was in America, that is, free to obey. Congress voted as Lincoln made it vote.[39]

Clerical newspapers were particularly scathing in their criticism of Northern democracy. Lincoln was a true dictator, claimed the Clerical *Union*.[40] The *Monde* charged that American democracy as described by Tocqueville would soon be only a memory. There was talk of electing a president for ten years. Why not for life? Then he would become hereditary. Nothing was so disastrous, claimed the Clerical newspaper, as that system of popular elections.[41] Clerical newspapers viewed the failure of democracy as inevitable because democracy as a social system was fatally flawed. Democracy aimed to absorb everyone in a monstrous unity with no place for liberty or individual initiative. Even worse, American democracy had no religious base, and no one had seen a nation formed without such a base. The United States, completely rationalist, was not able to endure. The war would lead to a military supremacy, a necessary consequence for the United States.[42] That newspaper hoped that Catholicism would have more influence in the United States because only Catholicism was able to remedy the vices of a social state so new and already so corrupted and so degenerate.[43]

Clerical *Union* made some pointed observations about European reaction to the Civil War. Three years of massacre and ruin had led politicians of the Old World to suspect that the United States was only a fortuitous establishment, and the American example seemed destined to give the lie to the "famous theory of modern society." The terrible cost of the war in casualties and money had also given the lie to extreme republicanism. In addition, the *Union* perceived an irony in European reaction to the "anarchy" in the United States. The guardians of monarchical order supported the liberty of the Southern states, while the defenders of "revolutionary right" supported the president of a republic desirous of establishing a regime of "dictatorship pushed to the last extreme of despotism."[44]

While the characteristics of American democracy fascinated the French, slavery was the feature of American society which attracted the most attention. Since Frenchmen were resolutely anti-slavery, Conservatives could scarcely praise the institution of forced labor in the South. Instead, Conservatives argued that Northerners were hypocritical on the slavery question. The Yankees really did not favor abolition, and they were racists in any event. Northern soldiers refused to fight alongside blacks, which "edified" one Conservative newspaper "sufficiently about the sincerity of the liberal and humanitarian protestations of the North."[45] The North was scarcely antislavery, claimed the *Pays*, since Yankees scorned, exploited, and detested blacks in the North.[46]

Northern society had other faults in the eyes of Conservatives. The war had produced "rascals." What other word was fitting for Senator James Lane of Kansas, who would not be satisfied until the last men of the South had been hung? "Marat is distanced by the generous Yankee," charged a Conservative newspaper in the Midi. Let people say that the North is the only representative in America of liberty and civilization. Such a beautiful representative, snorted the Midi journal, "which has in its ranks a Butler, scourge of women, and a James Lane celebrating the glories of assassination."[47] The money-grubbing Yankees even failed to do a good job of managing their national finances. Midas had changed into gold everything that he touched; the American Congress had changed gold into paper, and such detestable paper.[48] As a result, the financial situation in the North got worse and worse.

Even some Liberal supporters of the North confessed to flaws in Northern society. One Liberal Frenchman who had traveled extensively in the North admitted, for example, that "often the black man's advocates and defenders don't really care very much, when all is said and done, what becomes of him." Except for a few intellectuals "to whose democratic consciences the whole idea of slavery is repugnant, the noisiest abolitionists do not, if the truth were known, feel much offended by slavery." A Northerner was angry about slavery not because slavery was a moral wrong or degraded blacks; rather, Northerners were concerned about the supremacy of their society over the society of which slavery was the cornerstone. "Nowhere is color prejudice more deeply rooted," wrote this blunt observer, "than in the regions permeated by abolitionist ideas."[49]

As the war dragged on interminably, a few Liberal newspapers became critical of Federal resolve. The *Presse* in June, 1863, saw the conflict as no more than a work of destruction inspired by a savage obstinacy. There was nothing more to be done than trace out the boundaries of the two separated states.[50] The *Siècle*, which resolutely supported the Northern cause throughout the conflict, did not know how Europe in the nineteenth century could find writers in the service of *esclavagistes*. Still, the *Siècle* was clearly disappointed that the North had done so little against slavery. If the North was not able to kill slavery, let the North at least mortally wound it.[51]

Other Liberal newspapers, however, continued to support Northern goals and institutions. The *Courrier du dimanche* claimed to see a campaign by the official press which systematically attacked the North. *Courrier* could not understand how someone could always hold the principles of 1789 in the mouth and hold the hand to slavery, how anyone could advocate the fall of "the most beautiful democracy that ever was."[52] In a direct rejoinder to Conservative charges that Northerners mistreated blacks, the *Revue des deux mondes* favorably reviewed John Bigelow's book, *The United States in 1863*, citing explicit examples of progress made by blacks under freedom. Certainly slavery had been struck a mortal blow.[53] The *Revue* concluded that the Northern cause was "the good cause, the cause that the sane intelligence of French interests recommends to our political sympathies."[54]

THE ELECTION OF 1864

In view of their differences on other aspects of the Civil War, it is not surprising that Liberals and Conservatives disagreed about the presidential election of 1864. In May of that year the Clerical *Monde* printed a report that even Republicans were turning against Lincoln and the chances of his re-election seemed to diminish day by day.[55] The Liberal *Opinion nationale*, on the other hand, claimed that the re-election of Lincoln appeared certain despite the opposition of Democrats and radicals.[56]

French newspapers had no difficulty finding evidence and arguments to support their divergent positions. The Conservative *Pays* argued that no paper in New York, Baltimore, or Washington would defend Lincoln. Northern people wanted peace; the peace party was growing except for Lincoln and hundreds of intransigents and furnishers of war materials.[57] After the nominations of Abraham Lincoln by the Republicans and George McClellan by the Democrats, one Conservative newspaper perceived clear differences between the two. Lincoln and the Republican party favored political centralization at Washington, conquest of the South, and maintenance of the Union, while Seward claimed that the issue of slavery had nothing to do with the war. McClellan and the Democrats favored political decentralization, recognition of the rights of the states, and maintenance of the Union by pacific means if possible and by war if necessary.[58] Even more succinctly the *Patrie* summarized a major difference between the two candidates: "the one [McClellan] is a gentleman while the other [Lincoln] is not."[59]

Liberals perceived the election in very different terms. To the *Siècle* Lincoln's election would encourage government, not of the Middle Ages, not of an official church, not of a hereditary aristocracy as in Great Britain, but rather of a great form of representative government. His election would provide encouragement to Europe.[60] The *Revue des deux mondes* noted serious divisions among the Democrats: copperheads who wished peace at any price, and McClellan who wished above all to maintain the Union, peacefully if at all possible. Republicans also desired to maintain the Union, but Lincoln had also carefully explained that he would not sacrifice the question of slavery in the interest of peace. Despite these issues, the *Revue* believed that the outcome of a battle between Lee and Grant would decide the election.[61]

News of Lincoln's electoral triumph elicited predictable assessments. One Conservative newspaper agreed with a British organ's prediction that the second administration of Lincoln would mark the transition between a democracy and tyranny. The election insured that the implacable war would continue unabated (*guerre à outrance*).[62] That war, bitterly charged a Conservative provincial newspaper, already had covered with ruins, had inundated with blood, the territory of the United States; four additional years of war would pile new ruins on smoking ruins and would increase the flood of blood that resulted from immutable policies.[63]

On the other hand, exulted a Republican newspaper in Marseille, the friends of liberty in Europe and in the world welcomed the news of the re-election of President Lincoln. A triumph of the Democratic party would have meant slavery and separation. The election of Lincoln was the most sure, the most practical way of putting an end to the struggle.[64] Thus Lincoln's election was "a grand and brilliant manifestation against the pretensions of the South."[65] To the *Courrier du dimanche*, the election of Lincoln showed that American democratic institutions were still strong and unshaken by the Civil War.[66]

The *Alabama-Kearsarge* Affair

Even before the election of 1864, French newspapers reported issues arising from the construction of Confederate commerce raiders in Britain. Such construction elicited serious protests by Federal officials. Ultimately, the British forbade the illegal practice of constructing warships for the Confederacy, but in the meantime the *Florida* and the *Alabama* had slipped out of British ports and wreaked havoc on Northern shipping. When such vessels entered French ports for repairs and supplies, they became a controversial topic in French newspapers.

The *Florida*, the first raider acquired by the Confederates, had been constructed in Liverpool; unarmed when it left Britain in March, 1862, it received some arms in Bermuda. Subsequently, it went to Mobile, Alabama, where it secured additional armament and then embarked on a very successful career as a raider, destroying some thirty-six Northern merchant ships. Needing repairs and supplies, the *Florida* sought refuge in the French port of Brest in August, 1863. In subsequent diplomatic maneuvering the French government strictly followed a very proper neutral policy by allowing repairs so that the Confederate warship would be seaworthy but likewise forbidding the enhancement of its armaments. Ultimately, the *Florida* evaded Union naval surveillance and slipped out to sea in February, 1864, and resumed its commerce raiding.[67]

As might be expected, the French press reacted to the Confederate commerce raiders along ideological lines. Calling such ships "pirates" and *corsairs*, or privateers, the Republican *Siècle* was sharply critical of the Confederate practice of burning captured ships without judgement by a court.[68] The *Journal des débats* argued that, while the Confederates did have belligerent rights and had the right to arm privateers, such vessels had no right to stop ships on the high seas, allow the captain to make judgement, and then burn captured ships. The Confederates must obey international law, and now was the time to obtain justice.[69]

Conservatives argued that the commerce raiders were not pirate ships or privateers, but rather were regular Confederate naval ships. They noted that the

Florida had been armed, manned, and commissioned in Mobile, Alabama. Agreeing with that contention, the French government inserted in the *Moniteur,* the official newspaper, a notice stating that the *Florida* was not a privateer but rather a regular warship forming "part of the navy of the Confederate States."[70]

Even more controversy ensued as a result of the dramatic naval encounter between the Confederate commerce raider *Alabama* and the Union warship *Kearsarge.* Constructed in Britain, the *Alabama* in July, 1862, slipped out of Liverpool and subsequently was equipped with armaments in the Azores. The *Alabama* then embarked upon a remarkably successful, two-year career as a commerce raider. She entered the port of Cherbourg on June 11, 1864, needing extensive repairs. Inhabitants of the city were sympathetic to the South and warmly welcomed the Confederate warship; "elegant society visited the *Alabama sans cesse.*"[71]

Upon the arrival of the Union warship *Kearsarge*, Captain John Winslow commanding, off Cherbourg, the Confederate captain of the *Alabama*, Raphael Semmes, challenged the Union ship to a duel. Subsequently, on June 19, Semmes sailed his vessel out of the harbor into international waters, where the two warships fought a ninety-minute engagement. In that naval battle the *Alabama* was sunk, while the *Kearsarge* suffered relatively minor damage. The *Kearsarge*, the British vessel *Deerhound*, and various small French boats picked up the Confederate survivors.[72]

Preparations for the engagement had been extensively discussed in the press. The result was that thousands of people in Cherbourg witnessed the naval battle fought barely beyond the three-mile limit. Hundreds of Parisians who had gone by special train to pass Sunday at Cherbourg were able, if not to follow details of the combat, at least to hear the cannonade and to see the *Alabama* disappear beneath the water.

Newspapers in all parts of France reported and commented on the naval battle. Frenchmen were clearly fascinated with the drama inherent in a naval engagement between foreign belligerents fought within sight of a major French port. In addition, many Frenchmen looked upon the Confederates as chivalrous and romantic underdogs. Conservative newspapers, in particular, were notably sympathetic toward the Confederates, as were most of the throng of observers. One provincial newspaper reported that before sailing out to meet the *Kearsarge* in "that most moving maritime drama," Confederate Captain Semmes proclaimed that the moment had come to vanquish or die. Thousands cried out: "Hurrah for the South! Long live Lee! Long live France!" In another sympathetic account, the *Patrie* claimed that the contest was unequal, since the *Kearsarge* was more heavily armed and more heavily staffed with men while the *Alabama* was in poor condition because of three years at sea. The *Alabama* tried to board the *Kearsarge*, but was foiled by evasive tactics of the latter. Nevertheless, the *Alabama* was winning until a *Kearsarge* projectile struck a mortal blow against the gallant Confederate warship. The French press and the French people, according to the Conservative account, perceived

> the sailors and officers of the *Alabama* as men going valiantly to death for their political faith, for their flag, for their country; each of us has rendered homage to that act of devotion, to that martyrdom![73]

In contrast to the heroism of the Confederates, charged Conservative newspapers, Union naval officers of the *Kearsarge* were delinquent in picking up survivors.

Finally, Conservative newspapers rejoiced in what they reported as overwhelming support by the French press for the heroic Confederates. To the honor of the French press only one newspaper, claimed the *Pays*, had "the distressing audacity to offend public emotion," to insult the vanquished in that chivalrous duel, and to salute with transports of inhumane joy the sacrifice of brave men "who died as all men of courage ought to wish to die."[74]

The Republican *Opinion nationale* proudly acknowledged that indeed it had rejoiced in the victory of the *Kearsarge*. The *Opinion* had no sympathy for the *Alabama* because "Where the right is not present, pity ought not to be present." Reserving its sympathies for the victor, the *Opinion* praised "the brave Captain Winslow who by his skill and by his courage has enhanced the honor of the great American republic."[75] Denying Conservative charges that the Yankees were slow in picking up Confederate survivors, the *Opinion* replied that Union commander Winslow promptly sent three lifeboats to rescue Southern sailors after their vessel sank.[76]

In a similar pro-Northern stance the *Siècle* was not at all impressed with either the Confederate warship or its commander. The *Siècle* saw the *Alabama's* challenge to the *Kearsarge* as an attempt by Semmes to rehabilitate a naval career that had not been brilliant.[77] Nor was the *Siècle* impressed with the claim that the *Alabama*, experienced in boarding procedures, would have won if it had succeeded in boarding the *Kearsarge*. While the *Alabama* had much experience in boarding unarmed merchants, this was, acidly observed the *Siècle*, the Confederate vessel's first and last encounter with a federal warship. The *Siècle* added that it was time to put an end to enthusiasm for Semmes which approached "the ridiculous."[78]

DIPLOMATIC ISSUES

Other diplomatic issues affecting French interests were less dramatic than the *Alabama-Kearsarge* naval battle and attracted less attention in 1863 and 1864. The Republican *Presse*, which in the past had shown itself as an outspoken advocate of neutral rights, continued raising objections to the blockade in 1863. Embracing an extreme pro-neutral rights stance, the *Presse* charged that Federal forces were maintaining a paper blockade, and "the governments of Europe have been dupes of a fiction which has caused immense prejudice to their nations." The *Presse* argued that private enemy property ought to be respected on the sea as on the land, and "the blockade OF COMMERCIAL PORTS ought to be prohibited even between belligerents."[79] Actually, this isolated outburst against the legality of the blockade by the *Presse* demonstrates that midway in the Civil War the blockade was no longer a major issue. As previously noted, alternate sources of supply were replacing Southern cotton, and the cotton *crise* was abating.

If the blockade was becoming a virtual non-issue by 1863, Conservative newspapers, nevertheless, continued to urge mediation and/or recognition of the South. French newspapers reported the maneuvers of the Englishman John Roebuck, who met with Napoleon III, to promote his plan of joint British–French recognition of the Confederacy. His maneuvers failed after Roebuck in the House of Commons publicly described his private meeting with Napoleon. The affair did, however, provide the occasion for French newspapers to argue for Southern recognition.[80] Indeed, one Liberal newspaper complained of a "campaign" by the official press in favor of the Southern states.[81] The *Patrie* in turn grumbled that the British were dragging their feet on mediation; if they did accept mediation, it would be "in tow" by France.[82]

The Clerical *Union* argued very strenuously for mediation. In an extended article, the *Union* summarized Conservative views about the Civil War: Northern traffickers and a tyrannical Congress were waging a war for tariffs and against Southern planters under the pretext of emancipation; the South was constitutionally justified in secession; it was pointless for the North to try to conquer the South; if conquered, the South would remain unreconciled, an Ireland, a Poland. The Clerical newspaper differed from other Conservative supporters of Napoleon III in calling for France to act alone, not in concert with Britain. Thus the opposition Clerical newspaper carved out a position consistent with its conservative views yet one that was in opposition to the policy of the French government,[83] which viewed cooperation with the British as essential to diplomatic initiatives in the Civil War.

Liberal newspapers meanwhile continued their opposition to French recognition and mediation. The *Siècle* noted that the *esclavagiste* newspapers in 1863 were spreading rumors of the near recognition of the South. Now it was to be done by England; now, by France. Now they were saying it would be done by both. Why recognize the South, queried the *Siècle*? France no longer had need of her cotton, whose cultivation was now widespread.[84]

The *Revue des deux mondes* took an even stronger position. *Revue* not only opposed French intervention, but also explicitly criticized the government for its pro-Southern stance. "Since the beginning of the Civil War," charged the Orleanist organ, the government

> has shown a disturbing partiality for the secessionist party. . . . That character of partiality has been all the more marked since our situation and our conduct presented the most strange contrast with the situation and conduct of England. England suffered more in its cotton industry than we from the closing of the Southern ports; England has a palpable political interest in the dissolution of the American Union; the English nation, by its traditions, by its instincts, by all the sentiments of the people, has been inveigled against the North and in favor of the South in that conflict. However, the English government has scrupulously avoided every act which would have been able to lead to an intervention between the belligerent parties and to a war against the North. France

> presents an entirely contrary aspect. The Civil War imposes on us less suffering than to the English; the maintenance of an integral republic of the United States is a cardinal point of our traditional policy; we contributed in the creation of that republic and we have drawn from that work the first inspirations of our revolution; the existence of that republic is a condition of maritime equilibrium in our favor. . . . Independent organs of public opinion have unanimously deplored as an attack against the interests of France everything which would lead to the dismemberment of the United States. . . . In England the government is obliged to struggle against the public in order to fulfill its duties toward the United States and prevent the armament of Confederate privateers in English ports; among us . . . mysterious naval construction, which appears to be done in our shipyards for the Confederate states, is spontaneously denounced by the liberal and democratic press. Nevertheless the government, against natural tendencies of our tradition of public opinion, has not had the prudence to thrust aside or to dissimulate its unfavorable ideas against the American republic. The extreme peril of that partiality is manifest if combined with the result of our Mexican affair.[85]

The cryptic phrase about "mysterious naval construction" refers to efforts by Confederates to construct a navy in Europe. After the British government blocked such efforts, Confederate officials turned to France. With the private encouragement of Napoleon III, Confederate officials contracted for six naval craft, to be constructed at Bordeaux and Nantes. When the American minister to France, William Dayton, received evidence of the destination of the ships, he protested to French officials, who took steps to block the delivery of the ships to the Confederates. Ultimately, one of those ships reached American waters but too late to participate in the war.[86] Two Parisian Republican newspapers, the *Opinion nationale* and the *Siècle*, published information on French construction of ships destined for the Confederacy. The *Opinion*, in particular, published documents providing proof of such activities.[87]

The failure of the Confederates to build a navy in Europe ultimately was dwarfed by other developments. As Grant and Sherman were preparing to deliver hammer blows against Southern armies at the end of 1864, the days of the Confederacy were numbered. Yet in 1864 and 1865 Liberals and Conservatives in France continued to disagree about events in the Civil War.

NOTES

1. A. Pouillard, (Charleville-Mézières) *Courrier des Ardennes*, January 10, 1863.
2. Papailhiau, (Albi) *Journal du Tarn*, July 18, 1863.
3. Chatard, *Presse*, October 18, 1863.
4. Plantade, (Cahors) *Courrier du Lot*, May 25, 1864.
5. Esparbié, *Courrier de Bayonne*, January 11, 1863.
6. (La Rochelle) *Charente-Inférieure*, March 12, 1863; Makaire, (Aix-en-Provence) *Écho des Bouches-du-Rhône*, March 1, 1863.
7. (La Rochelle) *Charente-Inférieure*, August 2, 1863.
8. Mac-Sheehy, *Union*, December 13, 22, 1863.
9. Barlatier, *Sémaphore de Marseille*, July 22, 1863.
10. C. Davisson, U.S. Consul at Bordeaux to William Dayton, Bordeaux, July 24, 1864, in Carl L. Lokke, "A Consular Report from Bordeaux: July, 1863," in *French Historical Studies*, 1 (1958), 101–102.
11. Weiss, *Journal des débats*, July 21, 1863, cited in W. Reed West, *Contemporary French Opinion on the American Civil War* (Baltimore, Johns Hopkins University Press, 1924), p. 130.
12. Husson, *Siècle*, July 10, 1863.
13. Assollant, *Courrier du dimanche*, November 1, 1863.
14. (La Rochelle) *Charente-Inférieure*, April 28, 1864.
15. Plantade, (Cahors) *Courrier du Lot*, May 25, 1864.
16. New York correspondence dated May 30, 1863, in *Moniteur*, June 17, 1864.
17. Rolin, (Bar-le-Duc) *Écho de l'est*, June 22, 1864.
18. Vattemaine, *Patrie*, June 2, 1864.
19. Dufaure, (Versailles) *Concorde de Seine-et-Oise*, July 7, August 14, September 4, November 24, December 4, 1864.

According to the *Index*, a pro-Confederate weekly published in London, Paris newspapers differed in their portrayal of military events in America. The *Siècle* and the *Opinion nationale* (both Republican newspapers) pictured Sherman as about to capture Atlanta. The *Constitutionnel, Patrie, and Moniteur* (all pro-Government newspapers) "know quite well that Sherman has neither occupied the centre, the circumference, nor, indeed, any part of the defenses of Atlanta; and that he was completely defeated by General Hood on July 22." *Index*, August 18, 1864, p. 522, cited in Ephraim Adams, *Great Britain and the American Civil War* (2 vols., London, Longmans, Green & Co., 1925), II, 236fn.

20. Gullaud, *Patrie*, December 19, 1864
21. Forcade, *Revue des deux mondes*, 51, June, 1, 1864, p. 748.
22. Chatard, *Presse*, June 18, 1864. Clearly, French newspapers were impressed by the large scale of military operations in 1864. Commenting on Grant's 1864 campaign, the *Presse* claimed that there had never been such an example of warfare previously: not the wars of the Red and White, the religious and political wars of France, the wars of Marius and Sulla, of Pompey and Caesar. Europe was profoundly moved by the events before Richmond. *Presse*, June 18, 1864.
23. Assollant, *Courrier du dimanche*, May 6, 1864.
24. Forcade, *Revue des deux mondes*, 53, September 1, 1864, 252.
25. Forcade, *ibid., 53,* October 15, 1864, 1017.
26. Duquesnel, (Saint-Malo) *Commerce Breton*, January 10, 1863.
27. Conil, (Saintes) *Courrier des deux Charentes*, February 12, 1863.
28. (La Rochelle) *Charente-Inférieure*, April 19, 1863.

29. Chantrel, *Monde*, January 31, 1863; Taconet, *ibid.*, May 28, 1864.
30. Chantrel, *ibid.*, June 3, 1864.
31. Conil, (Saintes) *Courrier des deux Charentes*, January 1, 1863.
32. Jourdan, *Siècle*, June 27, 1863.
33. Chatard, *Presse*, June 18, 1864.
34. Ernest Duvergier, *A Frenchman in Lincoln's America* (2 vols., Chicago, Lakeside Press, 1975), I, 105–106.
35. Conil, (Saintes) *Courrier des deux Charentes*, January 1, 1863.
36. Gaches, *Journal de Saint-Étienne*, January 11, 1863.
37. Barnard, (La Rochelle) *Charente-Inférieure*, October 6, 1864.
38. Mouttet, *Courrier du Havre*, January 27, 1863.
39. Aucaigne, *Patrie*, May 22, 1864.
40. Moreau, *Union*, March 22, 1863.
41. Taconet, *Monde*, May 31, 1864.
42. Chantrel, *ibid.*, June 3, 1864.
43. *Ibid.*, June 6, 1864.
44. Mac-Sheehy, *Union*, September 9, 1864.
45. Figuery, (Lons-le-Saulnier) *Sentinelle du Jura*, March 13, 1863.
46. *Pays*, November 7, 1863.
47. Gault, (Montpellier) *Messager du Midi*, April 23, 1863.
48. Taconet, *Monde*, May 3, 1863.
49. Ernest Duvergier, *A Frenchman in Lincoln's America*, II, 557–58. In the United States, Duvergier heard "on everyone's lips that God made America for the white man and not for the blacks." Duvergier believed, on the contrary, that Americans must realize that by striking a death-blow at the slave system they had set upon a path which could only lead to full equality of the races. Duvergier, *A Frenchman in Lincoln's America*, p. 560.
50. Chatard, *Presse*, June 24, 1863, cited in West, *French Opinion*, p. 135. A year later the same newspaper supported the Union cause, writing with approval of the goals of nationalism and abolition; Chatard, *Presse*, June 18, 1864.
51. Jourdan, *Siècle*, June 27, 1863. A year later the *Siècle* expressed more confidence that the North was fighting to abolish slavery. In any event, the South would not abolish slavery if independent (as argued some Conservative newspapers). As evidence for that assertion, the *Siècle* cited Confederate Vice President Alexander Stephens's famous "cornerstone" speech and his statement that an independent South would try to spread slavery. Jourdan, *Siècle*, August 31, 1864.
52. Delpart, *Courrier du dimanche*, August 9, 1863. Two months later, a writer for the *Courrier* despaired that a Union victory would mean a garrison state; better lose Union than liberty!; Assollant, *Courrier du dimanche*, November 1, 1863.
53. Élisée Reclus, "Les Noirs américains depuis la guerre," *Revue des deux mondes*, 44, March 15, 1963, 364–94, 719.
54. Forcade, *Revue des deux mondes*, August 1, 1863, 748.
55. Taconet, *Monde*, May 21, 1864.
56. Malespine, *Opinion nationale*, April 6, 1864.
57. Lomon, *Pays*, September 1, 1864.
58. Gullaud, *Patrie*, October 10, 1864.
59. *Patrie*, November 24, 1864, quoting the London *Daily Telegraph*.
60. Martin, *Siècle*, October 15, 1864.
61. Forcade, *Revue des deux mondes*, October 1, 1864, 766–67. Actually, Sherman's capture of Atlanta helped Lincoln win the election.
62. Plantade, (Cahors) *Courrier du Lot*, November 23, 1864.

63. Chuquet, (Bar-le-Duc) *Écho de l'est*, November 23, 1864.

64. Carle, *Sémaphore de Marseille*, November 22, 1864.

65. Bédollière, *Siècle*, November 23, 1864. The Legitimist *Monde* caustically observed that French democratic newspapers applauded all riots, all insurrections directed against the most legitimate governments but those same newspapers treated the South as rebels; Coquille, *Monde*, November 23, 1864.

66. Delpart, *Courrier du dimanche*, November 27, 1864.

67. For diplomatic activities related to the *Florida's* sojourn in Brest, see Case and Spencer, *Civil War Diplomacy*, pp. 483–92.

68. Bernard, *Siècle*, August 14, 20, September 25, 1864.

69.

pp. 312–33. Barlatier, *Sémaphore de Marseille*, August 15, 1863, professed to see a happy contrast: the Confederates approved privateering, while Lincoln refused to allow it. The Republican newspaper was incorrect. The Northern Congress had authorized privateers in March, 1863; because of the effectiveness of the Union navy and limited Southern seagoing commerce, however, no letters of marque were issued, though some Northern privateers had actually operated early in the war; Randall and Donald, *Civil War and Reconstruction*, p. 448.

70. *Moniteur*, September 16, 1863, cited in Case and Spencer, *Civil War Diplomacy*, p. 487.

71. Sacy, *Journal des débats*, June 21, 1864.

72. For a scholarly appraisal of the battle, see Warren Spencer, *The Confederate Navy in Europe* (University of Alabama Press, 1983), pp. 184–90. Spencer suggested that Semmes offered the challenge to the Union vessel because the Confederacy was "drawing to a close" and he could not permit his gallant ship to "cringe behind the neutrality of France." Spencer hypothesized that the *Alabama* lost the battle to the *Kearsarge*, a vessel about equal in size and speed, because of poor marksmanship and the deterioration of the vessel's powder.

73. Gullaud, *Patrie*, June 21, 1864; Grenier, *Pays*, June 21, 22, 1864; Limayrac, *Constitutionnel*, June 21, 1864; *Journal d'Alençon*, June 21, 1864; Dufour, (Bourg-en-Bresse) *Courrier de l'Ain*, June 21, 1864.

74. Grenier, *Pays*, June 22, 1864.

75. Labbé, *Opinion nationale*, June 25, 1864.

76. Malespine, *Opinion nationale*, June 21, 1864.

77. Delord, *Siècle*, June 25, 1864.

78. *Ibid.*, June 27, 1864.

79. Paignon, *Presse*, February 4, 6, 19, 1863.

80. Perroud, (Le Puy) *Moniteur de la Haute-Loire*, July 14, 1863.

81. Delpart, *Courrier du dimanche*, August 9, 1863.

82. Aucaign, *Patrie*, June 5, 1864.

83. Riancey, *Union*, June 16, July 6, 1864. Abolition in principle was part of Riancey's proposal.

The issue of slavery was a problem for Conservative newspapers. Slavery contributed to the prolongation of the war by depriving the South of moral support. European governments were denying recognition to a government that had all of the marks of a *de facto* government because of conscience over slavery. When that was resolved, there would be "nothing in the way of recognition." Horn, *Revue Contemporaine*, September 14, 1863, cited in West, *French Opinion*, p. 136.

84. Delord, *Siècle*, June 29, 1863.

85. Forcade, *Revue des deux mondes*, September 15, 1863, p. 488. Watson, *Siècle*, November 25, 1863, hoped that in case of war between France and Russia, that the American government would not tolerate violations of neutrality by construction of warships for the Czar. It was a good time, said the *Siècle*, for France "to put an end to such construction."

86. For Confederate efforts to build a navy in France, see Owsley, *King Cotton Diplomacy*, pp. 437–49, Spencer, *The Confederate Navy in Europe*, pp. 147–76, and James D. Bulloch, *The Secret Service of the Confederate States in Europe* (2 vols., reprint New York, 1959), II, 21–67. For the diplomacy relating to the Confederate ships, see Case and Spencer, *Civil War Diplomacy*, pp. 427–79. John Bigelow, *Retrospections of an Active Life*, II, 56ff. Blumenthal, *Franco-American Relations*, p. 151, believed that Napoleon's encouragement of the program to construct Confederate ships had "an outright sinister character." He dated Napoleon's support for such activities as October, 1862, a date that coincided with his major mediation offensive.

87. Malespine, *Opinion nationale*, March 10, 28 and 29, July 5, December 4, 1864; Labbé, *ibid.*, May 14, 1864. Watson, *Siècle*, November 25, 1863; Delord, *ibid.*, August 22, 1864. Bigelow reported that *Opinion nationale* in April 29, 1864, "printed conclusive evidence that vessels of war building at Nantes and Bordeaux . . . are destined for the Confederates." He had heard that the government prohibited other journals from making any allusion to the revelations. No subject had occupied "more of the attention of social and political circles for some days past, [yet] no other print has had a reference to the subject." Bigelow, *Retrospections of an Active Life*, II, 181–82, 184.

Gullaud, *Patrie*, March 29, 1865, reported construction of the *Stonewall* at Bordeaux. That vessel was first sold to Denmark, which refused delivery. Subsequently the vessel went into Confederate service, reported the *Patrie*.

Chapter 8

The End of the War

> When I think what the Anglo-Saxons [Northerners] have done by cupidity, by the aid of a liberal, hypocritical mask, to spread floods of blood of our Frenchmen [Southerners]; of those same Frenchmen chased from our country and principally from La Rochelle, as a result of the revocation of the edict of Nantes; when I think that their children were worthy of them in fighting for their independence and their constitutional liberty, I blush with shame to see them insulted and vanquished in a heroic struggle falsely attributed to slavery and that [Northerners] conquered them to preserve that cadaver of liberty, the Republic of the United States!
>
> A. T. Barnard, (La Rochelle) *Charente-Inférieure*, May 11, 1865

> America is not only America, one place or one race more on the map; it is yet and especially the model school of liberty. If against all possibility it had perished, with it would fall a great experiment.
>
> Eugène Pelletan, *Courrier du dimanche*, January 1, 1865

In January, 1865, the days of the Confederacy were numbered. Ulysses S. Grant's army, encamped outside Richmond and Petersburg, was waiting for more favorable weather and the inevitable weakening of the badly outnumbered Southern army commanded by Robert E. Lee. At the beginning of the year William T. Sherman's force, resting at Savannah, was preparing to resume its march, this time northward into the Carolinas and toward an eventual junction with Grant's forces. Grant made his decisive move in April, cracked Confederate lines, forced the evacuation of Richmond, and later in the month placed his army squarely in front of Lee's decimated forces and compelled Lee to surrender on April 9, 1865. Rejoicing over the Union triumph turned into horror and dismay with John Wilkes Booth's assassination of Abraham Lincoln and concern over leadership by an untried President, Andrew Johnson.

In France these dramatic developments elicited predictable reactions. Early in 1865, Liberal and Conservative newspapers continued to differ about the nature of American democracy and the causes of the Civil War. After Lee's surrender, Conservatives grieved over the Confederate defeat, while Liberals rejoiced in the Union triumph; they also differed on the significance of the Union triumph. While both factions lamented Lincoln's death and praised his personal traits, Liberals made special note of Lincoln's achievements in securing freedom and preserving a democratic republic. Finally, French Liberals and Conservatives differed on responsibility for the assassination and on the leadership to be expected from Andrew Johnson.

In 1865, French attitudes toward the nature of American democracy and the causes of the Civil War were closely related—and familiar. Conservatives continued to view Northern society as vindictive, greedy, and racist. As a result, they argued that the Civil War occurred because of Northern aggression, which in turn was motivated by economic reasons; racist Yankees used abolitionist goals only as a hypocritical mask to hide their sordid economic aims. The Conservative *Patrie* cited the passage in Lincoln's second inaugural address that the war would be continued until "every drop of blood drawn with the lash shall be paid by another drawn with the sword." The effort, charged the *Patrie*, to make Europe believe that slavery was the cause of the war was belied by the declarations of Northern generals and especially by the conduct of Sherman, who parked the Negroes in swamps along the coast of Georgia. Those actions proved that the war was only a question of "political ambition and not a moral affair."[1] The North always used "the same lie." Early in the war, bitterly charged one provincial Conservative newspaper, while hoping to persuade the South to return to the Union, Northerners said slavery was not at all the goal of the war; "today they say the war was brought about only by slavery."[2]

Liberal newspapers perceived America and the war in very different terms. The true, the only cause of the war, claimed the Orleanist *Courrier du dimanche*, was slavery, which Lincoln had crossed out with a stroke of the pen. Thus Lincoln founded America a second time and merited the recognition of the entire world.[3] The Republican *Presse* believed the causes of the war originated in the antagonism between aristocracy and democracy as well as the antagonism between plantations with forced labor and factories with free labor. The interests threatened by Lincoln's election refused to obey the decision of the majority and seceded with states rights as their justification.[4] The *Revue des deux mondes* directly tied the Northern cause to French liberal democracy and patriotism. A Northern triumph, it claimed, would be a "great moral victory for the liberal democracy of France, which remained faithful to the principles and best traditions of our patriotism and never doubted the powerful vitality" of the United States.[5]

Curiously, at this late stage in the war, certain Conservative journals were still weighing the merits of European intervention in the conflict. Citing a report that Lee proposed using black troops, the *Pays* said that such an action would make the war in America assume immediately a character of savage energy, "which would decide without doubt a friendly and official intervention of Europe in the interest of humanity."[6] Another semi-official newspaper, the *Patrie*, however, implicitly acknowledged that French intervention was impractical. Responding to the regret expressed by the Clerical *Gazette de France* that the French government had not taken a more "determined attitude" toward America, the pro-Governmental Patrie argued that the failure to intervene could not be blamed on the French government. "The imperial government," asserted that Conservative organ, "has done everything for three years to lead Europe to take steps which would have certainly put an end" to the American war. Russia and England, however, did not wish to cooperate, and it would have been unwise for France to act alone.[7]

If by 1865 it was too late for European intervention in America, both Conservatives and Liberals expected American intervention in Canada and Mexico upon conclusion of the Civil War. The British were particularly worried that the United States would invade Canada.[8] The Conservative *Patrie* darkly warned that the British navy could ruin American commerce in the event of war.[9] The Orleanist *Courrier du dimanche,* on the other hand, was quite content that the Yankees would look south after the war and would enter Mexico two days after the departure of French soldiers from Vera Cruz.[10]

Conservatives and Liberals continued to disagree, however, about military operations in the last months of the war. Conservatives gave a pro-Southern interpretation to these operations. The capture of Savannah by Sherman in December, 1864, was not important from a commercial or military point of view, claimed the Conservative *Patrie.*[11] In February, 1865, the Clerical *Union* summarized the results of the war: Grant had lost 100,000 men and was not as close to Richmond as McClellan had been in 1862; Sherman had lost 50,000 men and could only claim the capture of Savannah; the Confederates had recaptured Atlanta; the Federals had seized Fort Fisher but not Wilmington.[12] The capture of Charleston and Columbia, South Carolina, according to the *Pays*, did not represent progress for Northern arms but rather a tactic of Southern armies, newly inaugurated by Lee, of not defending advanced ports or cities in favor of concentrating armies.[13] The Confederates did not lose but rather evacuated Charleston, Savannah, and Wilmington, agreed the Legitimist *Monde*; their defenders were better employed elsewhere, especially since the blockade made possession of the forts useless. The Southern press had never shown more determination or confidence in victory, the *Monde* added.[14]

Even the fall of Richmond did not mean an end to the war, according to Parisian Conservative newspapers. The *Patrie* approvingly quoted the London *Times*' prediction that events now would show whether the American conflict was a "revolt" or a "revolution." If it was a revolt, then it was ended; if it was a revolution, then the war was not ended but rather would change character. The conflict would, declared the *Patrie*, become "yet more disastrous, more terrible in its relentlessness, more deadly in its material results. . . . One disperses an army, one triumphs in an insurrection, but one does not conquer an entire people!" The

Union was no longer possible, claimed the *Patrie*; it ceased to exist when two American armies found themselves face to face. An alliance could not be reconstituted in blood! Thus the true difficulties of the North were going to commence, "a conflict relentless, incessant" as in Spain and Italy at the beginning of the nineteenth century.[15] The fall of Richmond, agreed fellow Conservative *Pays*, could only be considered as ending one of the most bloody periods of the war. "However, one must not," warned the *Pays*,

> draw the conclusion . . . that the conflict is terminated and the South is going to put down their arms. . . . The war will only change aspects: it will be a guerrilla war, terrible, inexorable, which will be as difficult to anticipate as to predict its end.[16]

A provincial Conservative journal was willing to admit "the worst," that the North would triumph. Yet, queried that skeptical newspaper,

> will it not be more embarrassed than satisfied by its victory? Will the yoke imposed be supported patiently by the Southern states? Will it not be shaken off violently one day or another? If that happens, it will be necessary to recommence the carnage, to make the beautiful provinces of America a cemetery, a desert. President Lincoln, that Brutus in a hazelnut jacket, will do just that, but will the nation disenchanted with blood and powder follow him?[17]

In sharp contrast to the bitter tone of the Conservative press Liberal newspapers in early 1865 rejoiced in the expectation of a Federal victory. "The triumph of the great liberal republic is near," proclaimed the *Revue des deux mondes*, "and it is not forbidden to hope that the year 1865 will see its accomplishment."[18] In their comments on military operations, Liberal newspapers put particular emphasis on Union General William T. Sherman. They repeatedly cited disparaging Conservative assessments of Sherman's operations. European newspapers favorable to the Southern cause ("they are in great number!") had predicted the annihilation of Sherman's army during its march through Georgia, reported the *Presse*.[19] English newspapers represented Sherman as another Attila, and they foresaw disaster after disaster as they anticipated another retreat from Moscow, reported the *Courrier du dimanche*. A retreat from Moscow, snorted the *Courrier*, "under the gentle skies of Georgia!"[20]

Perhaps as a result of such pessimistic assessments, Liberal newspapers took particular relish in reporting Sherman's triumphs. The *Revue des deux mondes* described Sherman's campaign in Georgia as not only "one of the most remarkable episodes in the American war," but also as one of the most decisive actions in that period of the war.[21] One of the results of Sherman's advance from Savannah, the fall of Charleston, was "the dramatic *dénouement*" of the war, added the *Revue*. Its capture produced a profound impression in France since Charleston was where the war had started. Charleston had wanted separation while rich

Virginia hesitated; now Charleston was in ruins.[22] Sherman's march north from Savannah was "irresistible," claimed the *Presse*, and it was impossible to stop him. For many weeks in the late stages of the war, awed Liberal newspapers gave more attention to Sherman than to Grant.[23]

The capture of Richmond gave Liberal newspapers further reason to rejoice. "All the news pales before the grand event [the capture of Richmond and Petersburg]," cried the *Courrier du dimanche*; "the supreme battle was accomplished. . . . [Lee] is in full retreat. . . . Peace is conquered." As for a prolonged guerrilla war, that was simply absurd. The necessity now was to obtain the best possible conditions.[24] With the capture of Richmond and the army of Lee half destroyed, one "could consider the war as finished," claimed the *Siècle*, adding that humanity rejoiced in the victory of liberty.[25]

After Lee's surrender, French newspapers turned to discussion of reconciliation. The Republican organ in Marseille graciously conceded that the South fought to the end with a courage worthy of a better cause.[26] The *Courrier du dimanche* saw a happy augury of the future in the surrender terms for Lee's army. The correspondence between Grant and Lee "did honor to the victor and the defeated. Nothing [was] more noble and at the same time more simple," added the *Courrier*, than the language of those two men who sought to establish a durable and sincere peace.[27] The *Siècle* reported that President Lincoln appreciated the difficulties of reconstituting the Union and he would find means of conciliation.[28] Conservative newspapers likewise welcomed the "very honorable" surrender terms and conciliatory statements by Lincoln as good auguries of the future.[29]

While trying to assess the significance of those momentous events in America, horrified Frenchmen learned of the assassination of President Lincoln by John Wilkes Booth. The news from America led the *Courrier du dimanche* to remark that sometimes in history nearly every hour was marked by an important event. That was true in 1815, and it was true of America in 1865, with the capture of Richmond, the surrender of Lee, and Lincoln's assassination.[30] Frenchmen—Liberals and Conservatives alike—responded with grief and indignation at the tragic news from America. The official *Moniteur* reported that the assassination

> aroused in France a movement of general indignation. Public opinion is unanimous in stigmatizing a crime as odious and to pay a tribute of regret to the memory of the president of the United States.[31]

The *Siècle* reported that the details of the assassination and of demonstrations in favor of the American union took up a large part of the columns of newspapers, not only in France, but in all of Europe.[32]

While Conservatives vied with their Liberal colleagues in condemning the assassination, there were significant differences in their appraisal of the event. Conservatives emphasized the enormity of the crime and the unanimous condemnation by Frenchmen of every political persuasion. The *Patrie* reported that the violent death had "thrown all spirits into a profound stupefaction."[33] All newspapers, whether or not partisans of Lincoln's policy, observed a provincial Conservative newspaper, were unanimous in branding in the most energetic terms the odious and horrible crime.[34] Everywhere the assassination provoked indignation among partisans of the South as well as those of the North, reported another provincial newspaper.[35] Conservatives also praised the personal traits of Abraham Lincoln. Although the *Pays* had disagreed with Lincoln on many occasions, nevertheless that Conservative journal found him "a good man, a man of faith, and by character a great citizen." He had displayed "an unshakable firmness and confidence at every test in the correctness of his mission and in the future of his course." While there had certainly been more intelligent Presidents, no one was superior to his spirit, vigor of patriotism, tenacity of will, and energy.[36]

Like their Conservative counterparts, Liberal newspapers expressed horror at news of the assassination. Europe was rejoicing in the peace until receipt of the frightful news of the assassination, reported the Orleanist *Courrier du dimanche*. Europe then "passed from joy to horror and consternation." Lincoln died at the moment when he showed himself animated with sentiments the most conciliatory and generous.[37] Liberals differed from their Conservative colleagues, however, in emphasizing the importance of Lincoln's political accomplishments, especially his contributions to liberty. According to the Republican *Siècle*, Lincoln was a martyr to the most holy of causes; he would "be mourned by friends of liberty and right, in the entire world."[38] The assassins were blind, claimed the *Presse*. "They think," charged the Liberal newspaper, "that they strike the cause which they detest, and it is always their own cause that they strike; it is their cause that they dishonor. . . the idiots!" Three American presidents would never be forgotten, added *Presse*: Washington, who refused the crown; Jefferson, who respected liberty; and Lincoln, who freed the slaves.[39] Indeed, the *Courrier du dimanche* saw Lincoln as belonging not just to Americans; he belonged to all humanity. The blow which struck Lincoln, asserted that Orleanist organ, had "been felt by all those who, in our old Europe, believe in liberty, law and justice."[40] In an extended discussion the *Revue des deux mondes* summarized Liberal views of the assassination. The Orleanist journal first recorded "a universal movement of stupor, of indignation, and of affliction" in response to that "heinous crime." Unlike its Conservative counterparts, however, the *Revue* explicitly placed the event in a Liberal political context: news from the United States had brought in fifteen days "the most grand political consolation that liberal opinion had received in fifteen years . . . and also one of the most lively griefs that the tragedy of human events might be able to cause to its moved spectators." The assassin struck down a president who sustained in "the most cruel tests" the democratic and liberal republic of the United States, who with tranquil firmness of soul saved his country from the calamity of internal dissolution, who had assured the integrity of the American republic, and who applied honest and scrupulous thought to the work of reconciliation of the parties and the reorganization of the great American homeland.[41]

The editor of the Liberal Catholic *Correspondant*, A. Cochin, was even more explicitly political in his reaction to the assassination. In a letter to John Bigelow, American minister to France, Cochin wrote that he intended for the assassination

> to provoke many articles. We cannot profit too much by this misfortune to bring back public opinion strongly towards the cause of the North, or at the same time render too much homage to the memory of this great man, whose name will be immortal.[42]

If Conservatives and Liberals differed about the significance of the assassination—Conservatives emphasizing personal tragedy, Liberals emphasizing Lincoln's contribution to democracy and freedom—they had even sharper differences over responsibility for the assassination. Many Liberals blamed Southerners or "slavery fanaticism,"[43] while Conservatives and Legitimists scathingly criticized Liberal claims that slavery or Southern partisans were responsible for the assassination.[44]

Conservative newspapers proposed various explanations for the assassination with some Conservatives blaming radical Republicans for the evil deed. Repeatedly, the *Patrie* charged that "the Booth brothers, habitants of the North and known by their relations with the exalted of the Republican party, were made the cowardly instruments of the passions of that party."[45] A La Rochelle newspaper agreed that ultra-Republicans were responsible for the assassination. Such crimes were "never the isolated work of fanatic sects or of an insane." Before attributing the crime to secessionists, readers should remember that secessionists were presumably aristocrats. But the assassin said *Sic semper tyrannis*. Were those the words of an aristocrat or of a frenzied radical, questioned the Conservative newspaper? Moreover, why would a secessionist plot the assassination of the three Northern statesmen who were the most conciliatory toward the Southern states: Lincoln, Seward, and Grant? Andrew Johnson, it was well known, represented "the ultra faction of the black Republican, or ultra Puritan, party." Why, asked the Conservative La Rochelle newspaper, would secessionists have conspired against the most clement statesmen and spared Johnson who was their contrary?[46] A vanquished South, with Lincoln conciliatory, argued the *Patrie*, "had everything to lose and the radical abolitionist party everything to gain by the death of Lincoln."[47]

A Conservative Rennes newspaper attributed the assassination to "the isolated work of an imagination distraught by the violence of political passions." As a result, that provincial journal sharply criticized Secretary of War Stanton's official report accusing Southern partisans of having organized a plot to assassinate the president.[48]

Another Conservative journal saw the assassination as both "a crime and a lesson" about American institutions and values. An act of fanaticism by a scoundrel, the assassination arose from lack of restraint and lack of belief in anyone or anything. Humans need "authority," a trait that this conservative journal found lacking in America.[49] The Legitimist *Union* also believed that the assassination was an index of the moral state of the United States. The deed reflected a corrupt society, where too often murder was the last resort of hatred. "Let us profit from the lesson of that democracy," intoned the very conservative newspaper; democracy "pushed to excess was only civilized barbarity."[50]

The Orleanist *Revue des deux mondes* drew a very different lesson about American democracy. We have heard in Europe, wrote the editor, declamations on the necessity of respect and on the principle of authority, declamations designed to make us adore absurd idols. The United States has shown, however, that the true principle of authority springs from the conscience of a free people, asserted the Liberal organ. True respect is inspired by leaders who have never wished to be imperial dominators of their country but have only been devoted servants until death.[51]

Liberals and Conservatives differed also in early appraisals regarding Andrew Johnson. While Conservatives placed Johnson in the radical Republican camp, which sought vengeance against the South, Liberals were hopeful that Johnson would follow Lincoln's moderate policy, "The sinister predictions" of the former enemies of the Union in France and England would not be proven true, the *Revue des deux mondes* predicted, and "no cruelty will tarnish the triumph of the Union."[52]

Finally, Liberals and Conservatives also differed profoundly on their assessments of the consequences of the war. The Legitimist *Monde* claimed that the war arose not from a misunderstanding but rather from a "well pronounced rivalry of contrary interests"; as a result, the causes would remain and conflict would continue. "The war proves, and nothing more," argued the *Monde*, "that the South was not sufficiently strong to defend its interests and its rights." Nor did the war solve the slavery issue. The North cynically used slavery as a "slogan," but Northerners did not like blacks; "their philanthropy," added the Legitimist organ, "is a mask which they will put aside when they will no longer have need of it."[53]

Other Conservative publications predicted that dire consequences would result from the conclusion of formal hostilities. One such journal claimed that Republicans, puffed up by their victory, would strengthen the Federal government and sacrifice the autonomy of the states. As a result, if the Republicans were successful, the United States would become a military despotism. If the Democrats, on the other hand, succeeded in maintaining local liberties, then the loose bonds of the central government would collapse with the slightest shock.[54] Another Conservative newspaper, the *Constitutionnel*, agreed; while the war was over, Northern troubles were just beginning. The Confederates would not really submit, and the occupation would be as expensive as the war. Emancipation had not worked, and blacks could not work under a free system.[55]

Thus Conservatives grudgingly acknowledged the Union victory while they remained hostile toward the North. The implacable *Patrie*, indeed, became even more bitter toward the North after the conclusion of hostilities. Benjamin Butler was a former slaveholder, gibed that ardent Southern supporter, while

Andrew Johnson was a former slave trader. The North wished to take away the slave monopoly from the South by an unjust war, added the Imperial journal.[56]

Exuberant Liberal newspapers described the significance of the war in very different terms. The Republican *Siècle* hailed the successful conclusion of the war as "the victory of liberty."[57] The Republican *Sémaphore de Marseille* asserted that the war would result in the abolition of slavery and a reordering of Southern society so that the poor whites, formerly dominated by the aristocracy, would be in a position where they ought to be.[58] The *Revue des deux mondes* saw the war as having great significance, not only for America but also for all of mankind. "When the wounds, today yet bloody will be healed," reported its American correspondent in July, 1865,

> one will see that the war has fortified more than it has weakened the Union. It has revealed to the American people all the depth of sentiment which they attach to it. In imposing terrible sacrifices on them, in condemning them to great griefs, the war has brought them at a blow from youth to maturity. The war has brought back to the federal constitution its original character, to the executive power the force which the democratic school had deprived by decrees; the war has put an end to the fatal contradiction between servitude and liberty; it has given to the nation more confidence in itself, in the grandeur of its destinies, in the nobility of its ideas purified and henceforth unalloyed. The war has shown that liberty is sufficiently strong, not only to sustain men against a tyranny but also to found institutions, a nation, a *patrie*.[59]

Many months after the end of the war, Eugène Forcade, editor of the *Revue des deux mondes*, made an even more flattering appraisal. He proclaimed American institutions the most just and reasonable that any human society had yet attained. He marveled at the peaceful disbandment of the huge armies and their prompt return to private life. He predicted an extraordinary expansion of democracy, "a consoling promise for the future of humanity."[60]

The end of the war also led to some very severe assessments of the role of the French government in the American conflict. Certain Liberal journals explicitly condemned what they perceived as a pro-Southern bias in French foreign policy. The *Revue des deux mondes* charged that "our diplomacy has shown itself . . . maladroitly inspired by sentiments partial for the Southern rebellion."[61] The *Courrier du dimanche* remembered clearly "that imprudent policy," the offer of mediation by France which "appeared to all the world, to Richmond as well as to Washington, a premature attempt of recognition of the South." The opposition had not ceased a single moment to signal the disadvantages of French policy toward the United States, argued the *Courrier*; those counsels, however, were given in vain for four years.[62]

Some Liberal newspapers also criticized French foreign policy in regard to Mexico. The end of the war pointed up the futility of French policy in trying to impose the Austrian archduke Maximilian as Mexican emperor. France had no interest in America, claimed the *Revue des deux mondes*, that could put in the balance difficulties with "our most natural ally, the American people." When Napoleon ceded Louisiana to the United States, he had superior intuition of that fundamental interest of France in America. The French government did not follow that principle in supporting Maximilian; nor did the government think of that principle in 1862, when French policy was based on the idea that the great American republic was doomed to irreparable disruption.[63]

At the end of the war in May, 1865, the Liberal *Journal des débats* charged that French and Catholic opinion had always been *esclavagiste*, that is, supportive of the slavery cause. That statement "astonished" the Conservative *Patrie*, which argued that French opinion had always been opposed to slavery and that the North reversed itself on slavery only under European pressure. The *Patrie* did agree that French and Catholic opinion had been pro-Southern [*suddite*] because neither had allowed itself to be surprised by American diplomacy and both knew what was fundamentally involved in the war: tariffs and material interests.[64]

That journalistic spat, so typical of Liberal-Conservative disagreement both about the causes of the Civil War and the reasons for French attitudes toward the conflict, nevertheless is revealing. French attitudes toward the American war as expressed in newspapers did follow patterns. Though these patterns were not determined by attitudes toward slavery nor French material interest, they can be related to *ideology*, *time*, and *events*.

Slavery was unquestionably an important issue to Frenchmen, but attitudes toward slavery were not related to French journalistic sympathies for the North or the South. Liberal newspapers interminably utilized the slavery question to justify support for the North, arguing that a Northern triumph would result in abolition. Conservatives rejected that contention. Conservatives argued that slavery was no longer "debatable" in France since all Frenchmen were opposed to that institution. Conservatives also argued, however, that the North did not make war for emancipation.[65] In short, opposition to slavery did not stop Conservatives from sympathizing with the Southern cause.

Material French interests also were a point of debate, but it is difficult to determine their role in influencing journalistic attitudes toward the war. Liberals held that a united America was vital to French interests, and a powerful United States was a necessary counterweight to British naval power. Conservatives saw in a powerful America a force contrary to French interests, an American which would seek hegemony over the New World. Conservatives also favored Southern independence in order to end the blockade and secure cotton for French industry. Liberals advocated the prompt return of the South to the Union in order to end the war and thus secure cotton. Thus the *crise*, like slavery, was a debating point and utilized to justify diverse views of French policy toward the American conflict. It is doubtful that either the *crise* or French material interests caused any French newspaper to change its fundamental stance toward the Civil War.

If attitudes toward slavery or material interest did not correlate with attitudes of French newspapers toward the Civil War, *ideology* provides a reliable guidepost. Republican and Orleanist newspapers favored the Federal cause and usually expected a Northern triumph. Imperial newspapers throughout almost all of the war favored the Southern cause and believed until the very end of the war that it would triumph. The least consistent pattern occurred among Legitimist newspapers. While the Parisian Legitimist newspapers favored the South, provincial Legitimist or Catholic newspapers were divided in their sympathy, with one provincial journal supporting whatever outcome would end slavery. The Liberal Catholic *Correspondant*, which favored the North, stands in marked contrast with the pro-Southern stance of Conservative Catholic newspapers.[66]

Civil War attitudes among French newspapers also were related to *time*. From the beginning of the secession crisis in 1860 until May, 1861, French newspapers were almost unanimous in regretting the crisis in America, in hoping that the United States would remain united, but also expecting a breakup of the American Union. In May, 1861, the Imperialist Parisian newspapers switched from supporting preservation of the American Union to support for Southern efforts to secede; this switch accompanied a similar change in official French policy. Certain Imperial provincial newspapers made a similar switch in attitude much later. In the summer and fall of 1862, a number of them changed from sympathy for the Union cause and a belief in a Union victory to advocacy of the Southern cause and a belief that the Southern cause would triumph.

In addition to slavery and time, attitudes of French newspapers were related to *events*. The most important were the Confederate triumphs in late spring and summer of 1862, which were crucial in changing the views of some Imperial provincial newspapers from support for the Union to support for the Southern Confederacy. Undoubtedly those events plus the cotton *crise* led pro-Southern Frenchmen to intensify support for mediation efforts by the French government, which reflected a pro-Southern policy. As late as 1863 and 1864 military operations continued to influence the views of Northern sympathizers: Union victories led to increased support and optimism for a Union triumph; Union defeats led to pessimism for a Union victory and fears that the American Union was disrupted.

Finally, the American student of the Civil War must understand that Frenchmen viewed events beyond the Atlantic through a French prism. Issues important in nineteenth century American, such as slavery, had a very different meaning and priority in France of the 1860s. In addition, not France but Frenchmen viewed the American conflict. While some Frenchmen described the Civil War in terms of American nationalism and abolition, others described the war in terms of Northern aggression and racism. Civil War events occurred in America, but diverse Frenchmen employed their own values and their own perspectives in their appraisals of issues in that conflict.

NOTES

1. Gullaud, *Patrie*, March 19, 1865.
2. (La Rochelle) *Charente-Inférieure*, March 23, 1865.
3. Pelletan, *Courrier du dimanche*, January 1, 1865.
4. Chatard, *Presse*, April 26, 1865.
5. Forcade, *Revue des deux mondes*, January 1, 1865, p. 252.
6. Voiseux, *Pays*, February 12, 1865.
7. Dréolle, *Patrie*, February 4, 1865.
8. Delord, *Siècle*, February 18, 1865.
9. Cucheval-Clarigny, *Patrie*, March 31, 1865.
10. Assollant, *Courrier du dimanche*, February 12, 1865.
11. Aucaign, *Patrie*, January 9, 1865.
12. Moreau, *Union*, February 14, 1865.
13. Voiseux, *Pays*, March 6, 1865.
14. American letter, March 1, *Monde*, March 20, 1865.
15. Dréolle, *Patrie*, April 20, 1865.
16. Chauret, *Pays*, April 16, 1865.
17. Bayvet, (La Rochelle) *Charente-Inférieure*, February 3, 1865.
18. Forcade, *Revue des deux mondes*, January 1, 1865, p. 251.
19. Chatard, *Presse*, January 5, 1865.
20. Chanut, *Courrier du dimanche*, January 8, 1865.
21. Émerig Szabad, "La Campagne de Géorgie et la fin de la guerre américaine," *Revue des deux mondes*, June 15, 1865, p. 998fn.
22. Forcade, *Revue des deux mondes*, March 15, 1865, 507; Chatard, *Presse*, March 5, 1865.
23. Chatard, *Presse*, April 4, 1865.
24. Chanut, *Courrier du dimanche*, April 23, 1865.
25. Delord, *Siècle*, April 16, 25, 1865. Bigelow, *Retrospections of an Active Life*, II, 502–507, printed extracts from various Parisian newspapers giving their reactions to the fall of Richmond.
26. Barlatier, *Sémaphore de Marseille*, April 26, 1865.
27. Millerin, *Courrier du dimanche*, April 30, 1865.
28. Delord, *Siècle*, April 25, 1865.
29. Figuery, (Lons-le-Saulnier) *Sentinelle du Jura*, April 28, 1865; Dufaure, (Versailles) *Concorde de Seine-et-Oise*, April 16, 1865; *Moniteur*, April 24, 1865.
30. Chanut, *Courrier du dimanche*, April 30, 1865.
31. *Moniteur*, April 28, 1865.
32. Bédollière, *Siècle*, May 2, 1865. Bernstein, *Essays in Political and Intellectual History*, pp. 130–33, emphasized that news of the assassination "released French popular feeling for the Northern cause." Even the French government "had to bow before the national sentiment."
33. Dréolle, *Patrie*, April 28, 1865.
34. Broise, *Journal d'Alençon*, April 29, 1865.
35. Dufaure, (Versailles) *Concorde de Seine-et-Oise*, April 30, 1865.
36. *Pays*, April 28, 1865.
37. Chanut, *Courrier du dimanche*, April 30, 1865.
38. Carle, *Sémaphore de Marseille*, April 27, 1865.
39. Girardin, *Presse*, April 28, 1865.

40. Target, Villetard, *Courrier du dimanche*, May 7, 1865.

Letters from France constituted a large part of the enormous volume of letters of condolence published by the American government in 1866, nearly all originating from Liberal sources: opposition press, Republicans of Paris and the provinces, etc. Karsky, "Les Libéraux français et l'émancipation des esclaves aux États-Unis," p. 589 fn61.

41. Forcade, *Revue des deux mondes*, May 1, 1865, p. 244. Cyrille Arnavon "French Images of President Abraham Lincoln," p. 8, noted "the ideological stir and partisan emphasis which will greet the final tragedy [the Lincoln assassination] in France."

42. A. Cochin to Bigelow, Paris, April 27, 1865, in Bigelow, *Retrospections of an Active Life*, II, 525–26.

43. Carle, *Sémaphore de Marseille*, April 27, 1865.

44. For examples of such criticism, see Laurentin, *Union*, April 29, 1865; Gullaud, *Patrie*, April 29, 1865.

45. Gullaud, *Patrie*, April 29, 1865. Dréolle, *Patrie*, April 30, 1865, insisted that the Booths were members of ultra-Republican families.

46. "J.," (La Rochelle) *Charente-Inférieure*, April 30, 1865.

In an obvious effort to exonerate secessionists from guilt for the assassination, a pro-Southern writer, Pequet du Bellet, asked the following questions:

Why were conservatives the targets?

Why did the police allow Booth to approach Lincoln?

Why was it possible for Booth to escape when the government ("an absolute dictatorship") controlled the telegraph lines and the railroads?

Why did Johnson find himself completely prepared to take the oath of office?

How did Stanton write that long letter?

47. Dréolle, *Patrie*, April 30, 1865.

48. Delaunay, (Rennes) *Journal d'Ille-et-Vilaine*, April 29, 1865.

49. Plantade, (Cahors) *Courrier du Lot*, April 29, 1865.

50. Riancey, *Union*, April 28, 1865.

51. Forcade, *Revue des deux mondes*, May 15, 1865, p. 513.

52. *Ibid.*, July 1, 1865, p. 239.

53. Vrignault, *Monde*, April 26, 1865.

54. *Revue Contemporaine*, April 30, 1865, cited in West, *French Opinion*, p. 146.

55. Joncières, *Constitutionnel*, April 19, 1865, and Martin, *ibid.*, July 4, 1865, cited in West, *French Opinion*, p. 145.

56. Aucaigne, *Patrie*, May 19, 1865.

57. Delord, *Siècle*, April 16, 1865.

58. Barlatier, *Sémaphore de Marseille*, April 26, 1865.

59. Auguste Laugel, *Revue des deux mondes*, July 1, 1865, pp. 411–12.

60. *Revue des deux mondes*, November 14, 1865, p. 529; November 30, 1865, p. 808; December 31, 1865, p. 253; all cited in Sears, "A Neglected Critic of our Civil War," p. 545.

61. Forcade, *Revue des deux mondes*, January 1, 1865, p. 251.

62. Millerin, *Courrier du dimanche*, May 7, 1865.

63. Forcade, *Revue des deux mondes*, June 1, 1865, 768–70.

64. Gullaud, *Patrie*, May 9, 1865.

65. *Ibid.*

66. The Lincoln administration counted on the support of Frenchmen who identified their own chances for political emancipation with democracy's success in America. Yet inconsistencies were common during this period in regard to ideology. The United States, long accused of disturbing the social order, in the Civil War was pursuing the conservative aim of maintaining the existing political structure. Law-abiding and traditional monarchists

of France, on the other hand, were supporting insurrection in the South at the same time that Napoleon was attempting to plant a monarchy in Mexico. Frenchmen who utilized the doctrine of nationality to justify support of the South violated that principle in Mexico. Blumenthal, *Franco-American Relations*, pp. 125–26.

Bibliographical Essay

All of the sources utilized in this study appear in the endnotes. Below are titles of particularly useful works.

BASIC SOURCES

French newspapers are the principal sources for this study. Paris newspapers are housed in the Bibliothèque Nationale at Paris; American depositories for microfilms of some files can be located in the Library of Congress guide to *Newspapers on Microform: Foreign Newspapers*. An untitled document, Archives Nationales, Paris, F18 295, lists Paris newspapers by political affiliation and gives their circulation figures for October 22, 1861. Various published histories of the French press are a readily available source for that information.

Files of provincial newspapers are housed at the Bibliothèque annex at Versailles. While few of those files are complete for the Civil War years, fortunately the files are most extensive for 1862, which was the most important year of the war from the French point of view. Two documents serve as indispensable guides for provincial newspapers. "Inventaire des journaux départementaux XIXe siècle," no author, no date, lists the holdings of the annex by department, by newspaper, and by year. (That document is located at the annex.) An untitled document in Archives Nationales, Paris, F18 294, lists provincial newspapers by department, by name, and by political affiliation, with circulation. (Much of that data may be found in the Pierre Albert work cited for Chapter 1.)

Studies of French newspapers and the American Civil War include W. Reed West, *Contemporary French Opinion on the American Civil War* (Baltimore, 1924); Serge Gavronsky, *The French Liberal Opposition and the American Civil War* (New York, 1968); Donaldson Jordan and Edwin J. Pratt, *Europe and the American Civil War* (Boston, 1931); Louis M. Sears, "A Neglected Critic [Eugène

Forcade, editor of *Revue des deux mondes*] of Our Civil War," *Mississippi Valley Historical Review,* I (1915), 532–45.

CHAPTER 1

For Franco-American relations, see Henry Blumenthal, *A Reappraisal of Franco-American Relations, 1830–1871* (Chapel Hill, 1959) and *France and the United States; their Diplomatic Relations, 1789–1914* (Chapel Hill, 1970); Marvin Zahniser, *Uncertain Friendship: American-French Diplomatic Relations through the Cold War* (New York, 1975); Crane Brinton, *The Americans and the French* (Cambridge, 1968).

For French views of America, see Denis Lacorne, Jacques Rupnik, and Marie-France Toinet, *The Rise and Fall of Anti-Americanism: A Century of French Perception* (New York, 1990); Jean-Baptiste Duroselle, *France and the United States from the Beginnings to the Present* (New York, 1990).

For the history of the Second Empire, useful works include George P. Gooch, *The Second Empire* (London, 1960) and Alain Plessis, *The Rise and Fall of the Second Empire, 1852–1871* (Cambridge, 1985). For Napoleon III and the Second Empire, see James M. Thompson, *Louis Napoleon and the Second Empire* (New York, 1967); Theodore Zeldin, *The Political System of Napoleon III* (London, 1971); William H. C. Smith, *Napoleon III: The Pursuit of Prestige* (London, 1991).

Studies of French newspapers for the Civil War era include Pierre Albert, *Documents pour l'histoire de la presse de province dans la seconde moitié du xixe siècle* (Paris, Centre de Documentation Sciences Humaines, 1973; Pierre Albert, Gilles Feyel, Jean-François Picard, *Documents pour l'histoire de la presse nationale aux xixe et xxe siècles* (Paris, Centre de Documentation Sciences Humaines, n. d.); Roger Bellet, *Presse et journalism sous le Second Empire* (Paris, Colin, 1967); Claude Bellanger, *et al*, *Histoire générale de la presse française* (5 vols., Paris, 1969–76), vol 2, 1815–1871 (l969); Henri Avenel, *Histoire de la presse française depuis 1789 jusqu'à nos jours* (Paris, 1900); Marc Martin, "Journalistes parisiens et notoriété (vers 1830–1870)," in *Revue historique*, 266 (1981), 31–74; Francis Choisel, "La Presse française face aux réformes de 1860," [the French press in relation to the reforms of 1860] in *Revue d'histoire moderne et contemporaine*, 27 (1980), 374–90. Works in English on the same topic: Irene Collins, *The Government and the Newspaper Press in France, 1814–1881* (London, 1959); Robert Justin Goldstein, *Censorship of Political Caricature in Nineteenth Century France* (Kent, 1989). Studies in English about individual journalists include Charles and Anne Marie Poinsatte, "Augustin Cochin's *L'Abolition de l'esclavage* and the Emancipation Proclamation," in *Review of Politics*, 46 (July, 1984), 410–27 and the Sears article about Forcade. For Confederate efforts to influence the French press, see Charles P. Cullop, *Confederate Propaganda in Europe, 1861–1865* (Coral Gables, 1969) and Frank Owsley, *King Cotton Diplomacy* (Chicago, 1931). For Union efforts to influence the French press, see John Bigelow, *Retrospections of an Active Life* (5 vols., New York, 1909–1913).

For French public opinion, see Lynn M. Case, *French Opinion on the United States and Mexico, 1860–1867* (Hamden, 1969).

CHAPTER 2

Literature on the American Civil War is too extensive for even a summary. James M. McPherson, *Battle Cry of Freedom* (New York, 1988), is an excellent one-volume survey with a good bibliography. French historians have not written extensively on the Civil War; for a bibliographical article on that topic, see Claude Fohlen, "Autour du centenaire de la guerre de sécession" [about the centenary of the War of Secession], *Revue historique*, 236 (1966), 69–78.

David H. Pinkney, "France and the Civil War," in Harold Hyman, ed., *Heard Round the World; The Impact Abroad of the Civil War* (New York, 1969), is a good summary, focusing on French attitudes toward the Civil War.

CHAPTER 3

Studies of the *Trent* affair include Gordon H. Warren, *Fountain of Discontent: The Trent Affair and Freedom of the Seas* (Boston, 1981) and Norman Ferris, *The Trent Affair: A Diplomatic Crisis* (Knoxville, 1977).

All major studies of Franco-American diplomacy during the Civil War describe the *Trent* affair. For historiography of the American policy of the Second Empire, which has elicited little interest among French historians, see Claude Fohlen, "Les Historiens devant la politique américaine du Second Empire," in *Revue d'histoire moderne et contemporaine*, 21 (1974), 127–34. Major works on Franco-American diplomacy include Lynn M. Case and Warren F. Spencer, *The United States and France: Civil War Diplomacy* (Philadelphia, 1970), a definitive study, largely from the French point of view ("indispensable from now on for every historian of Franco-American relations," according to French historian Claude Fohlen). Daniel Carroll, *Henri Mercier and the American Civil War* (Princeton, 1971), describes the activities of the man who was French minister to Washington during much of the war. For the American side of Franco-American diplomacy, see Glyndon G. van Deusen, *William Henry Seward* (New York, 1967); John Bigelow, *Retrospections of an Active Life*; and Frank Owsley, *King Cotton Diplomacy*.

Other useful studies of diplomacy include David P. Crook, *The North, the South, and the Powers, 1861–1865* (New York, 1974); Norman B. Ferris, *Desperate Diplomacy: William H. Seward's Foreign Policy: 1861* (Knoxville, 1976); Ephraim D. Adams, *Great Britain and the American Civil War* (2 vols., New York, 1925); Howard Jones, *Union in Peril: The Crisis over British Intervention in the Civil War* (Chapel Hill, 1992); Brian Jenkins, *Britain & the War for the Union* (Montreal, 1974).

CHAPTER 4

For views of French liberals about slavery, see Barbara Karsky, "Les Libéraux français et l'émancipation des esclaves aux États-Unis, 1852–1870," *Revue d'histoire moderne et contemporaine*, 21 (1974), 575–90, and Gavronsky's study of the French liberal opposition.

CHAPTER 5

The basic work on the cotton industry is Claude Fohlen, *L'Industrie textile au temps du Second Empire* (Paris, 1956). See also, Frank Owsley, *King Cotton Diplomacy*; Arthur L. Dunham, *The Anglo-French Treaty of Commerce of 1860 and the Progress of the Industrial Revolution in France* (Ann Arbor, 1930); Claude Fohlen, "La Guerre de sécession et le commerce franco-américain," in *Revue d'histoire moderne et contemporaine*, 8 (1961), 259–70.

CHAPTER 6

Many of the studies listed for Chapter 3 describe the French mediation proposals. Case and Spencer, *Civil War Diplomacy*, is particularly useful.

CHAPTER 7

For Confederate naval activities in France, see Warren F. Spencer, *The Confederate Navy in Europe* (University of Alabama Press, 1983). For Confederate activities, see James D. Bulloch, *The Secret Service of the Confederates in Europe* (2 vols., New York, 1959); for the Union side, see Bigelow's *Retrospections*. Previously cited works by Owsley, *King Cotton Diplomacy*, and Case and Spencer, *Civil War Diplomacy*, extensively cover this topic.

FRENCH NEWSPAPERS

The Parisian newspapers are listed alphabetically by title. The provincial newspapers are listed alphabetically by city, with the city where the provincial newspaper was published in the parentheses preceding the name of the newspaper, except where the title of the newspaper includes the name of the city.

Paris Newspapers

Constitutionnel
Courrier du dimanche
Correspondant

Journal des débats
Monde
Opinion nationale
Patrie
Pays
Presse
Revue des deux mondes
Siècle
Temps
Union

Provincial Newspapers

(Aix-en-Provence) *Écho des Bouches-du-Rhône*
(Albi) *Journal du Tarn*
(Angers) *Ami du peuple*
(Arras) *Courrier du Pas-de-Calais*
(Aurillac) *Moniteur du Cantal*
(Bar-le-Duc) *Écho de l'est*
(Besançon) *Franche-Comté*
(Blois) *Avenir*
(Bordeaux) *Gironde*
(Bordeaux) *Guienne*
(Bourg-en-Bresse) *Courrier de l'Ain*
(Boulogne) *Impartial*
(Bourges) *Journal du Cher*
(Caen) *Ordre et la liberté*
(Cahors) *Courrier du Lot*
(Cahors) *Journal du Lot*
(Chalon) *Courrier de Saône-et-Loire*
(Châlons) *Journal de la Marne*
(Charleville-Mézières) *Courrier des Ardennes*
(Chaumont) *Écho de la Haute-Marne*
(Colmar) *Journal du Haut-Rhin*
(Compiègne) *Écho de l'Oise*
Courrier de Bayonne
Courrier de La Rochelle
Courrier du Havre
Courrier de Verdun
(Digne) Ami de l'ordre
(Dijon) *Journal de la Côte-d'Or*
(Évreux) *Courrier de l'Eure*(Grenoble) *Courrier de l'Isère*
Journal d'Alençon
Journal de Beaune

Journal de Clermont
Journal d'Elbeuf
Journal de Rouen
(Limoges) *Courrier du Centre*
(Lons-le-Saunier) *Sentinelle du Jura*
(Lyon) *Progrès*
(Lyon) *Salut public*
(Maçon) *Journal de Saône-et-Loire*
(Le Mans) *Chronique de l'ouest*
(Marseille) *Nouvelliste*
(Montpellier) *Messager du Midi*
(Montauban) *Courrier de Tarn-et-Garonne*
(Nancy) *Impartial de la Meurthe et des Vosges*
(Pau) *Mémorial des Pyrénées*
(Périgueux) *Écho de Vesone*
(Privas) *Écho de l'Ardèche*
(Quimper) *Impartial du Finistère*
(La Rochelle) *Charente-Inférieure*
(Saint-Étienne) *Mémorial de la Loire*
(Saint-Malo) *Commerce Breton*
(Saintes) *Courrier des deux Charentes*
Sémaphore de Marseille
(Soissons) *Argus Soissonnais*
(Tarbes) *Ère imperiale*
(Toulouse) *Aigle courrier du Midi*
(Troyes) *Aube*
(Valence) *Courrier de la Drôme*
(Versailles) *Concorde de Seine-et-Oise*
(Vesoul) *Journal de la Haute-Saône*
Vigie de Cherbourg
(Yvetot) *Écho*

Index

The Parisian newspapers are listed alphabetically by title. The provincial newspapers are listed alphabetically by city, with the city where the provincial newspaper was published in parentheses preceding the name of the newspaper, except where the title of the newspaper includes the name of the city. A computer generated the pages listed in the index for provincial newspapers; their names appear in the endnotes and sometimes—but not always—in the text.

Adams, Charles Francis, 35
(Aix-en-Provence) *Écho des Bouches-du-Rhône*, 28, 41, 122
Alabama, Confederate commerce raider, 109, 117–19
Alabama-Kearsarge naval engagement, 109–10, 117–19
(Albi) *Journal du Tarn*, 122
Journal d'Alençon, 106, 124, 139
Algeria, 6, 74
Alsace, 7, 77, 79, 97
American Revolution, xi, 2–3, 32, 63, 88 n.61, 102
(Angers) *Ami du peuple*, 20, 37, 43, 55, 49–50, 56, 61, 69–70, 107
Antietam, battle of, 57, 62, 98, 110
(Arras) *Courrier du Pas-de-Calais*, 107

Atlanta, Georgia, Civil War campaigns, 111–12, 122 n.19, 123 n.61, 129
Attila, 130
Aucaigne, Felix, 14–15
(Aurillac) *Moniteur du Cantal*, 85

(Bar-le-Duc) *Écho de l'est*, 106–7, 122, 124
Courrier de Bayonne, 122
Beaufort, South Carolina, 92
Journal de Beaune, 56, 70
Beauregard, Pierre Gustave T., 38, 111
Bell, John, 27, 29
Bellet, Paul Pecquet du, 30, 96, 139 n.46
(Besançon) *Franche-Comté*, 108
Bigelow, John, 16 n.3; appointed consul at Paris, 14; and French construction of Confederate naval vessels, 125 n.87; and influencing French opinion, 14–15, 21 n.56, 70 n.39, 133
(Blois) *Avenir*, 51, 54–56, 105–6
Blumenthal, Henry: on construction of Confederate naval ships in France, 125 n.86; on corruption in the French press, 21 n.56; on the cotton *crise*, 84, 87 n. 46; on the effect of the Civil War on French trade, 84; on French worker sympathies on the Civil War, 88 n.64; on journalistic sympathies on the Civil War, 21 n.58; on strains in Franco-American relations, 16 n.2
Booth, John Wilkes, 131, 133, 139 n.46
Bordeaux, 11, 111, 121, 125 n.87
(Bordeaux) *Gironde*, 11–12, 91, 104, 108
(Bordeaux) *Guienne*, 61, 70, 107
(Boulogne) *Impartial*, 59, 70, 85
(Bourg-en-Bresse) *Courrier de l'Ain*, 43, 56, 85, 106, 124
(Bourges) *Journal du Cher*, 106
Bragg, Braxton, 95, 111
Breckinridge, John C., 27, 29, 111
Brest, 38, 117, 124 n.67
Brissot, Jacques, 24
British Indies, 97
Brown, John, 25, 28
Buchanan, James, 25, 34
Burnside, Ambrose E., 102
Butler, Benjamin, 115, 134

(Caen) *Ordre et la liberté*, 70, 107
(Cahors) *Courrier du Lot*, 70, 85, 106, 122, 124, 139
(Cahors) *Journal du Lot*, 81, 88, 106
Calhoun, John C., 26
Canada, 96, 129
Case, Lynn: and belief that the French press did not reflect public opinion, 12; on the concern of Napoleon III about public opinion, 8
Case, Lynn and Spencer, Warren: and belief that the Confederates set a trap in the *Trent* affair, 54 n.1; on French diplomatic dependence on Britain, 6; on French proposal of mediation, 98, 106 nn.42, 43; on plans by French diplomacy to resolve economic problems from the Civil War, 91–92; on Thouvenel's note in the *Trent* affair, 49, 55 n.24;
Catalonia, 75
(Chalon) *Courrier de Saône-et-Loire*, 56–57, 70–71
(Châlons) *Journal de la Marne*, 54
Chancellorsville, 106
Charlemagne, 93
Charles X, 2
Charleston, South Carolina, 35, 45, 129–31
(Charleville-Mézières) *Courrier des Ardennes*, 107, 110, 122
Chattanooga, battle of, 110–11
(Chaumont) *Écho de la Haute-Marne*, 85, 107–8
Cherbourg, 38, 110, 118
Clay, Henry, 26
Journal de Clermont, 88
Clovis, 36
Cobden Treaty, 1860, 80, 87 n.46
Cochin, Augustin: on American democracy, 36; on Lincoln's assassination, 133; on slavery, 40 n.10, 70 n.34, 71 n.42
(Colmar) *Journal du Haut-Rhin*, 43
Columbia, South Carolina, 129
(Compiègne) *Écho de l'Oise*, 70, 72

Constitutionnel, 19 n.34; on *Alabama-Kearsarge* affair, 118–19; on American democracy, 26; on American society, 24; on causes of the Civil War, 37–38; and belief that the South would attain independence, 31, 33; on Charlemagne, 43; classification of, 8–9; on consequences of the war, 134; as defender of Napoleon III, 20 n.47; on economic problems from the Civil War, 74; on election of 1860, 28–29; on John C. Fremont, 63; on French national interests, 93; on Lincoln, 27, 29, 33, 38; on mediation, 81, 95; on military operations, 58, 122 n.19; on secession, 30, 33; on slavery, 30, 37, 62–63, and support for the Northern cause, 23, 30, 32–33, 37; and support for the Southern cause, 33, 37; on the *Trent* affair, 48, 50, 52, 93; on William Walker, 25
Continental System, 2
Correspondant: on American democracy, 25–26, 36, 39, 40 n.9, 53; on the assassination of Lincoln, 133; and belief that the South would achieve independence, 39; on the causes of the Civil War, 41 n.32; on the cotton famine, 52, 75, 84 n.10, 85 n.21, 86 n.36; on economic problems from the Civil War, 85 n. 21; on French mediation, 51; on French national interests, 51–52; on Lincoln, 53; on racism in America, 71 n.47; on recognition of the South, 106 n.41; on slavery, 39, 52, 106 n.41; on subscriptions to help the unemployed, 89 n.69; and support for the Northern cause, 36, 51, 137; on the *Trent* affair, 52–53
Courrier du dimanche: on American democracy, 39, 58, 117, 127, 137; assassination of Lincoln, 131–32; causes of the Civil War, 39, 128; belief that the South would attain independence, 39, 132; classification, 9; consequences of the war, 111, 123 n.52, 131; criticism of French government policies, 135; economic problems from the Civil War, 81; French national interests, 51; intervention, 51, 81; Lincoln, 117, 131–32; Mexico, 129; military operations, 58, 130–31; recognition, 51, 132; slavery, 39, 58, 115, 128; support for the Northern cause, 58, 115; suspension, 13, 20 n.45; tariff, 39; *Trent* affair, 39
Crimean War, 4, 6

Davis, Jefferson, 41 n.37, 45, 64, 101
Dayton, William, 14; and mediation in November, 1862, 102, 106 n.45; and construction of Confederate warships, 121; and Thouvenel, 38, 105 n.38;
(Digne) *Ami de l'ordre*, 33, 42, 106
(Dijon) *Journal de la Côte-d'Or*, 42, 84, 85
Douglas, Stephen, 26–27, 29, 34
Drouyn de Lhuys, Edouard: and January mediation, 102–4; and October mediation, 99–101

Elbeuf, 83
Journal d'Elbeuf, 89
Emancipation Proclamation: final, January 1863, 65–69; preliminary, September 1862, 57, 62, 65, 99;
(Évreux) *Courrier de l'Eure,* 57, 60, 70, 72, 96, 106, 108

Farragut, David, 112
Ferry, Jules, 79
Flers, 80, 82
Florida, 117–18, 124 n.67
Fohlen, Claude: on the Cobden treaty, 80; on the consequence of high wheat prices, 80; on the cotton *crise*, 81; on the effect of the Civil War on French trade, 85 n.16; on the failure of King Cotton theory, 86 n.36, 88 n.64; on reasons for the high price of cotton, 79
Forcade, Eugène: on American democracy, 39, 135; on French economic problems, 77; on French

mediation proposal, 103; on French policy during the *Trent* crisis, 94; on French worker sympathy for the North, 88 n.64; on Union military failure, 59
Forrest, Nathan B., 111
Fort Fisher, capture, 129
Fort Sumter, 34–35, 42 n.68, 45, 73–74, 92
France: and abolition of slavery within France and colonies, 40 n.10, 70 n.33; American attitudes toward, 1–4, 16 n.2, 18 n.20; and anti-American sentiment, ix, 16 n.2, 17 n.6; and economic problems arising from the Civil War, ix, 7, 73–88, 92, 98; and economy of the Second Empire before 1860, 7; and foreign policy of Second Empire before 1860, 6, 18 n.21; and John Brown, 25; and political history, 1815–1852, 2–3; and political groups in the Second Empire, 5; and political structure of the Second Empire, 5; and postal service with America, 19 n.34; and pro-American sentiment, ix, 1, 16 n.2, 17 n.6; and pro-Northern sentiment, 19 n.29; and pro-Southern sentiment, 18 n.28; and relations with America before 1860, 3–4, 7, 17 n.8, 18 n.20; and traditional policies toward America, 16 n.3, 70 n.39. *See also* Newspapers; Mexico; France, official policies
France, official policies and actions arising from the Civil War: the blockade, 55 n.23, 91–92; construction of Confederate warships, 121; mediation , 92, 98–99, 102; partiality toward the North, 1, 38; partiality toward the South, 6, 38, 120–21; recognition of Southern belligerency, 35; relief for economic distress, 83, 91–92, 98, 102; treatment of Confederate warships in French ports, 117; the *Trent* affair, 46, 49
Franklin, Benjamin, 36, 39, 50
Fredericksburg, battle of, 102, 110
French Revolution, 2, 5, 97, 101

Gavronsky, Serge, on French Liberal support for the North, 10, 20 n.41
Georgia, 128, 130
Germany, 60, 76, 97
Gettysburg, battle of, 110–11
Grant, Ulysses S.: and appointment as General-in-Chief, 111; and Chattanooga, 110–11; and Forts Henry and Donelson, 95; and Lee's surrender, 131; and Lincoln's assassination, 133; and Virginia campaign in 1865, 121, 127, 129, 131; and Wilderness campaign, 11, 111–12, 116, 122 n.22
Great Britain: 2, 18 n.21,32, 40 n.10, 79, 93, 116; and the blockade, 93–94; and conservative views on the Civil War, 17 n.13; and Confederate commerce raiders, 117–18; and economic problems from the Civil War, 75, 76–77, 82, 85 n.21, 86 nn.36, 45; and French diplomatic dependence on, 6, 8, 18 n.19, 38, 55 n.24, 120; and mediation, 98, 99, 107 n.46, 100, 102, 104; and recognition of the South, 93, 97, 104; and Southern belligerency, 35; and the *Trent* affair, 45–53, 55 nn.23, 24; United States as makeweight against, 18 n.20, 19 n.29, 50-52, 61, 93–94, 104. *See also* Cobden Treaty
(Grenoble) *Courrier de l'Isère,* 56, 108

Hamilton, Alexander, 2
Le Havre: and commerce with America, 38; and cotton, 75, 78–79; and relief for the unemployed, 82
Courrier du Havre, 86, 91, 123
Holy Land, 6
Hood, John B., 111, 122 n.19
Hotze, Henry, 15, 21 n.56
Hugo, Victor, 25
Hungary, 36, 96

India, 75, 79, 97, 102, 104
Indochina, 6
Italy, 130; and cotton, 76; and French

troops protecting Papal domains, 6, 98; and independence, 28, 38

Jefferson, Thomas, 39; and followers corrupting American democracy, 25–26, 40 n.9; and views of followers on the French Revolution, 2; on the importance of New Orleans, 31; on liberty, 132; on slavery, 63
Johnson, Andrew, 127–28, 133–35, 139 n.46
Journal des débats: on the *Alabama-Kearsarge* affair, 118; on the attitude of the unemployed regarding the Civil War, 81; on the causes of the Civil War, 31, 70 n.42; on Confederate commerce raiders, 117; and belief that the North would maintain the Union, 29; on the election of 1860, 29; on the firing on Fort Sumter, 35; on French national interests, 94; on intervention, 92; and Laboulaye, 16 n.3, 70 n.39; on Lincoln, 29; on mediation, 97, 103; on military operations, 111; on recognition, 94; on secession, 29; on slavery, 25, 29, 31, 70 n.42, 136; on the tariff as a cause of the Civil War, 31; on the *Trent* affair, 48, 52, 94

Kansas, 25, 28, 115
Kearsarge, Union warship, 110, 117–19, 124 n.72
King Cotton theory: and its failure, 86 n.36, 88 n.64; and Southern embargo of cotton, 78; and Southern belief in, 86 n.36

Laboulaye, Edouard: on American democracy, 17 n.63, 63; on the Civil War, 70 n.39; on French intervention in the Civil War, 105 n.1; and Napoleon on Louisiana, 16 n.3; on slavery, 62; and the Statue of Liberty, 17 n.6
Lafayette, Marie Joseph, Marquis de, 1–2, 101
Lancashire, 79, 83, 102
Lane, James, 115
Latin America, 3, 6, 17 n.8, 18 n.20, 25
Lee, Robert E., 118, 128; and Grant, 111, 116; and military operations in 1865, 127, 129, 131; and Peninsular campaign, 12, 57, 60, 68, 95; and surrender, 127, 131; and Wilderness campaign, 112
Leon, Edwin de, 15, 21 n.26
Lille, 77
(Limoges) *Courrier du Centre,* 106
Lincoln, Abraham, 61, 82, 96, 101, 110, 124; and arbitrary actions, 114; and assassination, 11, 127, 131–33; and blockade, 35, 50; and early life, 26–27; and election of 1860, 28–29, 36, 38; and election of 1860, 28–29, 36, 38; and election of 1864, 116–17, 123 n.41; and Emancipation Proclamation, 57, 59, 65–69, 128; French assessments of, 128, 130, 132, 139 n.41; French images of, 12 n.1; and Fort Sumter, 35, 42 n.68; and inauguration in 1860, 23, 30, 33–34, 74; and mediation, 92, 104; and personal characteristics, 27; and slavery issue, 11, 39, 57, 62, 64; and *Trent* affair, 47, 49, 52–53
(Lons-le-Saunier) *Sentinelle du Jura,* 123, 138
Lorraine, 77
Louis Philippe, 2, 4–5, 9
Louis XVI, 2, 16 n.3, 51, 70 n.39, 99, 101
Louis XVIII, 2
Louisiana, 73; French heritage in, 3, 24, 32; and Napoleon's sale to America, 2–3, 16 n.3, 104, 136
(Lyon) *Progrès*, 34, 42
(Lyon) *Salut public,* 71

(Maçon) *Journal de Saône-et-Loire,* 56, 71, 96, 106, 108
Manchester, 50, 79, 81–82, 86
(Le Mans) *Chronique de l'ouest,* 56
March to the Sea, 111
(Marseille) *Nouvelliste,* 70–71
Sémaphore de Marseille, 31, 42, 70,

84–85, 89, 101, 105, 107, 109, 122, 124, 135, 138–39
Maximilian, 6, 135–36
McClellan, George B., 51, 105, 129; and the Peninsular campaign, 12, 57–61, 92, 95, 98; and the election of 1864, 116
Mercier, Henri, 18 n.20, 56 n.50, 94
Mexican War, 3
Mexico, 30; and American intervention in, 96, 129; and French intervention in, 3, 6, 18 nn.18, 28, 98, 135, 140 n.66
Middle East, 4, 6
Missouri, 29
Mobile, 112, 117
Monde, 124 n.65; on American democracy, 30, 34, 114; on American society, 30, 36, 114; on causes of the Civil War, 36, 100, 112–13, 134; and belief that the South would win, 40, 58, 85 n.25, 129; classification of, 9; on consequences of the war, 134; on cotton famine, 79; on economic problems from the Civil War, 83; on the election of 1864, 116; on the Emancipation Proclamation, 68–69; on French mediation, 87 n.54; on French national interests, 51, 93; on Lincoln, 34, 53, 68–69, 100, 116; on military operations, 58, 129; on slavery, 36, 68–69, 100, 113, 134; and support for the Southern cause, 8, 40; on the tariff as a cause of the Civil War, 112; on the *Trent* affair, 47–48, 51, 53, 54 n.19, 76, 93
Monroe Doctrine, 3, 96
(Montauban) *Courrier de Tarn-et-Garonne*, 60, 70, 85
(Montpellier) *Messager du Midi*, 123
Morrill Tariff, 64, 74

(Nancy) *Impartial de la Meurthe et des Vosges*, 107
Nantes, 121, 125 n.87, 127
Napoleon I: and French tradition, 3, 70 n.39, 93, 99; and sale of Louisiana to America, 2–4, 16 n.3, 104, 136
Napoleon III, 1, 13, 16 n.1; and American anger over actions in the New World, 4; and concern over public opinion, 8, 92; and Conservative supporters, x, 5, 8, 12, 15, 18 n.28, 30; and construction of naval ships for the Confederacy, 121, 125 n.86; on cooperation with the British, 91; and domestic economy, 7; and foreign policy, 6, 17 n.17, 18 n.19; and John Roebuck, 120; and Liberal opponents, x, 5, 10, 12, 15, 19 n.29, 20 n.41; and mediation, 5, 78, 92, 95, 98–99, 102, 106 nn.42, 44; and Mexico and Maximilian, 6, 18 n.21, 98, 140 n.66; as president of the Second Republic, 4; and proclamation of himself as emperor, 3, 4; and pro-South sentiments, 6, 8, 38, 98, 105 n.1; and pro-Union sentiments, 1, 8, 16 n.1; nd role in French government, 4, 6; and workers, 88 n.65, 102, 106 n.44;
Newspapers: General: circulation data for, 9–10, 18 n.25; Civil War sources and coverage of, 10–11, 19 n.34; and classification by political orientation, ix, 8–9, 11–12, 18 n.25, 19 n.38, 21n.58; and conventions in endnote citation, xi–xii; and corruption, 12, 14–15, 20 n.53, 21 n.56; importance of, 16, 20 n.50, 21 n.59; and principal characteristics, 8–11; provincial press, 11–12, 19 n.38; and validity of views, 12–16, 20 n.43
Newspapers, Clerical/Legitimist: on American democracy, 30, 36, 40, 114, 134; on American society, 30, 114, 134; on the assassination of Lincoln, 134; on the causes of the Civil War, 36, 40, 64, 69, 100, 112–13, 134; and belief that the North would maintain the Union, 40, 60–61; and belief that the South would attain independence, 58, 60–61, 95, 120; on consequences of the war, 114, 134; on cooperation with Great Britain, 8, 103, 120; on the cotton famine, 79; and criticism

of French government policies, 120, 129; on economic problems from the Civil War, 99–100; on the election of 1864, 116; on the Emancipation Proclamation, 68–69; on French mediation, 61, 95, 99–100, 103, 120; on French national interests, 50–51, 61, 93; on Lincoln, 36, 53, 68, 100, 114, 116; on military operations, 110–11, 129; on racism in America, 61, 134; on secession, 30; on the semi-official press, 69 n.1; on slavery, 36–37, 49–50, 61–62, 68–69, 93, 100, 113, 133–34, 137; and support for the Northern cause, 37, 62; on the tariff as a cause of the Civil War, 112, 120; on the *Trent* affair, 47–51, 53, 54 n.19, 76, 93–94

Newspapers, Imperial journals: on the *Alabama-Kearsarge* affair, 118–19; on American democracy, 26, 34, 51, 59–60, 104, 114, 128; on American expansion in the New World, 96; on American society, 24, 30, 113–14, 128, 133–34; on the assassination of Lincoln, 131–33, 139 n.46; and belief that the North would maintain the Union, 59–60; and belief that the South would achieve independence, 31–33, 58–60, 95, 99, 137; on the blockade, 81, 94, 136; on Booth, 133; on the causes of the Civil War, 30, 37–38, 40, 64, 112, 128, 136; on Confederate commerce raiders, 117–18; on the consequences of the war, 113, 117, 134; and construction of Confederate warships, 125 n.87; on the cotton famine, 78, 84, 86 n.45; on economic opportunities from the Civil War, 32, 38, 74, 76, 82, 99; on economic problems from the Civil War, 32, 73–78, 94, 96, 99–100; on the election of 1860, 27–29; on the election of 1864, 116–17; on the Emancipation Proclamation, 65–67, 69; on the firing on Fort Sumter, 35; on freedom of the press, 14; on French mediation, 81, 93, 95–96, 99–100, 102–04, 106 n.32, 120; on French national interests, 50, 93–94; on intervention, 93–95, 99, 107 n.45, 128–29; on Johnson, 133, 135; on Lincoln, 26–27, 29, 33–34, 38, 41 n.19, 50, 66–67, 96, 114, 116, 131–33; on military operations, 19 n.35, 58, 96, 110–11, 122 n.19, 129–30; on racism in America, 38, 64–65, 96, 114–15, 128, 134; on recognition of the South, 58, 76, 93, 96, 120, 124 n.83; on recognition of Southern belligerency, 36; on secession, 29–34; on the "semi-official" press, 38, 105 n.5; on slavery, 25, 28–30, 32–33, 37–38, 60, 62–67, 82, 91, 94, 114–15, 128, 134, 136; on subscriptions to help the unemployed, 77, 83–84; and support for the Northern cause, 8, 12, 19 n.40, 32, 37, 40, 50–51, 59–60; and support for the Southern cause, 8, 12, 14, 19 n.40, 32–33, 37–38, 40, 59–60, 127, 136–37; on the surrender of Lee, 131; on the tariff as a cause of the Civil War, 64, 74, 76, 112, 136; on traditional French policies, 94, 99; on the *Trent* affair, 47–48, 50–53, 76, 93–94; on workers' reactions to economic distress, 82

Newspapers, a Liberal Catholic journal *See under Correspondant*

Newspapers, Orleanist journals: on the *Alabama-Kearsarge* affair, 118; on American democracy, 26, 32, 39, 40 n.9, 117, 132, 134–35; on American expansion in the New World, 17 n.8, 25, 129; on American society, 35; on the assassination of Lincoln, 132; and belief that the North would maintain the Union, 58, 59–60, 112, 130–31; and belief that the South would achieve independence, 31–33, 58–60, 95, 112, 137; on the blockade, 93; on the causes of the Civil War, 39–40, 63, 71 n.42, 128; on Confederate commerce raiders, 117; on the consequences of the war, 123 n.52, 135; on the construction of Confederate warships, 121; on the cotton famine, 75, 79, 81, 84, 86 n.45, 93, 97, 120; and criticism of French government policies, 20 n.47, 103, 120–21, 135–36; on economic problems from the Civil War, 74, 77, 79, 81, 104, 111; on the election of 1860, 27–29; on the election of 1864, 116–17; on the Emancipation Proclamation, 66, 68–69; on the firing on Fort Sumter, 35; on freedom of the press, 13, 20 n.45; on French national interests, 70 n.39, 94, 101, 136; on French traditional policies, 70 n.39; on intervention, 92, 120; on Johnson, 134; on Lincoln, 26–27, 29, 34, 41 n.19, 66, 68, 104, 116–117, 128, 132; on French mediation, 81, 97, 101, 103–104; on military operations, 58, 111–12, 130–31; and pro-Union views as a cloak to attack Napoleon III, 15; on recognition of the South, 93–94, 96–97; on secession, 29, 31; on the "semi-official" press, 8; on slavery, 11, 25, 29, 31, 34, 39, 63, 66, 68, 97, 115–17, 128, 136; on subscriptions to help the unemployed, 77; and support for the Northern cause, 32, 37, 40, 58–59, 116; on support for the Southern cause,136; on the surrender of Lee, 131; on the tariff and the Civil War, 31, 39; on traditional French policies, 121; on the *Trent* affair, 46–48, 51–52, 94; on *Uncle Tom's Cabin*, 40 n. 11; on William Walker, 25; on workers' reactions to economic distress, 81

Newspapers, Republican journals: on the *Alabama-Kearsarge* affair, 119; on American democracy, 26–27, 34, 52–53, 115; on American expansion in the New World, 129; on American society, 24, 50; on the assassination of Lincoln, 131–33; on the blockade, 97, 101, 104, 119; and belief that the North would maintain the Union, 31, 59, 111, 131; and belief that the South would achieve independence, 31, 61, 92, 115; on the causes of the Civil War, 31, 39, 63–64, 103, 113, 128; on Confederate commerce raiders, 117; on the consequences of the war, 135; on the construction of Confederate warships, 121, 124 n.85, 125 n.87; on the cotton famine, 75, 79, 104, 120; and criticism of French government policies, 20 n.47, 104; on economic problems from the Civil War, 53; on the election of 1860, 27–28; on the election of 1864, 116–17; on the Emancipation Proclamation, 67–69; on freedom of the press, 13; on French mediation, 49, 81, 92, 94, 97, 101, 103–04; on French national interests, 104; on intervention in the Civil War, 81, 97; on Lincoln, 26–27, 34, 41 n.19, 65, 68, 101, 116–17, 131–32; on military operations, 11, 109–12, 122 n.19, 130; and pro-Union views as a cloak to attack Napoleon III, 15, 21 n.57; on racism in America, 64, 115; on recognition of the South, 32, 81, 97, 104, 120; on recognition of Southern belligerency, 36; on secession, 29, 31, 34, 104; on slavery, 19 n.35, 25, 27–28, 31, 34–35, 39, 63–65, 68, 74, 97, 100–101, 103–104, 113, 115, 117, 123 n.51, 128, 132–33, 135–36; on subscriptions to help the unemployed, 83; and support for the Northern cause, 11, 59, 61, 97, 115, 123 n.50; and support for the Southern cause, 32; on the surrender of Lee, 131; on the tariff, 74; on traditional French policies, 97; on the *Trent* affair, 46–47, 49–50, 52–53, 93

New Orleans, 25; capture of, 58, 78, 111; and commerce with France, 31, 76; Seward opens port in 1862, 92

Normandy, 7, 77, 79–82, 86 n.44, 87 n.46

Opinion nationale: on the *Alabama-Kearsarge* affair, 119; on Alexander Stephens's "cornerstone speech," 70 n.41; on the causes of the Civil War, 31; classification of, 9; on construction of Confederate warships, 121, 125 n.87; on the election of 1864, 116; on Lincoln, 34, 116; on military operations, 122 n.19; on the *Presse*, 10; on recognition of Southern belligerency, 36; on slavery, 31, 34; on the *Trent* affair, 52

Oregon, 3

Owsley, Frank L., on reasons for the cotton *crise*, 80

Patrie: on the *Alabama-Kearsarge* affair, 118; on the assassination of Lincoln, 131–33; on the causes of the Civil War, 64, 128, 136; classification of , 8–9; and confidence in a Southern victory, 33, 58, 129; on consequences of the war, 129, 134–35; on construction of Confederate warships, 125 n.87; and corruption in journalism, 14–15; on the election of 1864, 116; on French mediation, 120; on Great Britain, 120, 129; on intervention, 129; on John Wilkes Booth, 133, 139 n.45; on Lincoln, 128; on military operations, 58, 111, 122 n.19, 129; on racism in America, 128; on recognition of the South, 38, 92–93; on the "semi-official" press, 8, 38; on slavery, 63, 128, 136; and support for the Northern cause, 8, 37; and support for the Southern cause, 8, 14, 37, 134; on the tariff in the Civil War , 50, 93; on the *Trent* affair, 50, 93

(Pau) *Mémorial des Pyrénées,* 61, 70, 106, 107

Pays: on the *Alabama-Kearsarge* affair, 119; on the assassination of Lincoln, 132; and belief that the South would succeed, 58; on the British cotton industry, 86 n.45; on the causes of the Civil War, 64; classification of , 8, 9, 20 n47; on consequences of the war, 130; on the cotton famine, 86 n.45; on economic problems from the Civil War, 85 n.33; on economic opportunities from the Civil War, 32, 74; on the election of 1864, 116; on French mediation, 99; on intervention in the Civil War, 129; on Lincoln, 33, 116, 132; on military operations, 58, 129–30; and Paul Pequet du Bellet, 30, 41 n.37, 95; on racism in America, 115; on recognition of the South, 32, 95; on slavery, 29, 66; and support for the Northern cause, 37; and support for the Southern cause, 30, 37, 41 n.37, 58, 69 n.4; on the tariff in the Civil War, 64, 74; on traditional French policies, 99; on the *Trent* affair, 47

(Périgueux) *Écho de Vesone,* 106–7

Petersburg, Virginia, 127, 131

Pierre angulaire, 63–64, 106 n.41

Pinkney, David: on efforts by North and South to influence French opinion, 21 n.56; on reasons for pro-Northern sentiment, 18 n.29; on reasons for pro-Southern sentiment, 18 n.28

Poland, 19, n.35, 109, 12

The Pope, 74, 89 n.69

Port Royal, South Carolina, 92

Portugal, 76

Presse: 43 n.86; on American democracy, 26; on American society, 24; on the assassination of Lincoln, 132; and belief in a Northern victory, 59; and belief in a Southern victory, 59; on the blockade, 79, 119; on the causes of the Civil War, 31, 63, 113, 115, 128; classification of, 9; and condemnation by *Opinion nationale*, 10; on the cotton famine, 81, 97; on economic problems from the Civil War, 79; on the election of 1860, 27–28; on the Emancipation Proclamation, 67–68; on French mediation, 96–97, 100–101; on

Lincoln, 23, 34, 39, 132; on military operations, 11, 19 n.35, 59, 69 n.10, 110, 112, 122 n.22, 130–31; on slavery, 28, 31, 39, 74, 100, 113, 132; on subscriptions to help the unemployed, 83–84; and support for the Northern cause, 10, 123 n.50; and support for the Southern cause, 32; on the tariff in the Civil War, 74; on the *Trent* affair, 45–47, 49–50, 52–53, 93–94
Prévost-Paradol, Lucien, 11, 13
Procureurs généraux, 8, 88 n.63
Puritans, 24, 114, 133

(Quimper) *Impartial du Finistère,* 51, 56

Republican party in the United States: and assassination of Lincoln, 133–34; and election of 1860, 27–28, 31, 62; and election of 1864, 116–17; and racism, 61; and slavery, 39
Revue des deux mondes: on American democracy, 26, 32, 39, 134–35; on American expansion in Latin America, 17 n.8, 25; on American society, 25, 135; on the assassination of Lincoln, 132; and belief that the North would maintain the Union, 59, 128, 130; and belief that the South would attain independence, 31, 39; classification of, 9; on consequences of the war, 134–35; on the cotton famine, 75, 79, 84, 86 nn.36, 45; and criticism of French government policies, 101, 103, 120–21, 135–36; on economic opportunities from the Civil War, 84; on economic problems from the Civil War, 77, 79; on the election of 1860, 28; on the election of 1864, 116; on the Emancipation Proclamation, 68; on French mediation, 101, 103; on French national interests, 136; on French worker support for the North, 88 n.64; on Great Britain, 86; on intervention in the Civil War, 120; on Johnson, 134; on Lincoln, 34, 116; on military operations, 59, 112, 130; on the Northern cause and French liberal democracy, 128; on racism in America, 115–16; on secession, 29, 31; on slavery, 31, 116; on subscriptions to help the unemployed, 77; and support for the Northern cause, 59, 128; on the *Trent* affair, 47, 94; on wheat, 87 n.47; on William Walker, 25
Richmond, 94, 135; capture of, 127, 130–31, 138 n.25; in 1864 and 1865 military operations, 111–12, 122 n.22, 127, 129; in Peninsular campaign, 12, 57, 60–61, 69 n.10, 95, 98
Rochambeau, 101
La Rochelle, 74, 76, 96, 127
(La Rochelle) *Charente-Inférieure,* 32, 35, 38–39, 50, 64, 66, 73, 75–77, 94, 96, 100, 110–11, 114, 127–28, 130, 133
Courrier de La Rochelle, 35, 42–43, 48, 50, 54, 56, 67, 72, 85
Rouen, 77, 82–83, 87 n.46
Journal de Rouen, 88
Rouher, Eugène, 13, 19 n.31
Russia, 4, 98–99, 107 n.46, 114, 125 n.85, 129

(Saintes) *Courrier des deux Charentes,* 57, 85–86, 89, 100, 107–8, 112, 123,
Saint-Étienne, 75
(Saint-Étienne) *Mémorial de la Loire,* 42–43, 85, 105
(Saint-Malo) *Commerce Breton,* 108, 112–13
Sancton, Thomas: on the "myth" of French worker support for the North, 82, 88 n.64
Savannah, 127, 129–31
Secession, xi, 23, 30, 34; as viewed in Britain, 17 n.13; as viewed in France in 1861, 29–32, 34, 38, 52, 91, 137; as viewed in France in 1862, 62, 70 n.39, 96–97, 104; as viewed in France in 1863, 114, 120
Second Bull Run, 92

Second Republic, 3–4
Seine-Inférieure, 81–83, 85 n.30
Semmes, Raphael, 118–19, 124 n.72
Seward, William H., 92, 116, 133; failure to secure Presidential nomination, 27; and French mediation proposal, 102–104, 106 n.45; and *Trent* affair, 46–47, 53, 55 n.25, 56 n. 50
Sheridan, Philip, 112
Sherman, William T., 19 n.35, 111–12, 121, 122 n.19, 128–31
Siècle: on the *Alabama-Kearsarge* affair, 119; on Alexander Stephens's "cornerstone" speech, 123 n.51; on American democracy, 15, 27; on the assassination of Lincoln, 131; on the blockade, 97; on the causes of the Civil War, 131; classification of, 8–10; on Confederate commerce raiders, 117, 121; and confidence in Northern victory, 111; on the consequences of the war, 131, 135; on construction of Confederate warships, 125 n.85; on the cotton famine, 120; and criticism of French government policies, 20 n.47, 101; on the election of 1860, 27–28; on the election of 1864, 116; on the Emancipation Proclamation, 66, 68; on freedom of the press, 13; on French mediation, 20 n.47, 49, 81, 94, 101, 120; on French national interests, 97; on the influence of American democracy on Europe, 116; on intervention in the Civil War, 20 n.47, 81; on lack of interest in the Civil War, 19 n.35, 109; on Lincoln, 34, 131–32; on military operations, 122 n.19; on recognition of the South, 81, 97, 120; on secession, 31; on slavery, 19 n.35, 28, 31, 66, 68, 94, 97, 113, 115, 123 n.51; on subscriptions to help the unemployed, 83, 89 n.69; and support for the Northern cause, 66, 111, 113; on traditional French policies, 97; on the *Trent* affair, 48–49, 52
Slavery: and abolition in France, 20 n.53, 40 n.10, 70 n.33; as an influence on French attitudes toward the Civil War, ix–xi, 13, 15. 19 n.29, 21 n.57, 136–37; as an issue in 1860, 23, 25–29; as an issue in 1861, 30–31, 36–40, 47, 49–52, 62–63, 74; as an issue in 1862, 12, 58, 60–69, 69 n.1, 70 nn.34, 39, 71 nn.42, 47, 49, 93–95, 97–98, 100–101, 103–4, 106 n.41; as an issue in 1863, 19 n.35, 88 n.64, 91, 113–16, 123 n.51; as a issue in 1864, 117, 124 n.83; as an issue in 1865, 127–28, 133–36. *See also* Emancipation Proclamation
(Soissons) *Argus Soissonnais*, 70–71, 107
South Carolina, 3, 30, 35, 92, 129
Spain, 75, 130
Spencer, Warren: on the *Alabama-Kearsarge* engagement, 124 n.72
Stanton, Edwin, 139 n.46
Stowe, Harriet Beecher, 50 n.11
Syria, 6, 98

(Tarbes) *Ère impériale*, 88, 106, 107, 108
Tariff, 80 n.16, 85; as a cause of the Civil War, 30–31, 39, 64, 74, 76, 80, 112, 120, 136
Temps: on Alexander Stephens's "cornerstone" speech, 70 n.41; on the blockade, 93; on British economic problems, 74–75; on the causes of the Civil War, 39, 63; classification of ,9; and confidence in a Northern victory, 69 n.10; on the cotton famine, 75, 79, 86 n.44, 93, 97; and criticism of French government policies, 101; on economic problems from the Civil War, 81; on the Emancipation Proclamation, 68; on freedom of the press, 13; on French mediation, 101, 103; on French national interests, 101; on intervention in the Civil War, 81, 97; on lack of interest in the Civil War, 19 n.35; on Lincoln, 66, 68; on military operations, 69 n.10; on recognition of the South,

93, 97; on slavery, 39, 48, 52, 58, 63, 71 n.49, 66, 97; on subscriptions to help the unemployed, 77, 83; on the *Trent* affair, 46, 52
Texas, 3, 36, 58
Thouvenel, Antoine, 38, 105 n.5; and the *Trent* affair, 45–46, 49–50, 53, 55 nn.24, 25, 56 n.50, 91
Tocqueville, Alexis de, 3, 17 n.16, 114
(Toulouse) *Aigle courrier du Midi,* 89
Trent affair, ix, 45–53, 54 n.1, 55 nn.24, 25, 57, 76, 91–94, 105 n.12, 143
(Troyes) *Aube*, 104, 108

Uncle Tom's Cabin, 25
Union: on American democracy, 114, 134; on American society, 114, 134; on the assassination of Lincoln, 134; on the causes of the Civil War, 120; classification of , 8–9; on the consequences of the war, 114; and criticism of French government policies, 120; on French mediation, 103, 120; on Lincoln, 114; on military operations, 110, 129; on the tariff in the Civil War, 120

(Valence) *Courrier de la Drôme*, 71, 107
Vallandigham, Clement, 103
Vendée, 97, 101
Vera Cruz, 129
Courrier de Verdun, 70
(Versailles) *Concorde de Seine-et-Oise,* 122, 138, 139
(Vesoul) *Journal de la Haute-Saône*, 42, 55, 71, 72, 107, 108
Vicksburg, 111
Vigie de Cherbourg, 39, 43, 54, 76, 85, 105
Virginia, 24, 29, 112, 131

Walker, William, 25
War of 1812, 2
Washington, D. C., 13, 18 n.20, 33–35, 45–50, 57, 59, 68, 91, 98, 104, 113, 116, 135
Washington, George, 5, 36, 39, 40 n.9, 101, 132
Webster, Daniel, 26
West, W. Reed, on French sympathies in the Civil War, x; on reversal of views of the "semi-official" press, 18 n.27
West Virginia, 114
Wilderness campaign, 11, 112
Wilkes, Charles, and the *Trent* affair, 45–48, 51–52, 54 n.1, 93–94, 127
William the Conqueror, 36
Winslow, John, 118–19

(Yvetot) *Écho,* 85

About the Author

GEORGE M. BLACKBURN is Professor Emeritus of History at Central Michigan University.